THE ISLAMIC THREAT TO THE SOVIET STATE

D1599797

CROOM HELM SERIES ON THE ARAB WORLD

EDITED BY P.J. VATIKIOTIS
School of Oriental and African Studies, University of London

THE INTEGRATION OF MODERN IRAQ
Edited by Abbas Kelidar

PALESTINE IN THE ARAB DILEMMA
Walid W. Kazziha

THE LIBYAN OIL INDUSTRY
Frank C. Waddams

THE COHESION OF SAUDI ARABIA
Christine Moss Helms

ISLAM AND POWER
Edited by A.S. Cudsi and Ali E. Hillal Dessouki

The Islamic Threat to the Soviet State

Alexandre Bennigsen and Marie Broxup

CROOM HELM
London & Canberra

© 1983 Alexandre Bennigsen and Marie Broxup
Croom Helm Ltd, Provident House, Burrell Row, Beckenham, Kent BR3 1AT

British Library Cataloguing in Publication Data

Bennigsen, Alexandre
    The Islamic threat to the Soviet state. — (Croom
    Helm series on the Arab world)
    1. Islam — Europe, Eastern — History
    2. Soviet Union — History
    I. Title   II. Broxup, Marie
    947   BP65

    ISBN 0-7099-0619-6

Typeset by Mayhew Typesetting, Bristol
Printed and bound in Great Britain

CONTENTS

TABLES

FOREWORD

Ever since the conversion of the Khan Özbek of the Golden Horde to Islam in the early fourteenth century, marking as it does the beginning of regular and close contacts between Russians and Muslim Turks, the Muslim factor has dominated Russian history. The first period was that of Muslim pre-eminence during the fourteenth and fifteenth centuries, when the Golden Horde Khans ruled over their Russian vassals. During the sixteenth and seventeenth centuries a certain equilibrium was achieved: the Russians captured Kazan in 1552 and in 1556 conquered Astrakhan, but in 1571 Crimean Tartars burned Moscow and in 1604 the Russians were badly defeated by the Daghestanis and the Ottomans on the banks of the river Terek. The eighteenth and nineteenth centuries saw the emergence of Russian supremacy. In the twentieth century, the attempt by the same Russians — turned Soviet — to consolidate their position and at the same time to solve, once and for all, the problem of the coexistence of two different civilisations in the same state seems set to fail. The mosaic of nationalities which makes up the USSR remains as hostile — perhaps even more so — to one another as it has ever been and the emergence of a 'Soviet' nation becomes more and more difficult to achieve. Only Soviet agitprop proclaims the advent of a mythical 'Homo sovieticus' (*Sovetskiy chelovek*), but few people in the USSR believe in this dream. A Soviet Russian remains a Russian, a Soviet Muslim simply a Muslim, not a 'Homo Islamicus', another mythical monster born out of the minds of some Western political scientists.

This book is an attempt to place the current problem of Soviet Islam in its historical perspective. We believe that the roots of this problem go back to the time of the Golden Horde, the conquest of Kazan, and also to the revolt of the Basmachis in 1920 and the 'Holy War' of Shamil. The history of Soviet Islam is long, glorious and tragic, dominated as it has been by seven centuries of conflict with Muscovy and later Russia and the USSR. This inheritance could never be annihilated by the Socialist Revolution. The past has not been forgotten, but on the contrary is still present, continuing to mould the *Weltanschauung* of the Soviet Muslims as well as that of the Soviet Russians, from the most sophisticated intelligentsia to the rural and urban masses.

We believe that a thousand years of history is crucially important to a proper understanding of the complex relationship between

Foreword

Russians and Muslims and outweighs the Marxist–Leninist 'Nationalities Policy' which has been tried out for fifty years and which now shows unmistakable signs of failing.

ACKNOWLEDGEMENTS

The authors would like to express their thanks to Madame Marianne Dumont for her sterling work in preparing the manuscript of this book and for her valuable advice, to Michael Broxup, a long-suffering husband who provided much support, as well as their good friends Robert and Caroline Scallon, who struggled to interpret the authors' foreign syntax and helped turn it into acceptable English.

INTRODUCTION

When this book is published, the Muslim population of the USSR will be between 45 and 50 million, making it the fifth largest in the world after Indonesia, Pakistan, India and Bangladesh, far ahead of Egypt, Turkey or Iran.

In the USSR, the term 'Muslim' is generally used to describe a people who before the 1917 Revolution belonged to the Muslim religion and culture. It has, therefore, a national and cultural significance beyond the purely religious one. A religious culture fourteen centuries old which is as deeply rooted in the popular lore as Islam, penetrating all aspects of everyday private and public life, could not and has not been destroyed in fifty years by massive anti-religious propaganda. It still permeates the psychology, the character and the behaviour of Soviet Muslims — including those who are officially considered as non-believers — and it makes them significantly different from the average Soviet Russian citizen.

Several sociological surveys conducted in recent years in the Muslim territories of the USSR have revealed the proportion of atheists among Soviet Muslims to be around 20 per cent of the population (among the Russians the figure is 80 per cent), with the remaining 80 per cent divided between various categories of 'believers': by personal conviction, by tradition or under the pressure of the family 'milieu'. But even those officially listed as 'atheists', such as members of the Communist Party, or the Komsomol, or high-level intelligentsia who are obliged professionally to fight 'obnoxious religious survival', maintain certain ties with the religion. In particular, the majority observe the three basic religious rites which mark the private life of every Muslim and which make his behaviour so different from that of his Russian or other non-Muslim comrades: circumcision, religious marriage and religious burial in a special Muslim cemetery. According to all recent surveys, these family rites are performed by 95 to 99 per cent of the Muslim population. The surveys revealing this curious phenomenon lend support to the theory that absolute atheists do not exist in Muslim lands.

Soviet Islam belongs to the very heart of the Muslim tradition. For a thousand years Central Asia and the Caucasus played a central role in the development of Muslim culture and the history of the *Dar ul-Islam*. These territories, part of the Turko-Iranian world, were the seat of

1

mighty empires and brilliant centres of learning as important for the historical development of Islam as a whole as Turkey, Iran or India. It is enough that Tamerlan had his capital in Samarkand, that literary Persian was first used in Bukhara and that the greatest Muslim philosopher, Ibn Sina, was a native of Khwarezm.

Islam was brought to the territory of the present-day Soviet Union, first to Eastern Transcaucasia (Albania of the Caucasus, then in majority Christian and Mazdean) as early as the seventh century — the first century of Hijra — by the conquering Arab armies during the period of the Medina Califate. In 642, the Arabs occupied Azerbayjan and in 685 they took Derbent, which was to remain for many centuries the extreme northern frontier town of Islam facing the world of the Turkic nomads. The conquest of the Eastern Caucasus was followed by a rapid and complete Islamisation with practically no opposition. Eastern Transcaucasia remained tied to the history of the Califate and of the Iranian world as late as the Russian conquest in the nineteenth century. When Shiism became the official religion of the Safavi dynasty in the late fifteenth century, Azerbayjan followed Iran and accepted Shiism as the dominant creed of Muslim Transcaucasia.

In the seventh century, Arab armies advanced into Central Asia, a region with an old civilisation deeply impregnated by Buddhist-Manichaean and Nestorian-Christian influences. In 673 they crossed the Amu Darya, conquered Bukhara in 676 and, in 751, on the banks of the river Talas, they routed a Chinese army sent by the Tang Emperor to buttress his distant Central Asian vassals. Between 706 and 716 they took the entire sedentary territory south of Syr Darya and finally in the tenth century Islam became the religion of Central Asia with just a small group of Bukharian Jews resisting the onslaught. From this time on, Central Asia became one of the most prestigious cultural centres of the *Dar ul-Islam*.

After the Arabs, the expansion of Islam in the territory of the present-day USSR continued for thirteen centuries, as the result of the diplomatic action of the Califate (conversion of the Volga Bulghars) and later of the Ottoman Empire. Later this process was assisted by the personal missionary activity of Sufi orders from Central Asia and the Caucasus. Paradoxically, the Russian conquest of the Muslim lands between the mid-sixteenth century and 1900 did not stop the progress of Islam; it went on with relentless dynamism until by the time the October Revolution broke out it was a conquering religion, steadily spreading in Eastern Russia and making new converts among the animist or superficially Christian Eastern Finnic population of the Volga.

Thus, for centuries, the Muslim territories of Central Asia, the Caucasus, Volga and Crimea maintained the closest possible contact with the rest of the Muslim world, sharing as they did the same culture and history, being ruled by the same dynasties and speaking and writing the same language. The Russian conquest did not fundamentally change this situation, for even as late as the nineteenth century ideas, political doctrines and individuals were constantly moving back and forth over the Tsarist Empire's southern borders with the Ottoman Empire, Iran and Muslim India. In 1917, Baku and Samarkand still belonged to the *Dar ul-Islam* and were closer to Tabriz and Isfahan than to Moscow or Petrograd.

Around 1924, an iron curtain was pulled down on Soviet Islam and for more than half a century the Muslim world has been deprived of one of its most vital constituents. Central Asia and the Caucasus were now cut off from the rest of the *Dar ul-Islam* and subjected to a complex process of modernisation and social engineering, the final outline of which is impossible to predict. Of course, the present-day rulers of Russia pretend that their treatment of Muslim territories has been a total success and that for the first time in history, former colonies exploited by an imperialist power have been integrated as equal and willing partners into a commonwealth of free socialist nations.

The same rulers claim that the new community is built on entirely novel foundations — socialist, proletarian and internationalist. All the religious, cultural, social and historical differences between partners have disappeared or should do so, to be replaced by a new Soviet culture. A new human being — 'Soviet Man' (*Sovetskiy chelovek*) will emerge, liberated from the past, free and happy. There will be no spiritual, intellectual or even physical difference between Russians and Uzbeks, Estonians and Kirghiz, they will share the same culture, believe in the same Marxism-Leninism, eat the same food and adore the same rulers. Soviet Man's culture will be the harmonious blending of all the best elements from all national cultures: Lenin and Andrei Rublev, Brezhnev and Ibn Sina. But in order to achieve this final solution, it is essential to protect the development of this new community, threatened as it was by various forces of evil: capitalist encirclement, clerical fanaticism, aggressive imperialists, reactionary bourgeois nationalists . . . always defeated but never totally destroyed. Soviet Muslim territories were therefore isolated from the rest of the Muslim world and Islam was condemned to disappear.

The present essay is an attempt to assess the result of the Soviet authorities' efforts over half a century to destroy the past and to create a new basis for relations so as to ensure the survival of the Soviet Empire — if not for ever — at least for a very long period. Have they already succeeded in building this new order as claimed by Stalin several times before his death and by Khrushchev before his removal? Or are they, at least, perceptibly moving towards the 'advanced form of socialism' where local loyalties will wither away to be replaced by one supranational loyalty to Communism and to the Party? Alternatively, are the Muslim territories of the USSR simply the last colonies of a European imperialist state, which will sooner or later confront Moscow with the same insoluble problems that have plagued all other colonial powers? Will the next two decades, therefore, mark the decline of the last colonial empire in the world — the Soviet Union?

In order to give an objective answer to these vital questions, it is necessary to view Russian-Muslim relations from an historical standpoint. In doing so, it is important to bear in mind that these go back to the mid-thirteenth century, and that the Muslim 'problem' inherited by the Soviets from their Tsarist predecessors has, even after several hundred years of trying, proved stubbornly intractable.

Russian-Muslim relations are not, of course, the exclusive preserve of Moscow. It is important also to analyse the reaction of the Muslims to Russian attempts to destroy a civilisation built over fourteen centuries, ending in the latest attempt to impose a sixty-year-old Russian blend of Marxist authoritarianism that seeks to control every aspect of public and private life.

1 RUSSIA AND ISLAM

1 The Protohistory (Ninth to Twelfth Centuries)

Russia's position on the eastern flank of Europe has often been compared to that of Spain on the western side. Both are seen as bulwarks of Christendom facing the hostile world of Islam, of civilisation facing 'barbary'. Russia exhausted herself in a heroic struggle of several centuries, but this sacrifice was not to be in vain, for Europe was saved and could go on to develop its brilliant civilisation well protected by the Russians. The price of this voluntary sacrifice was heavy, since in order to survive and finally to overcome the 'Asian barbarians', Muscovy was obliged to adopt their ways, such as tyranny, despotism, serfdom and lack of liberty. Such is the picture that is painted in nearly all Russian and Soviet historical works. Far-fetched as it is, there are deep reasons for defending this absurd concept. According to the Russians, 'they have suffered more than any other people' and have 'played the role of protectors and saviours', a kind of St George killing the Asiatic dragon and rescuing the European princess. This exclusive position 'gives the Russians certain messianic rights', in particular the right to assume the leadership over their lesser European brothers and to 'civilise' the wild Asiatics.

The reality is of course far from this Manichaean approach to history. When the ancestors of the Russians first came into contact with Asia in the ninth century they were the 'Barbarians', not the highly civilised Muslims.

In the early tenth century, the borderline between 'Civilisation' and 'Barbary' followed more or less exactly the frontier which today separates the Slavic 'European' people of the USSR from the areas populated largely by Muslims: Middle and Lower Volga, North Caucasian mountains, Derbent, Syr Daria. However, 'Barbary' at this time was represented by the 'Europeans', ancestors of the Russians. (There are those who believe that the position has altered little over time.)

For the Muslims, the 'Rus' were wild and primitive natives, purveyors of rare blond slaves and such precious raw materials as fur and ivory. But they were dangerous neighbours and their plundering expeditions (912 and 941–4 raids in the Caspian Sea, the destruction of the Khazar Empire in 945 and the 985 expedition against Bulghar) were described in gruesome detail by early Muslim chroniclers.

During 942–4 the 'Rus' devastated all Muslim Transcaucasia. Berdea, the most prosperous city of Azerbayjan, was completely destroyed and its inhabitants slaughtered. According to Ibn Hawkal, from the 1,200 merchants which existed in the town before the Russian invasion, only 5 remained. In 1850, a Russian historian, Grigor'ev, wrote:

> When anarchy, fanaticism and barbarity were disputing the domination of Europe, the Khazar Empire was a centre of law, order and religious tolerance, a refuge for all those who were persecuted for their belief. It was like a brilliant meteor over the dark horizon of Europe.

In the tenth century, when Russians were still mostly pagans, Islam had already penetrated Eastern Transcaucasia and Daghestan. It had conquered the whole of Turkestan south of Syr Darya and the King of Bulghar in the far north had adopted the religion of the Prophet. Except for the Bulghar Kingdom, all these territories had long been settled with highly developed urban societies going back to the second millennium BC. Even the nomadic Turks of the Caspian steppes — the Khazars — whose feudal nobility had adopted Judaism as their official religion, had attained a higher level of political and cultural development than the ancestors of the Russians, their vassals in the eighth and early ninth centuries.

During the eleventh and twelfth centuries political and cultural equilibrium was established between the sedentary Kievian Rus, Christianised and civilised by Byzantium and the nomadic Qypchaqs (Polovtsy) — heirs to the Khazars who ruled over the Steppe territories between the Dniepr and the Aral Sea.

Contrary to the commonly accepted but totally misleading version put forward by Russian historians, relations between sedentary Russians and nomadic Turks were not limited only to plundering expeditions and punitive counter-expeditions, but included wide cultural and diplomatic exchanges between partners who treated each other as equals. Moreover, during this period Turkic princesses often married Kievian princes. (It is a well known historical fact that the vassal seeks the hand of his suzerain's daughter.) This happy period ended with the Mongol invasion, but not before a considerable number of Turkic, Iranian and even Arabic words synonymous with advanced societies were borrowed and have become so thoroughly Russified as to make it nearly impossible to recognise their Asiatic origins: *chugun, bulat, topor, sablia, saray, bumaga, khram, terem, yazyk, ochag, cherdak, loshad', chemodan, bogatyr, magazin, karandash, karaul*, etc. In contrast, Slavic vocabulary made no impression on Turkic languages — at least until the nineteenth century.

In the eleventh and twelfth centuries, the equilibrium which existed between the sedentary Kievian civilisation and the steppe nomads in the Black Sea–Caspian Sea area could be likened to an outwardly similar situation between the sedentary Irano-Turkic and nomadic Turko-Mongol worlds along the line of Syr Daria. To draw any sort of parallel would, however, be wrong. In Central Asia, Bukhara of the Samanids and the Empire of the Seljuqs were the great centres of world culture at that time and the defence line on Syr Daria marked the border between civilisation and barbary. There could be no borrowing of Mongol-Turkic or Manchu words from the Qara Khitay by the Persians or the Seljuqs and a Samanid king or a Khwarezm shah would never dream of marrying the daughter of a nomad chieftain roaming the Mongolian outback.

One element only was common to both: lack of any religious problem. This stemmed from the nomads' tolerance towards religious matters and willingness to drop their ancestral Shamanism for the more enlightened Islam in Turkestan and Christianity in the West.

2 The Tatar Yoke (Thirteenth to Fifteenth Centuries)

The dramatic arrival of the Chingissid Mongols destroyed for ever the equilibrium between the settled peoples and the nomads in Eastern Europe. The Mongol invasions in Iran, China and elsewhere all began with a decisive blow against sedentary peoples, with wholesale destruction of the urban way of life, massive slaughter of inhabitants and displacement of important groups such as soldiers, scholars and craftsmen.

If one were to compare the destruction wrought by the Mongols in China, Iran and Russia in terms of cities destroyed and people massacred, China would easily take first place, Iran and Central Asia would come second, with Russia trailing far behind. If, on the other hand, the yardstick used were the scars left by the invasion, then Russia would come first. In China and Iran, the Mongol invasion was only one — even if the most dreadful — of many major catastrophes which befell these two countries. Their urban civilisation was too deeply rooted to be destroyed even by the Mongols. Thus the wounds healed with an astonishing speed and life and culture went on.

The level of civilisation, whether in Kubilay's China, the khanate of Chagatay or in Iran under the Ilkhans, was certainly not inferior to that of the pre-Mongol era. The same cannot be said, however, for Russia, not just because of the collapse of the old order, but mainly because the new Russia did not participate in the extraordinary, century-long, economic prosperity brought by the 'Pax Mongolica' to all the countries between the Black Sea and the Pacific Ocean bordering the main commercial highways linking Europe to China (Silk Road) and to India (Spices Road). Southern Russia was so thoroughly ruined and depopulated that it never recovered, while Northern Russia was by-passed in the economic exchange between East and West.

The three centuries of the Mongol yoke proved an era of economic hardship for the Russians, but one of relative political and cultural freedom. Mongol rule was exercised indirectly. The Golden Horde rulers quickly learned to rely entirely on their vassals. Even when the ruling elite of the Golden Horde became Muslim, it maintained the traditional religious tolerance of Chingiz Khan.

All Russian historians have commented on the impact of the Mongol–Tatar yoke on Russia's historical development. Almost all of them explain Russian cultural backwardness, social inequality, the despotism of the rulers and the abject servility of the subjects by the Mongol example. Absolute monarchy, serfdom, arrogant messianism are presented as the direct legacy of the Golden Horde. While discussion of these phenomena is outside the scope of this book, it is interesting to speculate why the same unfortunate legacy was not left to other countries such as China, Iran, Turkestan, Georgia or Armenia under direct Mongol rule and which during this period enjoyed exceptional peace.

The real impact of the Mongol rule on Russian history must be sought elsewhere. It gave the Russians a deep respect for the political superiority of the Tatars and, as a corollary, a long-lasting inferiority complex towards their former masters which survives to this day and gives Russian-Muslim relations their unique character. These relations are not those of a classical 'colonial' type, where the European master, hated as he may be, was, at the same time, respected for his better organisation, greater technical skill and superior military power. The native Muslims in the USSR, even when obliged to recognise and to yield to the supremacy of their Russian 'Elder Brother', do not feel inferior in cultural or political matters. Ayaz Iskhaki, a Tatar pre-revolutionary historian, summed it up in one question: 'How did it happen that we became slaves of our former slaves?'

One among many consequences of this strange relationship where the 'Elder Brother' has an inferiority complex toward his 'Lesser Brother' is the deeply rooted, almost atavistic, hatred of the Russians towards the Muslims in general and toward the Turco-Tatar Muslim in particular. It has survived for centuries and it makes the cultural or biological symbiosis between different Soviet nationalities a hopeless dream.

3 Russian Conquest of Muslim Lands — 1552–1900

The expansion of the Russian Empire in the Muslim lands lasted 348 years. It started in 1552 with the conquest of Kazan and came to a temporary halt only in 1900, with the occupation of the Pamirs. Halted for 79 years, the drive forward of the same empire under Soviet guise was resumed in December 1979, with the invasion of Afghanistan by the Soviet Army and the extension, *de facto* if not *de jure*, of the Soviet political border as far as the Khyber Pass.

Russian expansion into the Muslim lands can be divided into three stages: first, the expansion of the Tsardom of Moscow, from 1552 to 1605, then the long period of relative quiet when Russia was expanding in the West, which began with the Time of Troubles and lasted practically until the reign of Catherine II and, lastly, the conquests under the Romanovs, from Catherine II to 1900, when Russia's expansion was directed towards Asia.

3.1 The Expansion of the Tsardom of Moscow — Sixteenth Century

Ivan the Terrible, whose reign saw the beginning of the conquest of the Muslim lands, inherited a twofold parallel and contradictory tradition of statehood. The oldest and the most deeply rooted was the heritage of Byzantium. Muscovy's ruler was the inheritor of the Greek Basileus and the Tsardom was modelled on the 'Second Rome', the Greek Orthodox Imperium. According to this legacy, which dominated the political 'ideology' of Ivan's father, Basil III, and grandfather, Ivan III, there was a perfect fusion between religion and state, between Orthodoxy and nationality. Moscow's realm corresponded to the expansion of the Russian Christian Orthodox world, and a subject of the Tsar could only be a *pravoslavnyi*. During this happy era, Muscovy was a nation state, or rather a religion-state, and had no nationality problem. Lithuanian princes and Tatar noblemen were free to come to Moscow to serve the Great Prince and to become Orthodox and Russian.

The other pervading influence was the result of Ivan the Terrible's personal *Weltanschauung*. In this the Tsar was the heir both to the Constantinople Basileus and the Great Khan of the Mongol Empire. He was therefore the most piously Christian sovereign, last warden of true Christian Orthodoxy, defender of the true faith against the Latin heretics in the West and the 'Busurmans' in the South and East. As such he had to be vigilant against heresy, heterodoxy and unbelief, and it was under his reign that the Church in Moscow became involved in missionary activity among the pagans still numerous in the northern territories and the new Muslim subjects of the Tsar. But as a successor of the Mongol Emperors and the Chingisside eucumenism, the 'White Khan' as he was called by his new Muslim subjects (this was the title of the ruler of the western part of the Mongol Empire, white being the colour of the West according to the traditional Turco-Mongol division of the world) was tolerant in religious matters and eagerly accepted Muslims as his loyal subjects — at least when they belonged to the upper level of the Tatar or Caucasian feudal nobility.

Ivan's second wife, Maria Temrükovna, was born Muslim and bore the beautiful name of Altynjan ('The Golden Soul') before her conversion to Christianity. The Tsar's father-in-law, Temrük, Prince of the Kabarda, remained Muslim, as did several brothers and cousins of the Tsarina, all of whom served the Tsar loyally in Moscow. At the court were many Nogay *mirzas* (relatives of Malhorub, the Tsarina's elder sister, who married the Chief of the Great Nogy Horde), as well as several Chingisside princes who descended from the Siberian, Crimean, Kazan and Astrakhan khans. What is more, the second more important figure in the Tsardom after Ivan was the Khan (Tsar) of Kasimov, Sain-Bulat (nephew of the Tsarina Maria Temrükovna). He turned Orthodox Christian under the name of Simeon Bekbulatovich only when Ivan decided to abdicate in his favour. The throne of Russia was thus momentarily occupied by a descendant of Chinghiz Khan (1575–6).

Ivan's extraordinary religious liberalism contrasts curiously with the intolerance of his own ancestors (especially that of his grandfather Ivan III), but even more so with the fanaticism which characterised Western Europe at the same time, when Catholics and Protestants were busily exterminating each other.

The spirit of religious tolerance in the newly conquered Muslim lands was imposed by the Tsar personally. The first bishop of Kazan, Mgr. Gurii, received a special order from Ivan to avoid brutality when dealing with the new Muslim subjects, and while conversion to Christianity was advisable, it had to be conducted 'with love and sympathy and never by force'. This religious liberalism of Ivan the Terrible — a ruler renowned as a bloodthirsty tyrant — was not only a unique phenomenon for his time, it is also a unique event in the history of Russia. After his death began a long era of religious intolerance which lasted practically until Catherine II.

Muscovy's drive eastward was rapid and, contrary to Russian and Soviet historiography, never took on the character of a crusade against Islam. Neither did Muslim resistance take on the aspect of a *jihad* or defensive 'Holy War' against the advance of Christendom. Muscovy's Muslim neighbours looked upon Ivan as 'one of their own', as a 'White' Khan, an inheritor of the Mongol Empire and his drive eastward as the 'gathering' of the western part of the Mongol Empire — the *ulu*s of Batu. Neither the Ottoman Sultan-Calife nor the Central Asian Shaybani rulers paid the slightest attention to Russian expansion. Only Devlet Giray, the Crimean Khan, tried in vain to oppose Moscow and save Kazan and Astrakhan, possibly because he too had his sights on the *ulu*s of Batu or was simply more discerning of the threat to the balance of power.

The expansion towards the Muslim lands began in 1552, with the conquest of Kazan. The fall of this strongest Tatar khanate, Muscovy's rival for more than a century, opened to the Russians the Volga road to the Caspian Sea and the door to Siberia. In 1556 Astrakhan, the weakest of Tatar khanates, fell to the Russians, followed by the khanate of Sibir in 1584. Crimean Tatars tried unsuccessfully to check the Russian advance by attacking Muscovy's southern border, but they lacked the support of the Nogay Horde, the mightiest Muslim military power in the area, who remained neutral and even showed some sympathy towards the Tsar of Moscow. In 1559, and once again in 1584, the Russians tried to complete the 'gathering' of the Western Mongol *ulu*s by attacking Crimea, the last surviving Tatar khanate. The offensive led by Muscovite armies, Don Cossacks and Western Cherkess tribes was repulsed by the Crimeans with the help of the Ottoman garrisons of Kefe and Azaq.

Although it went practically unnoticed in the contemporary Muslim world, the conquest of Muslim territories along the Volga and in Western Siberia was a major economic and political set-back for Islam. The possession of the Volga highway and the West Siberian forests gave to the Russians a world monopoly of the fur trade (which was at the origin of Kazan's wealth and power), and from 1552 onwards Moscow became the centre of this market. Trade with the Ottoman Empire and the Safavi Iran, the principal consumers of northern furs, especially priceless sable, earned Moscow large quantities of precious metals without which Muscovy could never dream of becoming a modern 'gunpowder' state able to subsidise a large sophisticated bureaucracy and a regular army. Politically, the set-back was just as disastrous. The conquest of Astrakhan and the appearance of the Russians on the shores of the Caspian Sea established a close link between Moscow and the Shia Safavi Empire in Iran. Since both powers were struggling against the same enemies, Ottoman Turks, Crimean Tatars and Shaybani Uzbeks, the link became close, culminating after Ivan's death in a full-blown diplomatic and military alliance against the Sunnis. The alliance was to have another dramatic consequence: the Russian lock on the Southern Volga together with the Safavi lock on the Caspian Sea cut the Muslim Sunni world in two and, despite all Ottoman, Tatar and Uzbek efforts (such as the 1569 unsuccessful Ottoman and Tatar campaign against Astrakhan) contact between the Western Turks (Ottoman and Tatars) and the Eastern Turks (Shaybani Uzbeks of Central Asia) could never be re-established. For the Ottoman Empire, this was to have long-lasting and ominous repercussions, although it was not understood as such at the time. Never again would the Ottoman rulers receive from Central Asia, the original homeland of the Turks, the support of the warlike tribes and clans which used to enlist under the banner of the Ottoman Sultan in the fifteenth century. For the Central Asian Turks it marked the beginning of total economic and political isolation, the closing of the Silk Road and the beginning of a long era of decadence in all fields — military, intellectual and economic.

Finally, three areas of the *Dar ul-Islam*, Middle Volga, Lower Volga and Western Siberia, were lost forever. It was, after the loss of Andalusia, the second great set-back for Islam, and it marked the beginning of the long retreat of Islam and the conquering advance of the Christian world.

Ivan the Terrible died in 1584. He was the first and only liberal sovereign in religious matters to rule Russia and to understand that Muscovy — a world empire in the making — belonged to two worlds, the Christian West and the nomadic Muslim East, and that it could only pretend to world leadership by following the tradition of the Mongol Empire. Ivan's son and successor Feodor, and Boris Godunov who succeeded Feodor, maintained the southward drive, but under a completely different ideological banner. Feodor, a pious Orthodox, behaved as the heir of Byzantium, the sovereign of the Third Rome, and was indifferent to the ideal of the Chingisside 'oecumene'. Under his reign the colonisation of the Tatar territory of the Middle Volga began.

The native Muslims were offered the choice of conversion or expulsion from major cities (including Kazan) and confiscation of their richest land for distribution among the Russian landed nobility, the monasteries and later the Russian peasants.

The Muslims were no longer treated as equals, as under Ivan the Terrible, but as 'second-rate' subjects to whom the rights reserved to Christians were denied. An intense missionary activity was launched by the archbishops of Kazan and the newly built monasteries brought to Christianity a relatively large group of Turkic natives, both animist and Muslim. They became Christian Orthodox, but maintained the use of their Tatar language (which also served as a liturgic language) and formed a separate isolated community — the Staro-Kryashens, in Tatar Taze Kryash — despised by Russians and Muslims alike. This community has survived until the present day.

Thus, under the reign of Tsar Feodor, Muscovy created for itself a 'nationality problem' to be handed on to the Imperial Russia of St Petersburg and later to the Soviet Union. Muscovy ceased to be a purely Russian Orthodox nation state and became a multinational Empire, in which one nationality or rather one religious group enjoyed privileged rights, the others being reduced to the rank of second-rate citizens. At the same time, Muscovy was unable to liquidate or to expel the Muslims from the newly conquered territories as the Spaniards had succeeded in doing in Andalusia.

However, in the sixteenth century the problem was still minor, since the Muslim native population was rapidly reduced to the status of a minority firmly set in the framework of Russian settlement. The policy applied by the Russian government was harsh: the former ruling classes were destroyed through economic ruin or conversion to Christianity, the activities of the religious establishment severely circumscribed and the masses submitted to strong attempts at cultural assimilation. The result was a series of violent uprisings led by the Tatar feudal aristocracy and, following their failure, the massive exodus of Tatars eastward, towards Bashkiriya, the Kazakh steppes and Turkestan. This has left the Tatars with a lasting hatred of Russia which they passed on to the other Muslim peoples similarly subjugated and which still survives, more than four centuries later.

Between 1584, the year which marked the beginning of the 'Time of Troubles' and 1605, Russian expansion was directed mainly south, towards the North Caucasus, the Kabardian territory and Daghestan.

The offensive began with the occupation of the Lower Volga valley and the building of several fortresses to prevent the nomads from crossing the Volga. In 1587, the Russians had already reached as far as the Terek in the Caucasian lowlands, and built the fortress of Terskii Gorodok which served as a springboard for further advance. In 1590, pushing further south, they built another fortress on the lower Sunzha river. They were thus ready for a major breakthrough into the Caucasus and nearer to their Iranian allies.

This time, realising the danger, the Ottomans and the Crimean Tatars reacted vigorously. In 1587, the Crimean Khan launched a major offensive against Kabarda, Moscow's ally, razing it to the ground.

In the same year, the Shamhal of Tarku, the most powerful ruler in Daghestan, who had hesitated between Moscow and the Ottomans, finally sided with the Turks and became their staunchest ally in the Caucasus.

In 1590, the Turks in their campaign against the Iranians in Trans-caucasia pushed northward to reach Derbent occupying Shirwan. In the process a Turkish galley fleet roamed the Caspian Sea for a while. In 1591, the Crimean Khan Bora Ghazi Giray II finally launched a major expedition against Moscow, but was severely defeated. In the same year, Russian troops reached the Sulak river and built a fortress, only to be driven out three years later by a joint force of Ottomans and Daghes-tanis. In 1595, however, the Russian hold on the Lower Volga area was strengthened by the construction of a fortress on the Yaik river. From this time onward the Russians were in control of the entire steppe terri-tory north of the Caspian Sea and could impose their will over the nomads.

In 1604, the Tsar Boris Godunov undertook a major offensive in the North Caucasus, the conquest of Daghestan, which would have opened to the Russians the road to Iran. A large expedition was launched which at first met with some success when Tarku, the capital of Shamhal, was taken by the Russians and destroyed. However, the attempt finally ended in disaster, when the Daghestanis, with the help of the Ottomans, routed the Muscovite army; all Russian fortresses on the Sulak, Sunzha and Terek rivers were destroyed and the Russian front line pushed back as far as Astrakhan.

Thus, Muscovy's offensive against Muslim territories ended, in the sixteenth century, with mixed results: a great success on the Volga and in Western Siberia but a significant set-back in the Caucasus. In a strategic move, the Ottoman Turks and the Crimean Tatars, realising the danger of the Russian advance, took steps to reinforce the presence of Islam among the mountain peoples in North Caucasus. Competition in Kabarda between Christianity and Islam ended with a total Muslim victory.

Hence, North Caucasus steadily became a Muslim stronghold and served in the nineteenth century as a bastion of Islamic resistance to Russian advance towards the southern seas.

3.2 Seventeenth to Eighteenth Centuries

The Time of Troubles completely ruined the Muscovite state and stopped Russian expansion in the East for almost two centuries. When in the middle of the seventeenth century Moscow recovered its power and dynamism under the reign of Tsar Alexis, it was no longer looking towards Asia but towards the West. For two centuries Russia fought Poland and Sweden, conquered Ukraine and the Baltic states until it 'opened a window to Europe' under Peter the Great.

Throughout this period Russia remained on the defensive along her southern borders. The main effort was to repulse the plundering expeditions of the Crimean Tatars and to avoid Ottoman expansion in the Ukraine. No attempts were made to conquer North Caucasus. Peter's efforts to reach the Black Sea ended in failure with the disastrous Prut campaign in 1711, with the result that Russian expansion in that direction was put off until the reign of Catherine II. Peter's expedition towards Iran met with temporary success: Derbent was occupied and so too were Ghilan and Mazanderan. But a few years later Nadir Shah forced the Russians to retreat to their former frontier on the Terek and to abandon further attempts at conquest.

It was in the steppe area, stretching from the Urals and the northern shores of the Caspian Sea to the Tian Shan mountains and across Siberian forests to the Aral Sea that the Russians continued their advance. This task was facilitated by the war between the Buddhist Mongol Jungarians and Kalmyks, established since 1613 in the Lower Volga area, and the nomadic Muslim Kazakhs and Nogays, which was to reduce the mighty Turkic hordes to a state of total impotence. Taking advantage of the anarchy reigning in the steppes, the Russians advanced slowly from Siberia, building fortresses on the way: Omsk in 1716, Semipalatinsk in 1718, Ust-Kamenogorsk in 1719. The Kazakh tribal federations, unable to resist the superior military might of the Jungarians, invoked Russia's help and asked for protection. This was accorded to the Lesser (Eastern) Horde in 1742. The Russian appearance on the scene coincided with the military decline of the Jungarians following their defeat by the Manchus. Henceforth no rivals could challenge Russian rule. The nominal protection accorded to the Kazakhs in the beginning was gradually transformed into virtual possession: Russian fortresses were built in the heart of the steppes and along the border with China in Semirechie, and little by little the Russians introduced their own direct administration alongside the old feudal system exercised by the native rulers.

From 1605 until the 1770s Russian influence over the Muslim territories of the Middle Volga, Urals, Western Siberia and Lower Volga–Caspian Sea area was steadily strengthened. Ironically the process was helped by waves of peasants fleeing serfdom in Central Russia to settle in the Muslim lands, thereby reducing the natives to the status of a minority threatened by a systematic policy of assimilation. The government in St Petersburg meanwhile was encouraging the inflow of foreign specialists, and was prepared to accept them as equals among the Russian nobility during the first half of the eighteenth century, to the extent that 'foreigners' virtually ran the state apparatus. While Russia allowed itself effectively to be governed by a foreign aristocracy of Catholic and Protestant persuasion, few of whom spoke Russian or considered themselves as anything more than servants of the Emperor, paradoxically the country was not seen by its rulers to be a multinational Empire but a Russian and Orthodox 'nation state'. The presence of a large body of Muslim Tatars a mere 200 miles east of Moscow was seen as an intolerable blight on this landscape which had to be eliminated, and their conversion to Orthodoxy was seen as the best way of solving this 'nationality problem'. From the reign of the first Romanov, the Tsar Mikhaïl, to that of Catherine II, Islam was treated as an alien, hostile body and various measures were taken to liquidate it completely: mosques were closed or destroyed (between 1738 and 1755, 418 out of 536 mosques of the Kazan *gubernia* disappeared); *waqf* property was confiscated by the state; special schools were opened for the children of the converted Tatars; intense missionary activity was instituted while Muslim counter-measures were punishable by death; Muslims were expelled from villages where groups of converts had been formed and deported to remote districts. The first half of the eighteenth century — the reigns of Peter the Great and his successors, especially that of the Tsarina Anna (1738–55) — could be compared in terms of the persecution of Muslims to the worst period of Stalin's anti-religious campaign in the 1930s. Notable among the consequences of these pressures were the continued exodus of the Volga Tatars towards Central Asia and Siberia and the active part played by the Tatars — Muslims and converted Kryashens — and the Bashkirs in the great popular uprisings of the seventeenth and eighteenth centuries (Stepan Razin and Pugachev respectively).

3.3 *The Expansion of the Russian Empire*

Russian expansion into Muslim Asia was resumed under the reign of Catherine II and continued unabated until shortly before the Revolution. In 1771, the Crimean Peninsula was occupied by Russian troops. In 1774, the Ottoman protectorate over Crimea came to an end and the khanate became officially an independent state, but in reality a Russian protectorate. In 1782, the last Tatar Khan, Shahin Giray, was expelled and the territory of the khanate annexed by Russia. The conquest of the North Caucasus began in 1783, but the Russians met with fierce resistance from the Mountaineers, organised by the Sufi Naqshbandi brotherhood, and it took almost a century to conquer this relatively small territory. In 1856, the surrender of the last Naqshbandi leader, Imam Shamil, signified the end of the Caucasian wars, although in the Daghestan and Chechen regions the Russians were obliged to maintain their presence by military means rather than by a civil administration. To this day they remain the most insecure territories of the Soviet Union.

Finally, as soon as the Caucasian wars were over, Russia embarked on the systematic occupation of Central Asia, where it met sporadic resistance. The native principalities, Bukhara, Khiva and Kokand, had long ago lost all their economic prosperity and political power and were thus unable, if not unwilling, to oppose the overwhelming might of the Tsarist Empire. The conquest which was to take almost half a century to complete began with the submission of Chimkent in 1855. Ten years later the Russians occupied Tashkent and in 1868, his army defeated, the Emir of Bukhara was obliged to sign a treaty placing his state under Russian protection. Khiva's turn came in 1873 after Russian troops had occupied the capital city of the khanate. Two years later the Russians invaded Kokand and in 1870 the khanate of Kokand was abolished and its territory placed under direct Russian military control as the 'Governorate-General of Turkestan'. The conquest of Central Asia was rounded off with the occupation of the Turkmen territory between 1873 and 1884 (in spite of strong resistance from the Yomud and Tekke tribes) and the annexation of the eastern part of the Pamirs in 1900.

The treatment of Islam by the government in St Petersburg and the status of the new Muslim subjects of the Empire changed significantly from the reign of Catherine II to that of Alexander III. Several 'models' were applied at different periods and in different areas, from the most liberal to the harshest.

Catherine II was personally interested in Islam and believed that it was a 'reasonable' religion, better fitted 'to civilise' the 'wild Asian populations' than Orthodox Christianity. Moreover, like her distant predecessor Ivan the Terrible, she had an 'imperial' approach towards Russia and understood that a multinational empire, in which the proportion of non-Russians was constantly and steadily increasing, could only survive if all subjects, notwithstanding their creed and cultural background, were treated as equal. In Crimea, the Muslims were guaranteed equal status with the Russians and the freedom to exercise their religion. The Tatar landed nobility retained its rights and prerogatives and was accepted into the hierarchy of Russian society without being obliged to adopt Christianity. The Muslim religious leadership also retained its wealth based on *waqf* revenues. Theoretically, the Ottoman Sheikh ul-Islam remained the head of the Crimean religious hierarchy and the name of the Turkish Sultan-Calif continued to be mentioned in all Crimean mosques during the Friday *khütbe*. Christian proselytism was forbidden and a non-assimilation policy was tried in Crimea. This liberal treatment assured the loyalty of the Tatar elite to the Romanov dynasty, if not to Russia itself.

However, equality between the Crimean Tatars and their new Russian masters could not last for long. From the first years of Russian rule, Crimea, the most pleasant land of the Empire, comparable with the French and Italian rivieras, received a flood of German, Baltic and Russian immigrants and the best lands, situated along the seashore, was requisitioned for the benefit of Catherine's numerous favourites. In the early nineteenth century Alexander I, a great admirer of Classical Greece, decided to make Crimea the new home for exiled Greeks. Crimea became the 'Government of Taurida' and all the major cities of the Peninsula were renamed with Greek names: Sebastopol, Simferopol and so on. Relegated to the most arid lands of Central Crimea and faced with ever worsening living conditions, the Tatars resorted to their only salvation — exodus. It is estimated that between 1783 and 1913 more than a million Tatars left Crimea for the Ottoman Empire, with the result that in their own homeland the Tatar community was reduced to a small minority submerged by the Russians.

Thus the nationality problem was not resolved by the assimilation of the natives by the Russians but by their expulsion and the transformation of Crimea into a Christian land. However, in 1913 a Tatar minority still remained in Crimea and it was therefore left to the Soviets to provide the final solution, which they did in 1943. There are no Tatars left in Crimea and the territory which played a considerable role in the history of the *Dar ul-Islam* is lost for ever to that world.

In the Volga Region, Catherine II was rewarded in her efforts to correct the dramatic errors of her predecessors from Peter to Elizabeth. The anti-Muslim campaign was halted, schools for Tatar converts were closed and permission was granted to the Tatars for the building of mosques. In 1783 the Tsarina established a Central Muslim Spiritual Board in Orenburg, chaired by the Mufti, to administer the religious life of her Muslim subjects (with the exception of Crimea). This astute policy of courting the Tatar religious and economic elite was a great success and for almost a century the Tatar merchant class became a loyal partner of the Russian government and of the young merchant bourgeoisie, to the great benefit of both sides. The Tatar merchant colonies served as 'scouts' in Siberia, China and Central Asia, which were still closed to the 'Infidels'. In return, the authorities helped the Tatars to build mosques and Quranic schools in Bashkir territory and the Kazakh Steppe.

Volga Tatars enjoyed this uniquely favourable position for almost a century. Their trading colonies spread throughout the Tsarist Empire and beyond to Western Europe, Scandinavia, Manchuria and Central Asia. They were wealthy, prosperous, active communities closely allied to their homeland by cultural and religious ties. In the nineteenth century, the Volga-Ural Tatar cities became important cultural centres and several Tatar *madrassah*s in Kazan, Ufa, Orenburg and Troitsk gained a world-wide reputation. The *jadid* movement, often called the 'Tatar Renaissance of the nineteenth century', was made possible by the extraordinary economic prosperity of the entire community.

This era of prosperity and co-operation came to an end after the Russian conquest of Central Asia eliminated the need for the commercial and diplomatic services of Tatar middlemen in Turkestan. The Russian and Tatar bourgeoisies, once allied, became competitors and new pressures were brought to bear by the Russian government on the Tatars as economic and religious rivals.

The Russian state again tried to solve the 'nationality problem' in the Volga region by assimilating the Tatar subjects of the Tsar. This time, however, the methods were less rigid — and consequently more efficient — than those adopted in the eighteenth century. Cultural Russification had proved counter-productive and was therefore given up, to be replaced by a new policy (elaborated in 1863 by Nikolas Il'minsky of the Religious Academy of Kazan) which aimed at the creation of a new Tatar intelligentsia, converted to Orthodoxy but speaking and writing Tatar. The process was confined to religion, for Il'minsky considered a non-Russian Orthodox a more reliable proposition than a Russian atheist. This new intelligentsia alone was to be entrusted with missionary work among Muslim Tatars, but it was invited to do so on the basis that their links with their cultural past would be maintained. This approach quickly achieved spectacular success (between 1865 and 1900 more than 100,000 Tatars are estimated to have been converted to Christianity), so much so that it was seen as a threat to the very survival of the Tatar Muslim community. At the same time, the policy created solid resentment among the stauncher members of the community and set them — elite and masses — against Russia and the Russians with lasting consequences.

In the Causcasus, conquered after a fierce resistance, the Russians applied a different policy. The status of nobility was granted to Kabardian, Ossetian and to some Cherkess feudal leaders not involved in the resistance movement, whilst it was denied to the Daghestanis, who had formed the backbone of Shamil's movement. Muslim Caucasians were not granted status as 'citizens' of the Russian Empire, but remained 'natives' (*inorodtsy*) not subject to military service. It would thus seem that the Russian government had no clearly defined strategy when dealing with North Caucasian Islam. Russian rural colonisation was encouraged in the lowlands and in the North-Western Caucasus, that is in the Cherkess territory. In the 1860s over a million Cherkess left the Caucasus for the Ottoman Empire. Their exodus left the Russians sole masters and reduced the native Muslims who remained to the status of a weak minority. On the other hand, the migration did not touch the North-Eastern Caucasus. The mountains of Daghestan and of the Chechen territory remained inviolate and no attempt was made to colonise them. The lowlands were, however, intensively colonised by the local Cossacks (Kuban, Terek, Grebenskie) and by new peasant settlers (*inogorodnye*) and the natives pushed towards the mountains, where the Russian presence made itself felt by a few scattered military posts. The Russian authorities refrained from interfering in the internal affairs of the country and limited their activity to the maintenance of law and order. No assimilation policy was introduced. Proselytism among the Mountaineers was strictly forbidden, except in Ossetia and Abkhazia where Christianity had sunk into animism and was threatened by Islam.

In the Kazakh steppes, Russian rule replaced that of the khans in the 1820s. At the outset the Russian authorities did not encourage the settlement of Russian peasants or try to assimilate the Kazakhs. The Kazakhs remained 'natives', preserved their customary laws (*adat court*) and even an embryonic self-government exercised by the tribal Councils of Elders. Until the reign of Alexander II missionary activity by the Orthodox Church was discouraged.

The Kazakh ruling class, the tribal feudal aristocracy, was granted a privileged status and, although not admitted into the Russian nobility, it remained rich and influential. The children of the Kazakh noblemen were accepted by the Russian military schools, notably in Omsk and Orenburg and by Russian universities. In the steppes, the Russians managed to avoid many of the blunders they committed elsewhere. In particular, instead of opposing the emergence of a national movement, they sponsored the birth of Kazakh nationalism led by the feudal nobility, only superficially Islamised and very proud of its nomadic Mongol origins. (Several of the Kazakh nationalist leaders, such as Chokan Vali Khanov and Ali Khan Bukeykhanov, were descendants of Chingiz Khan.) The Kazakhs were fervent 'Westernisers'; they studied Russian rather than Turkish or Islamic models and were keen to modernise and secularise their people. This impelled them to advocate co-operation with the Russians who were to respond, after 1865, by supporting Kazakh efforts to reduce Tatar and Bukharian influence in the steppes and their efforts to reinforce Islam among the nomads. The Russians also did their best to encourage the revival of traditional Kazakh culture, which was based on Kazakh literary language: Kazakh epic songs were published, anthropological and historical research was encouraged, and from 1841 on, Russian-Kazakh schools were opened.

This praiseworthy effort to establish real co-operation between the Russian state and the Kazakh nomads was not the result of any carefully conceived plan drawn up in St Petersburg, but represented a novel approach on the part of the Russian administrators on the spot who had fallen in love with the romantic aspect of a nomadic society. It was to be short-lived. The immense territory of the steppes with its scarce nomadic population seemed to offer a tempting solution to the eternal problem of pre-revolutionary Russia: the peasants' land hunger. In 1891 the first wave of Russian and Ukrainian settlers reached the steppes, not as in the eighteenth and early nineteenth centuries a disorderly rush of peasants spurred by the prospect of rich land and freedom from serfdom, but an organised migration, planned by the administration. By 1914, over a million Slav peasants from Central Russia and the Ukraine had settled in the richest areas of the steppes along the Chinese border and on the northern fringe of present-day Kazakhstan. The nomad Kazakhs were ruthlessly driven into the poorest areas of Central, Western and Southern Kazakhstan; and with the loss of their pastures and consequently their livestock, their standard of living plunged catastrophically.

By the end of the nineteenth century the Utopia of Russian Kazakh partnership was shattered, and in spite of the mutual goodwill of the local Russian administration and the Kazakh elite conflict between Russian settlers and nomads became a characteristic feature of steppe life. The tragic end came in 1916 when the nomad tribes attacked the settlers, only to be slaughtered by a joint force of Russian military and armed peasants. The survivors were forced to take refuge in China. The deterioration of relations was further accelerated at the turn of the century, when Orthodox missionaries were allowed to operate among the Kazakhs.

As in Crimea, the 'nationality problem' in Kazakhstan had not been solved by Russia. In 1917, the Kazakhs still represented the majority in their land, though the Russians formed a powerful, dynamic and fast-growing minority. The final solution to the problem in the Kazakh Steppes was, as in the Crimea, left to the Soviets to complete. The first attempt began in the 1920s when the Soviets slaughtered the nomads' livestock in an effort to destroy their way of life, which resulted in one and a half million people dying of hunger between 1926 and 1939. Another was made in the 1950s, when Kazakhstan was invaded by a huge wave of Russian rural and urban settlers which reduced the native Kazakhs to the status of a minority.

Muslim Transcaucasia, present-day Azerbaijan, was conquered by the Russians in the late eighteenth and early nineteenth centuries without any serious resistance on the part of the local population. The occupation liberated the territory from the misrule of the Qajars and put an end to a long and bloody period of unrest. Life in Transcaucasia after the conquest continued much as it did before; there was no rural colonisation, the Muslim landed nobility retained its wealth and prestige and the local merchant bourgeoisie profited by the Russian peace. The Russian presence was represented only by the army together with some administrative officials, and missionary activity was forbidden to the Russian Orthodox Church. The Muslims of Transcaucasia were politically and culturally orientated towards the Ottoman Empire in the case of the young progressive intelligentsia, or towards Iran as far as the more religious and conservative older Shia generation was concerned. The 'main enemy' of Islam in Transcaucasia was not the Russians, but the Armenians, whose superior economic power and dynamism threatened to reduce Muslims to the rank of an under-privileged community lagging far behind the ruling Russians and the wealthy Armenians. It was in Azerbaijan that the Tsarist administration was most successful in its endeavours to solve the national problem. This was achieved by using the method of *indirect rule*.

In Turkestan, the last land to be conquered, the Russians applied an altogether different approach: that of a traditional colonial power. In a country of over-populated oases, rural colonisation was impossible, so the numbers of Russian peasants who migrated to Turkestan were insiginificant. On the other hand, a relatively large number of Russian and other 'European' urban elements (civil servants, engineers and workers) settled in the cities, forming 'white' colonies in quarters specially built for them. The general lines of the 'national policy' to be applied in Turkestan were devised by the first Governor-General of the country, General Kaufman. It was somewhat on the lines of the apartheid policy in South Africa, with the natives neither treated as 'citizens' nor drafted into military service. They were isolated from the Russians and the country was cut off from any outside influence, Turkish and Tatar as well as Russian. The aim of this simple strategy was to maintain Turkestan — once one of the most brilliant cultural areas of the Muslim world — in a state of medieval backwardness and deep economic and social stagnation. Proselytism was strictly forbidden to the Russian Orthodox Church and the local Russian administration sought to preserve the most archaic form of Islamic culture. The Tatar modernist (*jadid*) teachers were banned from Central Asia, and the Quranic schools remained true to the most conservative *qadymist* type. No schools along the lines of the Russian-Kazakh model were organised. The Muslim 'clergy' remained wealthy, numerous and influential, and were supported against the Tatar and Turkish reformists, and the more dynamic and xenophobic Sufi brotherhoods, by the Russian authorities. Needless to say, the dream of keeping the immense territory of Central Asia isolated and 'protected' from all exterior influence was an illusion. Foreign influence (Tatar, Turkish, Iranian and even Afghan) played an important role in the political awakening of Turkestan.

It is difficult to recognise any sort of common thread running through Tsarist Russia's treatment of the Muslim problem. The approach varied according to the period, the territory, the 'ideology' prevailing at a given time in Moscow or in St Petersburg and to the extent of the opposition of the Muslim population to the conquest of their lands by the 'Infidel' invader. Russian policy towards the people themselves also varied greatly: the Tatars and the Bashkirs were citizens of the Empire; the Kazakhs and the Turkestanis remained the *inorodtsy*; the Kabardian and the Azerbayjani aristocrats were accepted with their ranks and privileges into the Russian nobility, whereas this was denied the Kazakhs and the Daghestanis; the Volga Tatars were submitted to strong pressure to convert to Christianity, whereas the Crimean Tatars and the Turkestanis were protected from any attempt at assimilation. However, during the three and a half centuries (from 1552 to 1917) during which Russians ruled over their Muslim subjects, various 'tactics' and methods were devised which enabled Moscow and St Petersburg to preserve their colonial empire. These may be classified into eight categories, from the harshest to the most liberal.

(1) Genocide by expulsion. Forced exodus − a crude but efficient policy − was successfully applied to the Western Cherkess tribes, the Abkhazian Muslims and partly to the Crimean Tatars who were forced to migrate to the Ottoman Empire in 1865. This left the rich Kuban lowlands open to Russian rural colonisation, while the Georgians colonised the Abkhazian coastal region.

(2) Genocide through slaughter was attempted later, unsuccessfully, by General Skobelev against the Turkmen tribes (massacre of the Teke tribesmen in Gök-Tepe in 1881).

(3) Genocide through extinction − 'dying out' (*vymiranie*) of a population completely cut off from all external influence and condemned to disappear through sheer 'backwardness'. The policy was applied with some success in the Volga Tatar territory during the sixteenth century, to the Bashkirs (seventeenth century) of the Southern Urals, in Crimea (eighteenth–early nineteenth century), in North-Western Caucasus (late nineteenth century) and finally in the Kazakh Steppes (late nineteenth–early twentieth century).

(4) Assimilation through conversion to Orthodox Christianity, but without cultural and linguistic Russification − a policy applied with great success to the Volga Tatars in the sixteenth century and again in the nineteenth. This same policy was applied to the Kazakhs in the early twentieth century and failed completely.

(5) Assimilation through conversion to Christianity and linguistic and cultural Russification, a policy applied in the seventeenth and eighteenth centuries (before 1783) to the Volga Tatars, with dubious results.

(6) Non-interference ('*laissez-faire*') policy, applied with good results in Azerbayjan in the nineteenth century.

(7) Co-opting of the elite and non-interference in the life of the masses. This policy was applied with some success in Kabarda and Ossetia, and produced results for a time in Kazakhstan.

(8) Policy of real political and economic partnership, applied with brilliant success by Catherine II to the Volga Tatars, and by Alexander II in the second half of the nineteenth century in the Kazakh Steppes.

4 The Soviet Empire — New Attempts to Solve the 'Muslim Problem'

The Soviet Union inherited the 'nationality problem'. For years Soviet leaders claimed that a 'problem' no longer existed in their country, or, if it survived, it was only as a remnant (*perezhitok*) of the pre-socialist era, i.e. of capitalism. The Soviet 'final solution' is claimed to be completely original, based on 'scientific Marxist–Leninist doctrine', owing nothing to the earlier models developed by the Tsarists. The reality, of course, is different; not only does the 'nationality problem' remain unsolved, but it appears more acute and threatening than ever, as the relative importance of the non-Russian element in the Soviet population grows rapidly and the Soviet Union loses its 'Russian character'.

It is true that the new strategy based on Marxist doctrine applied by the Bolsheviks to the nationality question, and to the Muslim minorities in particular, was original. But very rapidly the strategy proved unequal to the task of bringing about a final solution, and the Soviet authorities were forced to find other more practical and less doctrinaire methods. Around 1924 they had already started to look back and in doing so discovered the numerous tactics devised by their Tsarist predecessors for dealing with the Muslims. As a result, Soviet policy towards the Muslim minorities of the USSR developed into a sophisticated blend of Marxism (as interpreted by Stalin) and of various pre-revolutionary Tsarist experiments. It may be summarised, greatly simplified, as follows.

(1) All Soviet citizens are equal. They are 'citizens of the USSR' enjoying the same personal rights and bound by the same duties. There is no religious discrimination. In the case of Soviet Muslims, there is no longer any difference between former Russian citizens (such as Tatars and Bashkirs) and former *inorodtsy* (Turkestanis, Kazakhs, North Caucasians).
(2) The Russians represent the 'Elder Brother', the guide, the model for all Soviet nations. They provide the basis of 'Soviet' culture. Russian patriotism is the basis of Soviet patriotism.
(3) All nationalities of the USSR are equal and enjoy the same collective

rights. This equality is, however, more theoretical than real; the more important groups such as Uzbeks, Tatars and Azeris enjoy some measure of equality with the Russians, but some of the lesser groups are deprived of literary written languages, which mean, among other things, that they can be submitted to a relatively rapid assimilation by the Russians or by some other strong nationality. Some of these groups are also deprived of a national territory.

(4) Religion in the USSR is a private affair and not a criterion for national determination. Therefore there cannot be such a thing as a 'Muslim nation'.

(5) The USSR is a proletarian Marxist–Leninist state, the fatherland of Communism. Communist ideology is compulsory and has no rival. It is more important than national traditions. In case of conflict between 'national' and 'Communist', the latter prevails.

(6) The Communist Party of the USSR is a supranational institution, the spearhead of the world proletariat, and therefore endowed with greater power than the Soviet government. In fact, the totality of the power belongs to the Communist Party.

(7) Soviet society is dynamic, engaged in building socialism and straining towards Communism amidst constant change and evolution. This process draws the different Soviet nationalities closer to each other (*sblizhenie*) and the final stage of this evolution will be the merging of all nationalities (*sliyanie*) into one 'Soviet' nationality with one 'Soviet' culture. A new human being, the 'Soviet man' (*Sovetskiy chelovek*) will emerge with a 'Soviet', 'international', 'proletarian' supranational consciousness. National differences will disappear, national cultures will survive only as folklore. All Soviet citizens will have — as prophesised by Kalinin in the 1920s — 'the *Weltanschauung* of the Petrograd worker'.

When it became clear in the early 1920s that the repetition *ad nauseam* of these seven points of Marxist–Leninist doctrine would not solve the nationality problem, or even hasten its solution, the Soviet leaders — and first of all Stalin — were forced to revert to more practical measures. These new measures, which are still being applied, have nothing to do with Marxism, have no ideological basis and in fact borrow heavily from the old tradition of the Tsarist imperial strategy in dealing with the Muslim 'alien body'.

These measures have never been put down on paper by any Soviet theoretician and must be deduced from over sixty years of Soviet practice. The main difference between the measures adopted by the government of St Petersburg and those of the Soviets lies in the latter's much greater brutality. They may be put into two main categories:

(1) the elimination of the Muslim 'alien body' by genocide or expulsion;

(2) the integration of the same 'alien body' into Soviet society through *Sovietisation* and/or *Russification*.

4.1 Genocide

This drastic solution was tried with varying degrees of success after the war by Stalin against certain Muslim nationalities which had been in contact with German armies or which, although remaining out of reach of the Germans, were nevertheless accused of preparing an anti-Soviet uprising.

It is a well known fact that during the war the non-Russian nationalities did not display great enthusiasm for the defence of the Socialist Fatherland. There were many who, for reasons of ideological conviction or simply the will to survive, preferred the German invader. But it is also true that there were many Russians who sided with the Germans and even fought with the German Army. It is absolutely impossible to establish a scale of 'anti-Sovietism' among different Soviet nationalities; we find Russians who formed the bulk of the 'Vlassov army', Ukrainians of Bendera who fought a guerrilla war against the Red Army long after the defeat of Germany, former prisoners of war, Tatars, Turkestanis, Kalmyks, Georgians, Armenians, Caucasian Mountaineers, etc., who formed legions used by the German High Command to fight resistance movements.

In this respect, the Ukrainians or the Kabardians did not behave differently from the Tatars, the Kalmyks or the Chechens. But even before the end of the war, the Soviet government had decided to single out some nationalities and, against all logic and evidence, declare them 'traitors'. The aim was to punish them collectively by suppressing their administrative national territorial units and deporting the entire populations to Siberia and Central Asia.

The punished 'treacherous' nationalities comprised the Volga Germans, the Buddhist Kalmyks and five Muslim nationalities: the Crimean Tatars, the Karachays and the Balkars (North Caucasian Turks), the Chechens and the Ingushes.

In two cases the genocide could be considered as successful, but in all the others the operation failed and proved counter-productive.

4.1.1. Successful Genocide

(a) Crimean Tatars. In 1941, the Crimean Tatars numbered some 300,000, rather less than 25 per cent of the population of the 'Autonomous Republic of the Crimean Tatars'. Though a minority in their national republic, they enjoyed a relatively favourable position; they participated in the government of their national territory and Crimean Tatar and Russian were the official languages of the administration and the schools.

During the occupation of the peninsula by the Germans during 1941-3, the Crimean Tatars behaved like all Soviet citizens placed under harsh German rule. Some fought in the underground resistance, others simply survived, and a minority actually co-operated with the German masters. Proportionately, the Tatar 'traitors' were certainly no more numerous — probably less so — than Russian or Ukrainian collaborators. When Crimea was reoccupied by the Soviet Army in 1943, the Crimean Tatars were singled out as 'traitors' to the Soviet Motherland — '*Rodina Mat*'. Their republic was liquidated by a decree dated 30 November 1945 and attached to the Russian Soviet Federated Socialist Republic (RSFSR). Later it was detached from the Russian republic and passed on to the Ukraine (Decree of 19 February 1954).

All Crimean Tatars — those living in Crimea or elsewhere, including soldiers and officers of the Soviet Army and even members of the MVD — were rounded up and sent under horrifying conditions to Siberia and Kazakhstan. The operation took place in 1944 and it is estimated that some 300,000 were deported. The territory of their former republic was invaded by Russians and Ukrainians, and — according to usual practice in the Soviet Union — the punishment of the present-day 'traitors' was projected into the past as well. The history of the peninsula was rewritten with no mention of the Tatar khanate: the new history simply jumps over centuries from the Greeks and the Russian Tmutarakan to Catherine II.

After Stalin's death, the victims of the 'cult of personality' were rehabilitated and allowed to go back to their homeland: their national territories were reinstated. There were only two exceptions: the Crimean Tatar and the Volga German republics.

The present situation of the Crimean Tatars cannot be explained by any moral, political or strategic reason. The only explanation is that Crimea has, since the deportation of the Tatars, been densely repopulated with Russians and Ukrainians. Were the Tatars allowed to return to their homeland, it would be necessary to expel these Slav settlers. In world history, no 'colonialist' power had ever treated its colonised subjects in such a ruthless way. The only possible comparison outside the Soviet Union is the case of the inhabitants of the Bikini Islands.

It is estimated by Tatar *émigré* writers that there are at present some 400,000 Crimean Tatars in the USSR. Most of them live in Uzbekistan and Kirghizia, where they mingle neither with the native Muslim and Turkic population nor with the Russians. They enjoy a very limited cultural autonomy — a newspaper in Crimean Tatar is published in Tashkent, a Tatar theatre and a few schools with Crimean Tatar included in the curriculum. They do not figure as a separate community in the three post-war Soviet censuses (1959, 1970, 1979). In the last census in 1979 only 15,000 'Tatars' have been listed in the Crimean region (*oblast*) of the Ukrainian republic, but this figure certainly includes a high proportion of Volga Tatars with whom they have probably been bunched. The descendants of the deported Crimean Tatars have never accepted their fate and have been struggling for the right to return to the Crimea ever since their deportation. It seems a hopeless endeavour. Soviet authorities have proclaimed officially that the 'Crimean Tatars *have rooted themselves* in their new Central Asian homeland', so that there is no reason for them to go back to the Crimea. The leaders of the Tatar political movement have been arrested and jailed, while others have been expelled from the USSR. As far as the Soviet government is concerned, the Crimean Tatar problem has been solved for ever. A nation which for over five centuries had played a major part in the history of Eastern Europe has simply ceased to exist.

(b) The Meskhetians. The second successful genocide was less spectacular and can be more easily explained — though not excused — as a military strategic necessity.

On 15 November 1944, without any apparent reason (there was no trouble, no incident in the area) Soviet authorities gathered a certain number of Muslim ethnic groups in the small Meskhetia region of Southern Georgia (mainly in the districts of Akhaltsikhe and Akhalkalaki) and deported them to Central Asia, in most cases to Kazakhstan and Uzbekistan. It has been estimated that, because of cold and hunger, at least 50,000 people died during transportation. The total number of the deported 'Meskhetians' has been estimated at between 100,000 and 200,000. They comprised a majority of ethnic Turks living in Southern Georgia and various non-Turkic minorities, but all of them exposed to a strong Turkish influence: Karapapakhs (a Turkmen tribe of Northern Armenia), some Kurds of Ajaristan, Khemshins (Muslim Armenians) and even some turkified Ajars (Muslim Georgians), Abkhaz and Laz.

As opposed to the other nationalities deported during the war (Kalmyks, Crimean Tatars, Volga Germans, Chechens, Ingushes, Karachays and Balkars), the Meskhetians have never been accused of collaboration with the Germans or the Turks. No reason at all was given for their deportation, which remained secret, and until 1968 total silence was observed by Soviet sources about the fate of the Meskhetians. Official Soviet publications between 1945 and 1968 make no reference either to the territory of Meskhetia nor to its people. The reason for the deportation, however, is easy to discover: late in 1944 the Soviet Union was preparing to launch a pressure campaign against Turkey. In June 1945 Molotov, then Minister of Foreign Affairs, formally presented a demand to the Turkish Ambassador in Moscow for the surrender of three Anatolian provinces, which were supposed to have belonged to Georgia (Kars, Ardahan and Artvin). Since Moscow was also preparing to support Armenian claims to several other Anatolian provinces, war against Turkey — or at least action in North-Eastern Turkey — seemed possible, and Stalin wanted to clear the strategic Georgian-Turkish border of a Muslim population likely to be hostile to Soviet intentions. The removal of several small and harmless nationalities was a simple safety device in an offensive plan against a neutral neighbour (a plan which was to be abandoned in June 1953 when Molotov renounced both Armenian and Georgian claims to Turkish border areas).

Unlike the other deported Muslim groups, the Meskhetians have been neither rehabilitated nor permitted to return to their homeland. It was only in 1968 that the Soviet government recognised that the Meskhetians had been deported. On 30 May 1968 a decree of the Praesidium of the Supreme Soviet of the USSR declared that the Meskhetians 'had taken root' in their place of exile and were therefore invited to remain in Uzbekistan and Kazakhstan and condemned to be assimilated in the long run by the local Muslims. This optimistic picture is contradicted by the violent but hopeless struggle of the Meskhetians to be permitted to return to their homeland. A small number of Meskhetians was allowed to settle in the Saatly district of the Azerbayjan republic, in the most inhospitable part of the Mugan Steppe. The bulk were listed in the 1970 and 1979 censuses as 'Turks' (*Turki*). They numbered 79,000 in 1970 and 93,000 in 1979, but their location was not indicated. The deported Meskhetian Turks remain deeply religious: according to the latest surveys, they are the most religious of all Central Asian Muslims. A curious process of 'nation building' has developed among them, with the various ethnic groups blending to form a unique

'Turkish' nation. This movement was given expression in April 1970, when the leaders of the Meskhetian Turkish national movement applied to the Turkish Embassy in Moscow for permission to emigrate to Turkey as citizens of the Turkish Republic if the Soviet government persisted in its refusal to allow their resettlement in Meskhetia. The Meskhetian Turks were the first Muslim group in the USSR to claim national allegiance outside its borders like the Soviet Jews and the Volga Germans. The reaction of the Soviet government was to arrest the Meskhetian leaders.

Up to the present time, no Meskhetian Turk has been allowed to emigrate to Turkey. As a national group, the Meskhetians deported to Central Asia have been deprived of all rights: there is no press in Turkish, no school using Turkish, not even the semblance of cultural autonomy which has been granted to the Crimean Tatars. Thus they are condemned to extinction.

4.1.2 Unsuccessful Genocide. The third attempt to solve drastically the Muslim problem through genocide took place in the North Central Caucasus. After the German armies had reached the territories of the Crimean Tatars, the Karachays and the Balkars, they remained for some time under German rule. The other territories of the Lower Volga (Kalmyks) and North-Eastern Caucasus (Chechens, Ingushes), however, had never been occupied by the Wehrmacht, so it is absolutely absurd to pretend that the deported peoples had collectively, or even individually, collaborated with the invaders.

The Chechens and Ingushes were rounded up in February 1944 and deported. On 3 March 1944 the Checheno-Ingush Autonomous Republic was liquidated and its territory annexed to the RSFSR.

The deportation of the Karachays and the Balkars took place almost at the same time. Their national territories were suppressed. The Karachay-Cherkess Autonomous Region was reduced to the Cherkess Autonomous Region, the Karachays districts being annexed to Georgia, and the Kabardino-Balkar Autonomous Republic became the Kabardian Autonomous Republic. The Balkar territory was annexed by the Georgian Republic.

It seems that together with the Karachays and the Balkars, the Soviets deported some Cherkess, Muslim Ossetians (Digors) and even some Daghestanis (Avars). The precise number of the deported North Caucasians is difficult to ascertain. The following figures may be accepted as minima:

Chechens	— 400,000 to 450,000
Ingushes	— 100,000 to 150,000
Karachays	— 85,000
Balkars	— 45,000

plus an unknown number of Adyghe-Cherkess, Kabardians, Muslim Ossetians and Avars.

A total of 800,000 seems reasonable, out of which probably 20 to 30 per cent disappeared during transportation. They were settled in the most forbidding areas of Siberia, Kazakhstan and Kirghizia, and an unknown number were sent to various death camps. The intention to solve once and for all the North Caucasian problem by liquidating the most obdurate adversaries not only to Communism but also to the Russian presence is obvious, especially if we remember that Chechen and Ingush soldiers and officers in the Red Army, members of the Communist Party and even members of the secret police were deported.

Contrary to the Crimean Tatar experience, the attempt at genocide of the North Caucasian Mountaineers failed. After Stalin's death, all four nationalities were cleared of the accusation of treason. Their national territories were restored (Decree of the Praesidium of the Supreme Soviet of 9 January 1957) and the deportees allowed to go back to their homeland. What happened? It is obvious that the rehabilitation of the victims of Stalin's 'cult of personality' cannot be explained by any sense of moral atonement on the part of the Soviet leaders. Other victims, such as the Crimean Tatars, the Meshketian Turks, the Volga Germans and even the Caucasian Greeks, though cleared of the accusation of collaboration and treason, remain deprived of their elementary national rights and are condemned to be absorbed by other nations. The real reason for the rehabilitation of the Mountaineers could reside in the extraordinary vitality and resistance of the deportees who refused to die out and fought back victoriously. North Caucasians displayed an exceptional capacity for survival under the worst possible conditions. By 1959, they had already partly compensated their losses, and since then the two last Soviet censuses noted their exceptional vitality, as shown in Table 1.1.

The high figures of increase of the exiled nationalities between 1959 and 1970, higher than the average achieved by other North Caucasians, proves that there was no assimilation of the deported Mountaineers either by the local Muslim population in Central Asia or — even less — by Russians in Siberia. The census data also prove that in spite of fifteen years of exile, deprived of national schools and press, the North

Table 1.1: North Caucasian Population, 1959–79

	1959	1970	Percentage increase 1959/70	1979	Percentage increase 1970/9
Chechens	419,000	613,000	46.3	756,000	23.4
Ingushes	105,000	158,000	49	186,000	18
Karachays	81,000	113,000	38	131,000	16
Balkars	42,000	59,000	40.3	66,000	10

Table 1.2: Percentage of North Caucasians Claiming their Language as their Mother Tongue, 1959–79

	1959	1970	1979
Chechen	98.8	98.7	98.6
Ingush	97.9	97.4	97.4
Karachay	96.8	98.1	97.7
Balkar	97.0	97.2	96.9

Caucasians have preserved the use of their native tongues. In 1959, 1970 and 1979 the proportion of North Caucasians who claimed the Caucasian languages as their native tongues remained stable (see Table 1.2).

According to all recent Soviet sources, North Caucasians, especially the Chechens, are the most religious of all Soviet Muslims. Soviet sources are forced to admit that this militant religious spirit was fostered by deportation. Islam, in its most conservative form, became for the exiles deprived of their national rights and threatened by genocide *the only basis of identity*. This astonishing evolution was due to the activity of two Sufi brotherhoods, the Naqshbandiya and the Qadiriya. These have dominated religious life in Northern Caucasus ever since the later eighteenth century and have inspired and directed all major resistance movements against the Russian conquest, from Imam Mansur, a Naqshbandi sheikh in 1783, to the last uprising against Soviet rule during 1941–3. The vitality of the Sufi brotherhoods among the Chechens-Ingushes is demonstrated by the fact that in the later 1940s and early 1950s a new Sufi *tariqa* — the brotherhood of Vis Haji — was founded somewhere in Kazakhstan by a deported Chechen, Vis (Uweis) Haji Zagiev.

This *tariqa*, a branch of the old Qadiriya, is the most puritan and xenophobic, but also the most popular, of all North Caucasian Sufi orders. At the same time, it uses the most advanced methods to promote its cause while remaining the most conservative in its 'ideology'. According to recent estimates of Soviet sociologists, 'more than half of all Muslim believers in the Chechen-Ingush republic are members of a Sufi order'. This would put the number of Sufi adepts at 150,000 or 200,000, while in 1926, Soviet sources counted some 60,000 adepts among the Chechens and 10,000 among the Ingushes.

When the Mountaineers were deported a unique experiment was tried in the Chechen-Ingush territory, whereby total destruction of Islam was attempted through suppression of *all* mosques which were not reopened when the exiles were allowed to return to their homeland. All recent Soviet sources now admit that this radical strategy failed to achieve the desired result. On the contrary, the closure of mosques only contributed to the growth of the clandestine Sufi brotherhoods and helped spread their virulent message to the Chechen and Ingush, with the result that they became more religious than ever. Clearly the Sufi brand of Islam began to pose a more dangerous threat to the Soviets than the official domesticated Islam. In 1978, the Soviet authorities acted to reverse their policy, with the result that two mosques were opened in the Chechen-Ingush ASSR and five more in 1980.

More dangerous for the stability of Soviet rule in Central Asia was the influence exercised by the deported North Caucasians on the local Muslim population, especially the Kazakhs.

The revival of Sufism among the Kazakhs and the Kirghiz — whose faith used to be fairly superficial — and the consequent strengthening of Islam among them is attributed by all Soviet sources to the presence of the Chechens and Ingushes.

Finally, the ordeal of the deported North Caucasians led to xenophobia. The Chechens and the other former exiles are the most violently anti-Russian of all the Soviet nationalities, with the Chechen-Ingush Republic being classified as the most insecure of all Soviet territories. Between 1959 and 1979, the number of Russians in the Republic declined spectacularly from 49 per cent in 1959 to 34.5 per cent in 1970, and only 29 per cent in 1979 (from 367,000 individuals in 1970 to 336,000 in 1979). Because of the xenophobia, Russians and other 'Christians' (Ukrainians, Armenians) are leaving the area, which is rapidly becoming more 'native' and more Muslim. The attempted genocide ended in total failure.

4.2 *The Exodus*

It is significant that the Soviet government has never opted for the second radical solution adopted by the Tsarist government in Crimea — the exodus of Muslims abroad. This solution had, however, been adopted on a limited scale for minorities of foreign origin, or considered as 'foreigners', such as Jews, Volga Germans and Greeks. The Meskhetians were not permitted to emigrate to Turkey and, with very few exceptions, dissenting Crimean Tatars were jailed rather than allowed to emigrate. Why, after all, should any Soviet wish to leave the Workers' Paradise?

4.3 *Destruction of the Muslim* Millet

The destruction of Muslim unity was not a goal in itself but a preliminary move towards the integration of Muslims into the Soviet sphere. From the beginning of the sixteenth century until the last day of the monarchy the Tsarist government treated Russian Islam as a whole as though it constituted one 'nation', though divided geographically, ethnically, linguistically and administratively. Some of the Muslims were assimilated by the Russians and considered as 'regular citizens of the Empire', subject to the same general obligations and enjoying the same rights as their Russian co-citizens. Other Muslims — the *inorodtsy* — were not considered as fully fledged citizens, but rather as 'protected', second-rate subjects of the Tsar.

In spite of these administrative and legal differences, all Muslims were considered as members of *one nation*, 'the Nation of Islam', the Russian equivalent of the Ottoman concept of *Millet*, which intermingles the notions of religion and nation, and of the old Turkish-Mongol concept of *Yurt*, incorporating the notions of state, country and nation.

Until the Revolution, the term 'Muslim' was officially in use in all administrative and legal documents. The linguistic and ethnic distinctions remained vague and secondary. Thus, the Azeri Turks were commonly called 'Caucasian Tatars'; the Kumyks of Daghestan went by the name of 'North Caucasian Tatars'. All the Central Asian sedentaries — Turks or Iranians — were designated as 'Sarts' ('merchants').

All the pre-revolutionary Muslim reformers, from Ismail Gasprinsky to young socialists like Ayaz Iskhaki and the future Muslim Communists Mulla-Nur Vahitov and Mir Said Sultan Galiev, were convinced 'pan-Islamists'. For them there could be no doubt about the unity of the Muslim *Millet*. All the ethnic groups formed one nation, belonged to one culture and were united by a common religion and historical tradition. The first signs of a political life in 1904–5 had a strong pan-Islamic rather than pan-Turkic flavour. The three Muslim congresses of 1904–5 (in Nizhni-Novgorod, St Petersburg and once more in Nizhni-Novgorod) were open to delegates from all Muslim regions and distinctly 'pan-Muslim' in character. The Muslim political organisation created at the first Congress was called the Muslim Union (Ittifaq al-Muslimin), whose aim it was to group all the Muslims of Russia; in this context it is worthy of note that non-Muslim Turks, Chuvashes, Yakuts, Altayans and Gagauz were not represented.

The Great Pan-Muslim Congress met in Moscow on 1 May 1917 with 900 delegates representing all the Muslim territories of Russia. The Congress stood by the pan-Turk and pan-Islamic ideal and the principle of the unity of the Muslim nation was not in doubt. However, for the first time, the unity of the Russian Muslim world foundered on a vital point: the question of a Muslim state. A minority of the delegates advocated one Muslim nation, with no specific Muslim state. All the Muslims of Russia were to enjoy an 'extra-territorial cultural autonomy' in a unified democratic Russian Republic. The majority, however, advocated a federal principle with the Muslim nation divided into several geographically separate states. The federalists won by 446 votes against 271, but the ideal of unity was so strong that the Congress organised an all-Muslim central agency: the 'Muslim Council' (Milli Shura) responsible for co-ordinating joint political action. The Congress also decided to create Muslim national military units composed exclusively of Muslims and recommended a single school system using the same common pan-Turkic language.

The ideal of unity was further reinforced at the second pan-Muslim Congress in Kazan in July 1917. This Congress confirmed the plan of Muslim military units and organised an 'Army Council' (Harbi Shura). It also established a Muslim provisional government, a 'National Board' (Milli Idare) which was supposed to prepare the meeting of a Muslim National Assembly (Millet Mejlisi) which came into existence at Ufa on 20 November 1917 after the Bolshevik take-over. It was, however, rapidly disbanded.

It was obvious that as long as the Muslim *Millet* remained as *one nation*, the Muslims of the Soviet Union constituted a powerful potential threat which could challenge Russian claims to leadership of the USSR. The destruction of Muslim unity was the essential first step which the Soviet government had to take in order to solve the 'nationality problem'. This was no easy task, since in the first years of the Soviet regime the new Muslim Communists (Tatars, Caucasians and Turkestanis) remained loyal to the pan-Islamic ideal of their predecessors. They considered that the Muslims of Soviet Russia formed one *nation* (*Millet*) geographically divided into a limited number of states and using three official languages:

(1) Tatar-Bashkir state in the Middle Volga region, stretching over a huge area from Simbirsk and Kazan in the West to Cheliabinsk and Troitsk in the East and harbouring a population of over 6 million people, the majority Muslim. Volga Tatar was to be the only written language.

(2) unified Turkestan, including Kazakhstan and the other Central Asian territories (Uzbek, Kirghiz, Turkmen and Tajik). Chagatay Turkic was to be the official written language of this immense territory.

(3) Muslim Caucasus, including Azerbayjan, Daghestan and the Central North Caucasus, a heterogeneous territory, where different languages were spoken (Turkic, Iranian and Ibero-Caucasian), with a population belonging to various religious backgrounds (Sunni North Caucasians and Shia Azerbayjanis), but unified by the use of the same written language (Azeri Turkic).

During the first six years of the new regime (from 1918 to 1923) the term 'Muslim' was used in official Soviet texts to designate all the Muslim nationalities of the USSR. A 'Muslim' Red Army and a 'Muslim' Communist Party were in existence for a short while. Muslim administration was carried out by 'Muslim Commissariats' (Muskom) and in 1918 the Central Muslim Commissariat in Moscow represented the embryo of a 'Muslim government'.

After 1923, the Muslim Communist leaders resisted Soviet plans for the division of the Muslim *Millet* into small 'modern' nations and proposed instead the amalgamation of the entire Soviet Muslim world into a unified Turkestan with the addition of the Middle Volga territories, Tatarstan, Bashkiria and the Turkic, Christian Chuvash Republic, the Muslim areas of North Caucasus, Azerbayjan and Daghestan. This was to be the 'Republic of Turan', whose population would have been 75 per cent Turkic and approximately 80 per cent Muslim. It was to have been an independent and sovereign state.

To the Bolshevik leadership this proposal was of course quite unacceptable, not just on ideological grounds but, more important, because the creation of a huge Muslim national state in the southern part of the Soviet Union would have isolated the Russian territories from the colonial world and, in the long run, would have permitted Soviet Muslims to become the arbiters of the World Revolution.

The Bolshevik leadership proceeded to break up the unified Muslim *Millet* and put the fragments together into new small 'modern' nations, each one with an exact territorial demarcation, its own written official language, generally specially elaborated for this occasion, its own state apparatus, economic interests and even historical background and cultural traditions. This last point of the programme was the most difficult to bring about because all the members of the Muslim *Millet* shared the same religion, culture and history.

4.3.1 Volga-Ural. The attack on Muslim unity began in the Volga-Ural district. At the time of the Revolution, the Bashkir and Tatar peoples of this area were well on their way to uniting into a single nation — Tatar in language and culture. The differences between Tatars and Bashkirs were minor; Bashkirs spoke a slightly different vernacular dialect but had always used Tatar as a literary language, and although leading quite distinct life-styles (Bashkirs being a community of peasant mountaineers whereas Tatars formed urban communities of traders, craftsmen and clerics), both shared the same historical and cultural heritage.

In May 1918, hard pressed by the White armies, the Bolshevik leadership was obliged to make concessions to their Muslim allies by endorsing the programme of the Muslim Communist leaders and accepting the principle of a Tatar-Bashkir Republic. But as soon as victory swung to the Red Army in the autumn of 1918, the Soviet leaders changed their attitude completely and the dream of the great Muslim state in the Volga-Ural region was shattered. Instead of a single state, Moscow decided on two small republics: Tatarstan and Bashkiria.

On 23 March 1919 an autonomous Bashkir Republic was set up and on 27 May 1920 the Tatar Republic was created. This first administrative stage was followed in 1923 by the elaboration of a literary Bashkir language. Since then, the evolution of the Bashkir nation has been slow. The new Bashkir literary language did not prosper either, and has failed to oust Tatar as the written or spoken language of the Bashkir Republic. In 1979, almost a third of the Bashkirs were speaking Tatar (307,800 out of 936,000) and in the same year Bashkirs represented little more than a third of the population (936,000 Bashkirs as against 1,548,000 Russians and 940,500 Tatars). The Soviet authorities have been unable to create a 'Bashkir culture' and even less a sense of Bashkir nationalism. Bashkirs still consider themselves as part of the 'greater Tatar nation'.

The destruction of Turkic Muslim unity on the Volga-Ural was a model to be followed later in other Muslim territories.

4.3.2 Northern Caucasus. The North Caucasus presented a different problem. It was a mosaic of ethnic groups which were separated from each other by high mountains, speaking dozens of different languages derived from three linguistic families: Turkic, Iranian and Ibero-Caucasian. They had different social structures, historical traditions and economic orientations. The Mountaineers were, however, united by Islam, by the vivid memory of the common fight against the Russian invader and the widespread use of two literary languages, classical Arabic and Azeri Turkic. There was also among them a clear understanding that only by remaining united could they resist the encroaching Russians who, in the nineteenth century, had pushed them out of the rich lowlands towards the mountains. The political unity of the Mountaineers' 'Nation' founded upon two, centuries-old, written languages and a common culture was the watchword of all national leaders of North Caucasus. They ranged from the most conservative religious elements who advocated the use of Arabic to the extreme left-wing radicals, including the future Muslim Bolsheviks, who were in favour of Azeri Turkic.

The Soviet authorities, who were at the outset forced to look for allies wherever these could be found and whatever their ideological programme, seemed willing to satisfy the demand for unity. On 20 January 1919 an Autonomous Mountain Republic (Avtonomnaya Gorskaya Respublika) was founded. It embraced all Muslim nationalities bounded by the area from the Black Sea coast to the borders of Daghestan: Cherkess, Kabardians, Karachays, Balkars, Ossetians, Abazas, Chechens and Ingush (the neighbouring Daghestanis were to set up an autonomous republic of their own in November of the same year).

The unity was short-lived, for as soon as the Civil War was over and the Chechen-Daghestan uprising came to an end in 1921, the Soviet authorities began to dismantle the Moutain Republic.

Five administrative national territories were eventually created, with the addition of eight small nationalities each with its own written language. These were:

(1) The autonomous Republic of the Chechens and the Ingush created on 5 December 1936 by the fusion of the Chechen Autonomous

Region (founded in 1922) and the Ingush Autonomous Region (1924). The Chechen language was promoted to written language in 1925 and the Ingush in 1923.

(2) The Kabarda Balkar Autonomous Republic, created in December 1936 by the fusion of the Kabarda Autonomous Region (1921) and the Balkar Autonomous District (1922). The Kabardian and the Balkar languages became written in 1924.

(3) The North Ossetian Autonomous Region was made into an Auto-nomous Republic in 1936. In the beginning the Soviet authorities seemed to take into consideration the hetero-religious character of the Ossetian people and created two Ossetian literary languages: 'Iron' spoken by the Christian Iron tribes and 'Digor' spoken by Muslim Digors. However, in 1936, the latter lost the status of a literary language.

(4) The Adyghe Autonomous Region created on 27 July 1922. The Adyghe language became written in 1928.

(5) The Karachay-Balkar Autonomous Region created on 22 January 1922, with three written literary national languages: the Cherkess (similar to the Kabardian), the Karachay (similar to the Balkar) and Abaza, a Cherkess dialect, promoted to the rank of a literary language in 1938.

Thus, in Northern Caucasus, the Soviet authorities pushed the prin-ciple of fragmentation to the utmost, ignoring the wishes of the local intelligentsia and creating micro-nationalities of tribal type. The opposite, logical solution demanded by the local political leaders — including the Communists — was that the Mountaineers should be divided in three groups, as the political and linguistic unity of the entire region was geographically impossible: *the Cherkess group*, comprising the Adyghes proper, the Cherkess, the Kabards and the Abazas with one (and not three) written languages, Kabard-Cherkess; *the Turkic group*, comprising the Karachays and the Balkars, speaking and writing a common language; *the Checheno-Ingush group*, speaking closely related dialects and using one written language.

In Daghestan the policy of linguistic fragmentation was applied even further. In this territory were lumped together two dozen communities belonging to several linguistic families: Turkic (Kumyks in the North, Azeris in the South), Ibero-Caucasians (Avars, Darghins, Laks, Tabas-arans, Lezghins, Rutuls, Tsakhurs, Aguls, Andis, Didos) and Iranian (Tates). The country had no economic or social unity and different cultural and historical traditions intervened to draw the various ethnic lingustic groups apart. None of the local languages had reached the level of an authentic literary tongue. Those which had a written form before 1917 might be called semi-literary.

In spite of the diversity of the population, all the pre-revolutionary political leaders had been convinced that a unification of Daghestan was not only desirable but possible. The conservative religious elements, following the tradition of Shamil's theocratic state, wanted to unify Daghestan around the Arabic language spoken and written by almost all educated Daghestanis and around Arab culture. The young modernist, secularist intelligentsia advocated the use of Azeri Turkic, spoken and written by the majority of Daghestanis living in the lowlands, as the official administrative language of Daghestan.

The Soviets began by banning Arabic as a 'reactionary', 'clerical' language constituting an 'obstacle to progress and modernisation' and decided at first to unify Daghestan around Azeri, which between 1920 and 1928 became the official language of the administration and the only academic language of the Republic. After 1928, the authorities decided to stop the Turkification of Daghestan and Azeri began to lose ground. In 1930, Moscow opted for the linguistic break-up of the country. In 1933, the Republic had eleven official literary administrative languages: Russian, Azeri, Kumyk, Nogay, Avar, Darghin, Lak, Lezghin, Tabasaran, Chechen and Tates. With the exception of the Azeri, all other languages were semi-literary (and remain such until the present time). In the following years, several languages disappeared from the administrative use such as Nogay, Chechen and Tates. Azeri was confined to the city of Derbent and to the southern part of the Caspian plain, where it is still used in the press and some schools. In practice, Russian is now the *lingua franca* of the Republic.

4.3.3 Central Asia. It was in Central Asia that Moscow's strategy met the strongest resistance and had to overcome the virtually united opposition of the entire intellectual class from extreme right to extreme Bolshevik left.

During the first seven years of the new regime, the Soviet leadership maintained the old administrative division of the area, which corresponded not to ethnic but to historical and geographical formations. The General Government of the Steppes changed its name to that of the Republic of Kazakhstan without any modification of its border, whilst the former General Government of Turkestan became within its former frontiers the Autonomous Republic of Turkestan. The two protected states — the Emirate of Bukhara and the Khanate of Khiva —

were merged to become the People's Republics of Bukhara and Khorezm.

This preservation of the Tsarist administrative picture of Central Asia corresponded not only to the wishes of the pre-revolutionary 'bourgeois nationalists' of pan-Turkic persuasion, but also to those of the first Central Asia Bolsheviks, whose leaders, the Kazakh Turar Ryskulov and the Uzbek Fayzullah Khojaev, believed that sooner or later all Central Asia would be unified into one state, Soviet Turkestan, and would form one nation, the 'Turkestani'. While there would be several spoken languages, for administrative purposes there would be only Chagatay, an academic, literary language which appeared in the later fifteenth century and was used until the 1917 Revolution in a more or less modified form by all Central Asian intellectuals, together with Persian.

But the unity of Turkestan was to last only until its dismemberment by Stalin in 1924, when the area was divided up along national lines (i.e. ethnic linguistic) into six states:

(1) the Uzbek Soviet Socialist Republic, created on 27 October 1924;

(2) the Turkmen Soviet Socialist Republic, created on 27 October 1924;

(3) the Tajik Soviet Socialist Republic, first created as an Autonomous Region on 14 October 1924, an Autonomous Republic on 15 March 1925 and on 15 October 1929 a Federal Republic;

(4) The Kirghiz Soviet Socialist Republic, created first under the name of 'Qara Kirghiz Autonomous Region' on 14 October 1924, Autonomous Republic on 1 February 1926; Federal Republic since 5 December 1936;

(5) Kazakh Soviet Socialist Republic, created first under the name of 'Kirghiz Autonomous Republic' on 26 August 1920, and became 'Kazakh Autonomous Republic' in April 1925, Federal Republic since 5 December 1936;

(6) Karakalpak Autonomous Republic, created first as an Autonomous Region on 16 February 1925, Autonomous Republic since 1936.

The administrative division of Central Asia was completed by a political division: instead of one 'Turkestani' nation, the Soviet authorities created several nations and nationalities, each with its own territory (except the Uyghurs and the Dungans) and written literary language:

(1) Uzbeks, written language (distinct from the Chagatay) since 1923;

(2) Kazakhs, written language since the mid-nineteenth century;

(3) Kirghiz, written language created in 1924;

(4) Turkmens, written language close to the Chagatay since the eighteenth century, 'modern' literary Turkmen created in 1924;

(5) Tajiks, old literary language since the ninth century;

(6) Karakalpaks, written language created in 1925;

(7) Uyghurs, literary language, 'Neo-Uyghur', close to the old Chagatay;

(8) Dungans, using Chinese transliterated into Cyrillic script.

We will examine in the last chapter whether the Soviet strategy of division has achieved lasting results and whether the Central Asian *Millet* has finally been broken up. We must remember that the imposition of Soviet policy met with fierce resistance from all Turkestani intellectuals — the pre-revolutionary militant nationalists who sided with the Bolsheviks as well as the young radicals who had joined the Communist Party during the Civil War. Among those who opposed Stalin's strategy and fought for the unity of Turkestan were the most prominent figures of post-1917 Central Asia: the writer Münevver Qari, the first People's Commissar for National Education of the Turkestan Republic in 1922, Manan Ramiz, the Commissar for National Education of the Uzbek Republic, the writer Abdurrauf Fitrat, the leader of the Young Bukharian Party before 1917, later Commissar for Foreign Affairs of the People's Republic of Bukhara and Professor at the University of Tashkent, Fayzullah Khojaev, Chairman of the Council of People's Commissars of the Uzbek Republic, the poet Cholpan, Batu, chairman of the Cultural Affairs department of the People's Commissariat for Education of the Uzbek Republic and dozens of others (all to be liquidated in the 1930s by Stalin as 'traitors' and 'bourgeois nationalists'). The bastions of their opposition were the numerous literary societies, important conduits for the spread of ideology. The most important was the 'Chagatay Society' (Chagatay Gurungi), founded in 1920 by the best pre-revolutionary writers for the defence of Chagatay as the sole literary and administrative language of Central Asia. The Chagatay Society was wound up in 1922, but the members kept their outside posts and renewed their activity in 1927 as an official literary association called the Red Pen (Qizil Qalam). The members of the Association did not hide their hostility towards the Russians and the formation of new literary languages. Qizil Qalam was proscribed in

1928 and its members liquidated.

4.4 Sovietisation and Russification

The destruction of administrative, lingustic and cultural unity and the creation of modern Muslim nations out of the debris of the *'Umma* could ensure only administrative, not political, equality between Russians and Muslims. It was but a preliminary, negative stage in the building of a happy new socialist world supposed to be the final goal in the evolution of mankind. It was a novel endeavour, based on Stalin's personal doctrine of nationalities, and while it has been often criticised – even within the USSR – it still forms the basis of Soviet policy.

The positive element of the doctrine was to be the building (*stroitel'-stvo*) of socialism, of the new Soviet world order – a necessarily complicated process because it encompassed not only the economic, political and social spheres but, above all, the spritual. For over sixty years, Soviet ideologues – indeed the entire apparatus of the Communist Party and state – have been struggling to create the 'Soviet man', *Sovetskiy chelovek*, for without the emergence of this new race, liberated completely from the past, the entire Soviet endeavour would fail. All Soviet theoretical works from Lenin to Brezhnev are unanimous on this theme. According to this premiss, Muslims, like all other Soviet citizens, were invited to discard their thousand-year-old culture and become 'sovietised'. Only by doing this could they 'acquire the psychology and the ideals of a Russian industrial worker from Petrograd', the aim as expressed by Kalinin.

The process of sovietisation is a complex one, with a double and contradictory aspect: a preliminary negative stage consisting in the liquidation of various survivals inherited from the pre-socialist past, including religious survivals, and a positive, constructive spect, including the creation of the new man.

Old Bolsheviks believed that the destruction of the old order would be an easy process, since Islam, like all other religous creeds, was but a superstition from the past, while Marxism represented scientific truth and the future. Such was the *naïveté* of the Bolsheviks, Lenin included.

4.4.1 Destruction of the Islamic Religion. The massive assault against Islam was launched around 1928, some years after the beginning of the anti-Christian campaign. Its avowed goal was the destruction of Muslim religion in order to bring about equality between Russians and Muslims, which would only be contemplated once all Soviet citizens were free from the psychological hangovers of the past, in particular from the

false ideologies propagated by the exploiting classes. Russian Bolshe-viks, as true Marxists, were of course doctrinally committed to fight all religions, 'superstructural phenomena of capitalist or pre-capitalist eras, deflecting the working masses from constructive tasks'. In the case of Islam, the fight had to be especially ruthless, because the staunch ad-herence of Muslim believers to the juridical and moral code of Islam erected psychological barriers between them and the non-Muslims.

Thus, for the first time in history, an important Muslim community was faced with the systematic challenge of atheism and its religion threatened with total destruction. This was by no means the first attempt by the Russians to uproot Islam from their Empire (attempts were made under Tsar Fedor at the end of the sixteenth century, again under Tsarina Anna in the first half of the eighteenth century, and finally at the end of the nineteenth century by Nicolas Il'minsky), but the aim of these earlier campaigns was to supplant Islam by Christianity. The ruthless methods employed in the eighteenth century were not very different from those used under Stalin and the anti-Islamic propaganda devised in the nineteenth century by the Orthodox missionaries of Kazan and by Nicolas Il'minsky was in certain respects comparable with the themes employed by Soviet agitprop, although somewhat more sophisticated.

The theme of anti-Muslim propaganda has varied little since 1924, when the seeds of the anti-religious campaign were first sown and may be seen as having two main thrusts.

(1) Marxist arguments directed against all religions. Islam is the 'opium of the toiling masses, distracting them from the social struggle against the exploiting parasites'; 'it has played — and is still playing — a reactionary role, being an instrument for the spiritual oppression of the workers'; 'it inculcates in Man the spirit of resignation and humility, thus distracting him from revolutionary activity'; 'it is a fanciful, fallacious and anti-scientific creed, projecting the dream of Paradise into an imaginary other world'; and finally, the main argu-ment used against all religions, 'Islam, a spiritual creed, is a hangover from the pre-socialist past, it is a mere survival doomed to disappear. It has no place in a Marxist socialist world, which is building paradise on this earth . . . Marxisim-Leninism and religious ideology are there-fore incompatible and irreconcilable . . . and the Communist Party cannot remain indifferent or neutral towards religion . . . it must fight it and it must defeat it.'

These arguments, already employed before the Revolution by

Russian Marxists, are still repeated in official anti-religious publications, in particular in the two leading atheistic organs published in Moscow, *Nauka i Religiya* (*Science and Religion*) and the more 'scientific' *Voprosy Nauchnogo Ateizma* (*Problems of Scientific Atheism*), a quarterly journal edited by the Institute of Scientific Atheism of the Academy of Social Sciences attached to the Central Committee of the Communist Party of the USSR.

These same arguments constitute the basis of atheistic education of all Soviet citizens and are fed to Soviet children of all nationalities from the moment they enter an educational institution at the age of four. During the first twenty years of the Soviet regime (until the war) this dull, boring scientific gruel was spiced by parallel violent, vicious (but often comic) propaganda against the clerics who were represented as greedy, gluttonous, treacherous parasites. Since the war, however, anti-clerical propaganda has practically disappeared except for a short-lived attempt to resurrect it under Khrushchev. At present, 'anti-clericalism' is used exclusively against religious groups that have no legal existence (Orthodox and Protestant sectarians and the Sufi brotherhoods), never against established churches.

(2) Atheistic arguments used specifically against the Muslim religion. Even a superficial comparison of Soviet anti-Muslim literature with pre-revolutionary anti-Islamic publications of the Kazan and Irkutsk Orthodox missions (the first specialised in polemics against the Volga Tatars, the second dealt with the Buddhists and the nomad Kazakhs) show that Soviet agitprop is heavily indebted to the Orthodox specialists, especially to the collection *Anti-Musul'manskiy Missionerskiy Sbornik* published in Kazan.

There are five main objections to Islam. Far from being the national religion of Soviet Muslims, Islam is said to be a foreign religion, brought to Central Asia and the Caucasus by alien invaders such as Arabs, Iranians and Ottoman Turks. Although Islam always had a strong anti-Russian character, this did not prevent its leaders from being entirely submissive to the Tsarist regime. This frequently stated criticism is directed simultaneously towards official Islam and the radical, fundamentalist 'Parallel Islam'.

Of all the religions, Islam is claimed as the most conservative (even reactionary) and the least 'social': it sanctifies the authority of the elders, humiliates women, inculcates in its followers fanaticism, intolerance and xenophobia; it sets 'Believers' against 'Infidels' and is therefore an obstacle to friendship between different peoples of the Soviet Union. Islamic rites and customs, such as circumcision and fasting during Ramadan, are criticised as 'primitive', barbarian and unhealthy. Islamic morals are thought to be opposed to Communist morals, with Islamic art and literature ossified and unable to evolve or progress.

In summary, Islam belongs to the past, not even to the capitalist stage of evolution, but to the feudal era. As such, it has no place in a society of 'advanced socialism'.

Anti-religious propaganda is considered in the USSR as the 'moral duty' of 'all honest Soviet citizens', especially of the members of the Communist Party, of the Youth Organisation (Komsomol), of the trade unions (Profsoyuz) and of the entire state, government and Soviet apparatus, from kindergarten to the highest university level. Lectures on atheism may also be delivered at the evening courses of the Ministry of Agriculture or at a scientific meeting of the Republican Academy of Science. All Soviet mass media, periodical and non-periodical press, theatre, exhibitions, museums, television, radio, tele-plays and of course thousands of public and private talks dwell extensively on atheism. A huge number of books and pamphlets are published in all languages, every year, in the Muslim republics of Central Asia and the Caucasus on the subject of improvement of anti-religious propaganda.

Soviet anti-religious propaganda represents a massive effort and is conducted by an enormous, costly bureaucratic machine employing tens of thousands of full-time and part-time specialists.

The Soviet authorities themselves constantly denounce its dull, bureaucratic, formal character and lack of effectiveness while at the same time insisting on the vital importance of atheism in the building of Communism. New ways to improve anti-religious propaganda are constantly being discussed, but the basic character of the propaganda is never questioned. The suggested improvements merely provide for more propagandists, more lectures, more books, more articles and so on. If we compare the gigantic Soviet anti-Islamic machine to the small teams of Orthodox missionaries of a century ago, it is difficult to avoid the conclusion, paradoxical as it may seem, that the Orthodox Church was far more efficient then than the Soviet bureaucracy is now, after sixty years of 'scientific socialism'.

Anti-religious propaganda is only one of the weapons at the disposal of the Soviets in the fight against religion, and the least important. Already in 1925 the Soviet government had begun to expropriate all clerical property (*waqf*) which guaranteed the Muslim clergy's economic power, and by 1930 the process was completed. Thereafter, mosques and schools were without independent means of support.

At the same time, an attack was directed against the Quranic (*Shariyat*) and customary (*Adat*) laws. After several years of pressure, all traditional Muslim courts were abolished in 1927.

The third step was an offensive against religious teaching — 'the vehicle of feudal, bourgeois and clerical culture'. Before the Revolution, in the General Government of Turkestan alone there were about 8,000 *mektep* (primary schools) and *madrassah*s (secondary schools). The last of them disappeared in 1928.

Finally, in 1928 the frontal assault began on the Muslim religious establishment, which still possessed an impressive façade. On the eve of the Revolution, Russia (Bukhara and Khiva excluded) had 26,000 mosques served by over 45,000 *molla*s — an average of one Muslim parish per 700-1,000 believers. In 1927, this establishment was still largely intact. The brutal assault of 1928 was spearheaded by an attack on the more extravagant features of Muslim observance, such as flagellation as practised during the Shia ceremony of *Ashura* and by a campaign to discredit the clergy, who were variously accused of ignorance, bribery, corruption and immorality.

The onslaught against religion lasted for more than ten years, during which time mosques were closed (in 1942 only 1,312 'working' Mosques remained) and the clerics and congregations of believers were hunted down and liquidated not only as 'parasites of society' but as 'counter-revolutionaries', and from 1935 on as 'spies' in the pay of Japan and Germany. On the eve of war with Germany the Soviet government, for obvious reasons, was obliged to reduce the administrative and police pressures against Islam and a period of relative tolerance was inaugurated which lasted until Stalin's death, when the number of 'working' mosques rose to 1,500.

The administrative and psychological offensive against Islam was resumed by Khrushchev in 1953 under his policy of 'back to Lenin', and was to last for more than ten years. During this little-known purge, the number of 'working' mosques was reduced to around 400, and the number of 'registered' clerics to between 2,000 and 3,000, but according to all recent Soviet surveys, far from destroying for ever the religious feelings of the Muslim population, it only gave a new impulse to the fundamentalist, conservative trend represented by the 'Parallel' underground Sufi Islam, as we shall see later.

The destruction of the Muslim religion was the essential element of a broader campaign that aimed to 'sovietise' the entire Muslim society, which in 1917 was just beginning to enter the capitalist stage of development. Other aspects of the campaign included attacks on the traditional patriarchal framework of the Muslim family, which was seen as a move to encourage Muslims to align themselves with the Russians socially and, in a second stage, to facilitates mixed marriages between Muslims and Russians. The eventual aim was to achieve a new Soviet society, based on the absolute equality of the sexes and generations and a monogamous family unit, creating a new Muslim 'Soviet man', liberated from the social and religious traditions of the past, capable of participating with his Russian comrades in the building of socialism. The government's efforts to alter the family structure met with some success. On the plus side is the more or less complete disappearance of polygamy, of early marriage of Muslim girls, of the *paranja* (the veil) and of several family customs, such as the levirate and the sororate, the *kaytarma* (obligation for the bridegroom to spend time in the bride's household to pay the price of her hand). Other customs and traditions, without disappearing completely, have weakened. Such is the case of the endogamic and exogamic taboos and of the *kalym* (purchase of the bride). The large joint family survives, but only in the most remote districts. The authorities' efforts have brought the Muslims of the USSR to the stage of a monogamous family.

On the other hand, sexual discrimination still persists. Sixty years after the October Revolution and after fifty years of efforts, Muslim women continue to occupy an inferior position in their national territories both among the masses and the so-called 'advanced elements' of the Communist Party. Soviet sources generally ascribe this state of affairs to insufficient educational propaganda and to the feudal attitude of men. More recently, however, some specialists with a more objective or clear-sighted view than average have recognised that the main reason for women lagging behind lies in their own conservatism; Muslim women are more traditionalist, more religious than men, and obstinately refuse to become modern and sovietised.

Another failure of official efforts is marked by the persistence of the 'patriarchal character' in the relations between generations. The Muslim community is still characterised by *aqsaqalism* — the extreme respect of the 'white beards', the excessive authority of elders. In the same way the remnants of the clan and tribal systems, often denounced by the Soviet sources as *mestnichestvo* (local favouritism), have not only survived but, paradoxically, have developed during Brezhnev's era.

Finally, Muslim society preserves a multitude of social and cultural traditions, regulating food and dress as well as other aspects of everyday life, which sets it apart from Russian society and makes biological symbiosis between natives and 'Europeans' more difficult.

4.4.2 Liquidation of the Pre-revolutionary Elite. An entire generation disappeared during the bloody Stalinist purges of the 1930s and was replaced by a new generation of intellectuals, bureaucrats and technicians, mostly of peasant origin, brought up in the Soviet mould and trained ideologically as Marxists. In this field, the efforts of the authorities to create a new *Sovietskiy chelovek* seem to have met with success, but on close examination this success is more apparent than real. The great majority of the new elite consider themselves as 'Marxist' and 'Soviet'. Officially, they have broken with the past, they claim not to be believers and yet they continue to observe certain traditional religious rites and customs (circumcision, religious marriage and burial). To all outward appearances they are 'European', but they have failed to adopt Russian as their principal language. Finally, the young generation of Muslim Communist cadres seems to hold national traditions, including Islam, in greater respect than the generation of their parents. They may be 'sovietised' on the surface, but they remain nationalists and Muslims.

It is interesting to compare the efforts of the Soviet government to create a 'Soviet Muslim man', national in appearance and using his own language yet 'socialist' Marxist at heart, with the attempt of Nicolas Il'minsky, a century ago, to convert Muslims to Christanity by giving them access to Orthodoxy in their own language while refraining from any attempt at Russification.

Il'minsky's efforts failed mainly because of the opposition of the Russian Church itself. The belief that only a Russian could be a fully fledged Orthodox was still deeply rooted in the ecclesiastical thinking of the Russian Church. The prospect of a Christian Orthodox priest performing the Holy Mass in the Tatar language was therefore a difficult pill to swallow. As far as Muslims were concerned, Il'minksy's efforts were in part successful. A Tatar convert was offered access to the culture and full wealth of Orthodox Christendom and some of the neophytes became sincere and authentic Christians. The Soviets, on the other hand, invite Muslims to give up their magnificent, fourteen-centuries-old spirital patrimony for the sake of dull and intellectually vulgar Marxism-Leninism, an ageing pseudo-culture which has few followers of real conviction in the USSR. The comparison between the brilliant past and the miserable present is too unpleasant, and the half-century-long effort of the Soviet authorities to destroy Islam is doomed to failure. The religion of Islam has victoriously survived all pressures; the Muslim family remains a closed world and the more the authorities attack and denounce Muslim patrimony, the greater the attraction it exercises.

At the end of the nineteenth century Il'minsky and the Orthodox Church were faced with a dilemma: what was better for the survival of the Tsarist Empire, a Tatar Orthodox or a Russian whose Orthodoxy had been watered down? Il'minsky chose the Tatar, while the majority of the Church leaders chose the Russian. During and immediately after the Second World War a similar dilemma faced Stalin: what was better for the Soviet Union, an Uzbek (or Tatar) Marxist or a non-Communist Russian or other Slav (Ukrainian or Belorussian)? The experience of the war was alarming. Russian Christians fought well for the defence of Mother Russia (if not for the salvation of Marxism-Leninism) and for a short time, during the first weeks of the German offensive, when the Soviet leaders — including Stalin — panicked and lost their heads, Sergius, the locum tenens of the Patriarch of Moscow, behaved as the real head of the Russian nation. As for the Muslim nationalities, their behaviour was unsatisfactory, to say the least. Some fought bravely, but in the Muslim areas occupied by the Wehrmacht the attitude of the local people and the elites was ambiguous. In 1943, almost all Muslim nationalities whose territories had been reached by German armies (Crimean Tatars, Balkars, Karachays), and even those whom the Germans did not reach (the Ingush and the Chechens), were collectively accused by Stalin of 'treason' and deported. There were no exceptions and the Communist cadres were liquidated together with the *mollah*s. As long as the archives of the KGB remain closed to Western scholars we will be unable to understand exactly what happened during the tragic months of 1942 when German units were marching towards the Caucasus. One thing is certain, however: Stalin personally preferred the Russians, whether Communist or Christian.

Immediately after the end of the war, a new emphasis was laid on the role of the Russian people, the 'Elder Brother' of the family of Soviet nationalities. From 1945 on a move towards 'sovietisation' of all nationalities was considered the right solution to the nationality problem. This was to be achieved through a complex, two-stage process of 'getting nearer' (*sblizhenie*), leading to the 'merging' (*sliyanie*). Volumes have been published on this process in the USSR, which for almost thirty years was supposed to be the universal panacea, but because of its vagueness it is not easy to trace its development exactly. It may, however, be summarised in the following way.

During the first stage (the 'getting nearer') all non-Russian nationalities were to be submitted to a strong, constant cultural assimilation with Russian, set to become 'second mother tongue' of all Soviet citizens, and the local literary languages enriched and modernised by a massive inflow of Russian words. Local literature was to be raised to a higher level of proletarian art by imitating Russian models such as Gorky, Sholokhov and Mayakovsky. The process even extended to the modernisation of Central Asian cities so that they would lose their oriental flavour and become similar to an average Russian town. A climate of friendship and brotherly love was to replace the former ethnic and religious hostility and migration in both directions (Russians and other Europeans to the Muslim republics and Muslims to European Russia and Siberia) would, it was felt, help promote mixed marriages between Muslims and Europeans.

In the second stage, a really new society was to emerge: the 'International Community' (*Mezhdunarodnaya Obshchina*), with a common 'Soviet' culture representing the quintessence of all the best elements of different national cultures and speaking the same language (Russian of course, though Soviet theoreticians remain vague on this point), with a unique historical tradition (also Russian) and one 'Soviet' patriotism.

Thirty-five years after the war it is possible to point to the failure of this programme.

First, the biological symbiosis which was the aim of the first stage has not taken place: the two communities coexist but do not mix, mixed marriages remain rare, and when they do occur, they follow the traditional pattern of the Muslim *Shariyat* law by which a Muslim man may marry a non-Muslim, but the children must be brought up as Muslims. The converse is strictly forbidden. A recent survey in Daghestan gives the picture for 1973, as shown in Table 1.3. The study also revealed that the Russians represented some 12 per cent of the total population of Daghestan in 1973 and that the percentage of mixed marriages is no higher now than it was sixty years ago.

Second, the dream of an ethnic amalgamation of different nationalities through migration never came true. The massive flow of Russian immigrants to Central Asia which took place in the 1950s and at one time threatened to submerge the native population has slowed down. In 1970, there were almost 12 million Russians and other 'Europeans' in Central Asia representing 37 per cent of the total population. But because of the tremendous natural increase in the native population, the proportion of Muslims has been growing steadily, even in Kazakhstan and Kirghizia. 'European' migration still continues, but Central

Table 1.3: Muslim–Russian Marriages in Daghestan, 1973

	Total Number of Marriages	Women With a Russian Total	Per-centage	Total Number of Marriages	Men With a Russian Total	Per-centage
Avar	2,343	3	0.4	2,445	55	2.2
Darghin	2,124	15	0.7	2,155	40	1.8
Lezghin	1,642	10	0.6	1,667	44	2.6
Kumyk	1,469	12	0.8	1,531	83	5.4
Lak	667	9	1.3	683	31	4.5
Tabasaran	463	1	0.2	514	16	3.1
Nogays	191	3	1.6	189	11	5.8
Agul	65	1	1.5	64	0	0

Source: S. Gadzhiev and Z. Yankova, *Daghestanskaya Sem'ia* (*Daghestan Family*, Makhach-Qala, 1979).

Asia as a whole is rapidly 'going native' (i.e. more Muslim and more Turkic) as the 1979 figures show, with the European element representing only 33 per cent of the total population. As for the Caucasian Muslim republics, where the 'psychological' climate of xenophobia is more pronounced than in Central Asia, Russian colonies have been reduced in absolute numbers, which means that the Russians are moving out of the area. Between 1970 and 1979, the Russian community in Azerbayjan was reduced from 570,000 in 1970 (10 per cent of the total population) to 475,000 in 1979 (less than 8 per cent). In Daghestan, the number of Russians fell from 214,000 in 1959 to 190,000 in 1979, and in the Chechen-Ingush Republic the decrease was even more spectacular, with a drop from 45 to 29 per cent between 1959 and 1979.

An emigration of Central Asians and Caucasians to European Russia and Siberia has not happened, in spite of an intense propaganda campaign. In 1979, 99.2 per cent of the Uzbeks, 99 per cent of the Kirghiz, 98.5 per cent of the Tajiks, 98.5 per cent of the Turkmens and 92 per cent of the Kazakhs lived in Central Asia and 94.6 per cent of the Azeris lived in the Caucasus.

Third, linguistic assimilation was defeated by the extreme loyalty of the Muslim population, intellectuals and masses to their own languages. In 1979, 98.7 per cent of the Turkmens, 97.8 per cent of the Tajiks, 97.5 per cent of the Kazakhs and 98.5 per cent of the Uzbeks declared their national language as their 'mother tongue'. Moreover, a most extraordinary development has taken place since the last war. Far from being invaded by the Russian vocabulary, non-Muslim words — Russian and international — are steadily being replaced by Arab and old Turkic terms.

Fourth, so far, all attempts to create a common 'Soviet' historical tradition have failed. Russians and Muslims have, after all, been enemies for centuries. For the Caucasians, Shamil, who fought the Russians, and even Uzun Haji, who led an anti-Soviet uprising, are national heroes. For the Central Asians, Timur, credited among other great deeds with the burning of Moscow, remains an incomparably great sovereign. To counteract the explosion of Russian patriotism during the war — one of the symbols being Prince Dimitri Donskoy who defeated the Tatars at the battle of Kulikovo — the Tatars tried in 1945 to rehabilitate their own national hero, Khan Edighe, another great Muslim warrior who had destroyed the city of Moscow. The Tatar intellectuals who attempted this move lost their jobs and were severely criticised.

Finally, the attempted 'friendship' between different Soviet nations never became a reality. Russians living in Central Asia consider the natives as subhuman, as 'Blacks' (*chernye*), or rather as 'Black-Bottoms' (*chernozhopye*). For the native Muslims, Russians are the hated and despised invaders. 'Wait until the Chinese come,' one hears often in Central Asia, 'we will paint our walls with your blood.'

For the Russians, Islam remains the alien body that it was a century ago in Tsarist Russia. Significantly, around 1976-7, the expression *sliyaniye* (merging) disappeared completely from Soviet political literature to be replaced by a new term — *'raztsvet'* ('flourishing'). The hope of merging has thus been abandoned and the *'rapprochement'* between different cultures is now expected to produce no more than a mutual *enrichment* of different cultures.

2 THE MUSLIMS AND RUSSIA

1 The Perennial Menace

Soviet Islam is a 'frontier world' located along the extreme northern and north-eastern borders of *Dar ul-Islam*, facing the hostile 'World of War' (*Dar ul-Harb*). This inhospitable location contrived to give the Muslims of what is now the Soviet Union their unique character, one which marks them out as so different from the Muslims of the Middle East and Africa.

After defeating the only attempt by the Chinese to reimpose sovereignty over their distant Central Asian vassals at the battle of the river Talas in 751, the Arab conquerors reached what was to remain for almost a thousand years the frontier of the Muslim world facing the realm of barbary: *Arz ul-Zolm* ('the World of Darkness'). The 'limes' (borders) of Islam followed the valleys of the rivers Terek, north of the Caucasus, and Syr Darya in Turkestan. South of this line, Islam rapidly became the dominant — and later the only — religion of an immense territory comprising an Iranian-speaking population which, centuries before the Arab conquest, had already reached a high level of urban civilisation. In this area had flourished Buddhist, Manichaean, Christian (Nestorian) and even Jewish cultures. Arab Islam absorbed and assimilated this sophisticated civilisation and the territories of Transcaucasia and Transoxania became one of the most brilliant centres of *Dar ul-Islam*, indeed its very heart.

North of Syr Darya and Terek stretched the steppes, where nomads roamed between the Black Sea and the Great Wall of China. This territory was to remain for centuries outside the realm of Islam, a part of the *Dar ul-Harb* which was to play host to barbary represented by various Turkic, Mongol, heathen, Buddhist and Nestorian tribes. Confronted with this nomadic world, Islam adopted a triple strategy.

(1) *To push their vanguards into enemy territory*, creating Muslim strongholds which later became the springboards for Islamisation. Their most spectacular success was the conversion of sedentary Turks in the Middle Volga-Kama area. By the ninth century the ruling elite of the kingdom of Bulghar, ancestor of the Kazan Khanate, had already accepted Islam as its official creed. This remote northern Islamic land was to remain for centuries a centre of brilliant Muslim

55

culture. It survived the Mongol invasion of the thirteenth century and the Russian conquest of the sixteenth; from there Islam was brought by Tatar merchants to the Bashkirs of the Urals and to the forest tribes of Western Siberia.

(2) *To civilise the northern 'barbarians'* by converting them to Islam. This was a difficult endeavour because Islam was basically an urban civilisation, and its hold on the nomads remained superficial. The gradual Islamisation of the nomads, a process which owes much of its success to the missionary activity of Muslim merchants and Sufi adepts, started in the eleventh century and went on for nearly a thousand years until the Russian Revolution.

(3) *To protect the 'limes'* — this was possible while the rulers of Turkestan and Caucasus were strong enough to keep the nomads at bay, as was the case during the reign of the Samanids of Bukhara (875–999) and again under the Seljuqs, whose empire extended from Nicomedia on the Sea of Marmara to the Amu-Darya but, more often than not, the nomads crossed the borders without much difficulty. Once established in Turkestan, the ruling class of the nomad Turks, either heathen or superficially Islamised, were rapidly 'Iranised' and became zealous Muslims. As a rule, they settled in Transoxania and were entrusted with the protection of the frontiers of *Dar ul-Islam* against their barbarian brethren (Turks) or cousins (Mongols). Between the tenth and twelfth centuries, wave after wave of nomad Turks crossed the Syr Darya and founded the brilliant Irano-Turkic dynasties. Such was the case of the Qarakhanids, of the Ghaznevids, of the Seljuqs . . .

However, this classical process of 'civilising the barbarians' and subsequently using them to protect the civilised world against other barbarians (a strategy adopted by the Roman Empire and — with better results — by the Byzantine Basilei) could succeed only when the invading 'barbarians' were not the bearers of a rival 'ideology'. Between the eighth and twentieth centuries the world of Islam was challenged at least six times by 'Infidels' wishing to impose a rival ideology who were equal or even superior to them in military and political might. These challenges came (in chronological order) from Jewish Khazars, Buddhist Qara-Khitay, heathen, Buddhist and Nestorian Mongols of Chingiz Khan, Buddhist Kalmuks-Oïrots, Christian-Orthodox Russians and finally the same Russians in Marxist guise.

From the standpoint of the Caucasian or Central Asian Muslims there was a continuity in the challenge of the 'Infidels', even down to the methods they employed: attempted genocide through wholesale massacres, massive or selective transfers of population, religious proselytism, biological or cultural assimilation and so on. The response of the Muslims to these challenges over the last ten centuries also reveals a common pattern.

1.1 The Khazars

The first well organised adversary encountered by the Arabs in the steppe land north of the Caucasus was the Turkic Khazars. These nomads were heathen, except for the merchants, who were mainly Christian and Muslim, and the Khagan and the upper level of the nomadic aristocracy, who had been Jewish since the middle of the eighth century. For three centuries the Khazars formed a block north of Derbent through which the Arabs never managed to break. They also represented a constant threat to Muslim possessions in Transcaucasia. However, Islam had already penetrated into the Khazar territory in the late seventh century and by the middle of the ninth century it had become the religion of the majority of the population, if not the dominant creed of the Khazar khanate.

The Khazar empire was destroyed in 965 by the Kievan Russians and disappeared completely in 1030.

1.2 The Qara-Khitays

In the early twelfth century, while the Crusaders were threatening Islam in the West, another more deadly enemy appeared on the eastern border of the Seljuq Empire. For the first time since the Arab conquest, the threat from inner Asia was not from heathen or superficially Islamised nomadic hordes, but from a well organised alien military machine: the Qara-Khitay. Some of these Mongol tribesmen appeared on the border of Semirechie in the early twelfth century, having been expelled by the Manchu Jurjät from Northern China over which they had ruled from 936 until 1122. They were deeply impregnated by Chinese culture and probably used Chinese as the official language of their administration. There were some Nestorian Christians and Confucians among them, but the great majority were Buddhists and particularly unyielding to Islam. Their intrusion in Central Asia represented, according to René Grousset, 'the first reaction of Inner Asia against Islamization'.

The Qara-Khitay penetrated into what is now Kazakhstan around 1130, after which they advanced on Transoxania and in 1136 inflicted a heavy defeat on the Qara-khanid ruler near Khojent (now Leninabad) in the Ferghana valley. After this victory they invaded the Seljuq territory and in 1141 won a major victory over Sultan Sanjar at Qatwan near Samarkand. The Seljuq army was routed and it was said that 30,000 Muslims fell in the battle. It was a foretaste of the Chingisside catastrophe of the next century.

The Qara-Khitays rapidly extended their domination over the whole of Central Asia with the exception of Kwarezm. Their rule was not exceedingly harsh (compared with the life under the Chingisside invaders it was remarkably mild), but it was nevertheless the first time that an important Muslim country had fallen to the 'Infidel'. But in the case of the Qara-Khitay, the 'Infidel' being Buddhist — a *bot parast*, an 'idol worshipper' — was especially repulsive. All Muslim chronicles reflect the utter horror of the Islamic world at this new and unexpected development. Worse was to come.

1.3 The Mongols

It was during the autumn of 1219 that the Mongol vanguards appeared in Central Asia. In less than two years they had conquered all Turkestan, Afghanistan and the Caucasus, inflicting a major disaster on Islam. All the great cities were taken by the conquering hordes, their entire populations slaughtered (with the exception of skilled craftsmen who were spared for work in Mongolia) and the cities then razed to the ground. Terror, unprecedented in history, hovered over the *Dar ul-Islam*.

Chingiz Khan was tolerant in religious matters and had no personal animosity against Islam, but the slaughter with which his name is linked was so overwhelming that the Mongol conqueror became the symbol of the deadliest danger that ever threatened Islam.

Central Asia remained under the rule of the 'Infidels' for more than a century. The son of Chingiz, Chagatay, the first Mongol ruler of Turkestan, was personally hostile to Islam, while his heathen successors were deeply influenced by Buddhist and Nestorian thinking. It was therefore not until 1326 that a Chagataid khan, Tarmashirin, was converted to Islam and another fourteen years before Islam emerged as the dominant creed of the *ulus* of Chagatay. Even then the Mongol khans remained nomads and highly suspicious of urban civilisation until the fifteenth century.

The decline in importance of the cities during the Mongol domination was also accompanied by the decline of the old Arab-Persian Muslim religious establishment which was so deeply rooted in the urban life of the time. As a result, the character of Islam in Central Asia changed dramatically, ceasing to be the religion of the ruling elite and becoming instead the religion of the poor rural masses. Mongol rule also saw the development of the Sufi *tariqa* in Central Asia. As Trimingham writes (*The Sufi Orders of Islam*, p. 167):

> It is during this period that the Sufis became for the people the representatives of religion . . . the shrine [of the holy *mürshid*] became the symbol of Islam. The shrine, the dervish house and the circle of *zikr* reciters became the outer forms of living religion.

In short, the Mongols provided the most serious of challenges that had ever confronted Islam.

1.4 The Kalmuks

The last invasion of Central Asia by 'barbarians' from the interior of Asia was probably the most dramatic. It began in the first years of the seventeenth century when an entire West Mongolian tribe, the Torgut, left Jungaria, crossed the whole of Central Asia from north to south and settled in the area of Southern Volga. These 'Kalmuks', as they were called, were Buddhists and they remained a militant alien body in a Muslim Turkic environment.

During a century and a half, the Volga Kalmuks and their cousins, the Oirots (who remained in Jungaria), systematically raided Central Asia. In 1603, the Kalmuks laid waste Khiva, and in 1639 they deported the Turkmen tribes of Mangyshlaq to the Northern Caucasus. In 1643 the Oirots conquered Semirechie, which became their springboard for further expeditions. Between 1681 and 1695 they advanced towards Syr Darya, destroying all the sedentary settlements of the area. In 1718, they clashed north of the Balkhash lake with the Middle Kazakh Horde and defeated them in a battle which lasted three days. Crossing Syr Darya, they won a second major victory on the banks of the river Arys, north of Tashkent. More was to come, from 1723 to 1725 (remembered in Central Asia as 'The Years of the Great Disaster' (*aqtaban shubrundy*)), when the Kalmuks from the West and the Oïrots from the North launched one raid after another with practically no interruption, destroying the cities of Tashkent, Sairam and Yassy.

It was not until 1728 that the Kazakhs on the banks of Lake Chubar Tengir won their first victory over the Oïrots, but in 1740 and 1742 their hordes were once more defeated by the Kalmuks and Oïrots. In contrast to their predecessors — the Mongols of Chingiz Khan — neither the Kalmuks nor the Oïrots had any intention of settling in Central

Asia — merely of destroying it. Their expeditions were in the nature of a 'Buddhist Crusade' — and such was the imprint of horror they left behind that the memory of the earlier Chingisside invasion was all but erased. They figure in all Turkic epics: in the Kirghiz *Manas*, the Uzbek *Alpamysh*, the Karakalpak *Qyrq Qyz*, where they appear as the heathen enemy of Islam, the 'Chinese' easily recognisable as Oïrot or Kalmuk.

Salvation came in 1757 when the Manchu armies invaded Jungaria and destroyed once and for all the power of the Oïrots.

1.5 *The Last of the Barbarian Invaders: the Russians (Christian and Marxist)*

The Russians conquered Kazan in the middle of the sixteenth century and were still advancing in Central Asia in 1900, the year in which Pamir was finally occupied. From the point of view of Islamic dogma, these new invaders appeared — in the beginning at least — more acceptable than the Chingisside Mongols and Buddhist Oïrots who preceded them. The Russians were *Ahl al-Kitab*, 'People of the Book' who had been favoured with a divine revelation, albeit limited and imperfect. Furthermore, the Russians had been the vassals of the Golden Horde for three centuries and thus were not a totally unknown quantity. The Muslims certainly felt no sense of inferiority towards these former slaves and, for their part, the Russians settling in Muslim territories neither behaved as colonisers nor considered that they had been entrusted by the Almighty to bring culture and civilisation to an underdeveloped inferior race. In short, the Russians never had a feeling of racial superiority over the Turks or the Caucasians.

Nevertheless Russians came in massive numbers and they came to stay. They did not mingle with the local people, spurned cultural contacts and refused to be converted to Islam; thus they remained an alien body in the midst of the Muslim population. In the Middle Volga-Urals their colonies rapidly outnumbered the natives. Elsewhere, in the Crimea, southern Russia between the Bug and the Lower Volga and especially in the Kuban area and the northern and northeastern part of the Kazakh Steppe, they reduced local Turkic and Cherkess populations either to the state of an insignificant minority (as in Crimea) or totally eliminated the Muslim autochtones. These territories have now ceased — probably for ever — to be part of *Dar ul-Islam*.

In all Muslim lands conquered by Russians between the sixteenth and the twentieth centuries the feeling of the native population was that the invaders were foreigners — 'Europeans', never 'Eurasians'.

However, the methods used by the Russians in their dealings with the local population during the conquest were basically not very different from those of the Mongols. Russian methods were certainly harsher and more brutal than those employed by any other European colonial power, employing massacre and expulsion of populations.

Massive slaughter of the resisting population took place, such as the murders during the storming of Kazan in 1552, the quelling of the Nogay tribes in the late eighteenth century, during the Caucasian wars of the nineteenth century (especially in the Chechen region and in Daghestan), in the Turkmen territory at the end of the nineteenth century (the extermination of the entire population of Gök-Tepe by General Skobelev in 1881), and the slaughter of the nomad Kazakh tribes in 1916 by the Russian Army and the Russian colonists.

During the Soviet period massacres reached an unprecedented level: slaughter of the Kokand population in February 1918 by the troops of the Tashkent Soviet; the massacre of over a million nomad Kazakhs during the brutal attempts at settling them in the 1930s; deportation of over a million Chechens, Ingushes, Karachays, Balkars and Crimean Tatars during the unsuccessful attempt at genocide in 1943.

Massive transfers or expulsions of population were practised by the Tsarist authorities. In the sixteenth century, Kazan Tatars were expelled from the main cities of the Middle Volga and from the best agricultural lands along the rivers. During the nineteenth century Russian and Ukrainian colonists expelled the Kazakh nomads from the richest areas of the northern and eastern parts of the Kazakh Steppes. The Caucasians, Chechens, Kabardians, Daghestanis, etc. were driven from the rich Caucasian lowlands. Between 1783 and 1914 more than a million Crimean Tatars, most of the Nogays and over a million Cherkess from the North-Western Caucasus emigrated to the Ottoman Empire.

The same policy was pursued by the Soviets who deported some 2 million Crimean Tatars, North Caucasians and Meshketian Turks, Buddhist Kalmuks and Volga Germans. To this day, many of the victims are still prevented from returning to their homelands.

To the horrors of mass murder and deportation (suffered by the Muslims of Central Asia since the time of Qara-Khitay and of the Chingisside Mongols) the Russians added a sinister refinement: assimilation through co-optation of the elites, mass colonisation of Muslim lands and conversion (often forced) to Christianity. This was without any doubt one of the deadliest dangers that Muslim *'Umma* had to face since the first encounter with the 'Outer World'. All the Tatar literature of the nineteenth century is there to testify that they were fully aware of the threat. However, from the Muslim point of view Marxist atheism appears not as a rival ideology or another competing spiritual creed, but as the latest manifestation of ignorance and backwardness (*jahiliya*). The word 'unbelief' (*dinsizlik*) designates a kind of collective blemish representing cruelty, dishonesty and lack of conscience. It is in the fullest sense pejorative and it is therefore difficult to imagine that any Muslim, Communist or otherwise, would claim to be non-believing or, say, enter into an association bearing this label (*Soyuz Bezbozhnikov*). To the Muslims a real atheist is not deemed to be a romantic rebel or a superior philosophical freethinker, but a subhuman of limited intellect unable to grasp the conception of God and therefore degraded to the level of bestiality (*hayvanat*), if not below. The Marxist-atheist challenge is therefore believed by Muslims to be less dangerous than that of Christianity.

2 Muslim Reaction

Unlike Spain after the *Reconquista*, Islam has survived the Russian conquest. The difference is easy enough to explain; in the southern provinces the Russians have never succeeded in displacing the native populations and thus the entire south-eastern belt of the USSR remains part of *Dar ul-Islam*. But demographic trends alone cannot explain the triumphant survival of Islam. Without the stubborn resistance of the population and a heroic tradition of struggle to preserve their identity, it is probable that Islam would have disappeared.

This resistance took many different forms, some of which appeared simultaneously, but they may be grouped into three main categories.

(1) efforts to preserve *Dar ul-Islam* by armed resistance and uprising against the 'Infidel' rule, from 'Holy War' directed by Sufi brotherhoods to revolts under the leadership of feudal lords generally of Chingisside origin;

(2) the defence of Islam against encroachment by rival ideologies, whether Buddhist, Christian or Marxist, through either conservative or modernist movements;

(3) co-operation with the 'Infidels' in the hope of eventually regaining lost power.

2.1 *Preservation of* Dar ul-Islam *by Armed Resistance*

Armed uprisings against Russian rule started as early as the middle of the sixteenth century in the Tatar country and went on during the seventeenth, eighteenth and nineteenth centuries in the Middle Volga, the Urals and the Kazakh Steppes. As a rule, they were led by the feudal nobility, often by the descendants of Chingiz Khan. In the eighteenth century feudal resistance was relayed by popular movements led by Sufi brotherhoods, first in the Caucasus, where it lasted until the late nineteenth century, and later on in Central Asia (Andizhan 1898 — a Muslim uprising led by the Naqshbandi Sufi tariqa in the city of Andizhan in the Ferghana valley.

Armed resistance continued under the Soviets, as evidenced by the Daghestan-Chechen uprising of 1920–3, the Basmachi movement of 1918–28, and the Chechen revolt of 1941–2. As far as Muslims were concerned, the 1917 Revolution meant no basic change either in their situation or in their relations with the 'Infidel' rulers. The regime of the *Dar ul-Harb* might have changed, but the enemy remained the same.

2.1.1 Feudal Resistance. The first Tatar uprising against Russian rule took place a year after the conquest of Kazan in 1553 and lasted until 1557. The leader of the uprising, a feudal lord, Seit Hussein, was finally captured and executed. The Tatar revolts continued in 1571–2, 1574, 1580, 1584 and 1608–10, simultaneously with the expeditions of the Crimean Khans against Moscow. All were led by the Tatar gentry, who had been deprived of their rights, and all were crushed with the utmost brutality.

In the seventeenth century both the Tatars and the Bashkirs played an important part in the revolt of Stepan Razin. After the defeat of this movement, Muslim armed resistance switched over to the Bashkir country in the Southern Urals. For over a century the Bashkir clans, led by Chingisside princes, descendants of Kuchum, the last khan of Siberia, fought an almost uninterrupted guerrilla war and participated in practically all the revolts in the Lower Volga, the Don and the North Caucasus. The most serious uprisings took place in 1678, in 1705–22 under the leadership of Kuchuk Sultan, and in 1735 under Kilmet Abyz and Sultan Aqay. In 1737, a new and important revolt of Bashkir clans and Kazakh tribes broke out in the Southern Urals led by *biys* Pepene and Tüngevür Kösep. The last rebellion, led by a descendant of Kuchum, Sultan Baybulat, was crushed in 1742 after two years of fierce fighting. Another Bashkir revolt led by the *molla* Batyrsha Aliev took place in 1755. Finally, Bashkirs and Tatars participated actively in the Pugachev movement. Pugachev's most trusted lieutenant was a

Bashkir chieftain, Salavat Yulaev, who died in Schlüsselburg prison in 1797.

All these movements were crushed with appalling violence and by the end of the eighteenth century the fighting spirit of the Bashkirs and Tatars was finally broken. Armed resistance then switched to the Kazakh Steppes, where it was also often headed by Chingisside princes. It started in north-eastern Kazakhstan (Semirechie), where nomad tribes led by Batyr Srym Datov resisted the Russian advance from 1783 until 1797. Quelled in Semirechie, the resistance was taken over by the tribes of the Middle Horde (Orta Zhuz). Their action was led by the Khan Sarzhan (1824–36) and after his death by his successor, the Khan Kenesary Kasymov (1837–47). Simultaneously a revolt against Russian rule broke out in the Bukey Horde (1827–9), led by the feudal lords Isatay Taymanov and Mohammad Utemisov. When the Bukey Horde was defeated, the rebellion switched to the Lesser Horde (Kishi Zhuz), where it was headed by the Khan Alla Kul (1838–9). By the middle of the nineteenth century, however, the power of the khans had been destroyed and the revolts led by the feudal aristocracy put down.

Elsewhere, the landed gentry played only a minor role in armed resistance movements. The Russians managed to co-opt practically the whole of the feudal aristocracy of Kabarda and Azerbayjan, while in Daghestan the powerful landed gentry hesitated between resistance and co-operation, only joining the 'Holy War' after the final defeat of the religious cohorts. The uprising of 1877–8 led by the Daghestani feudal nobility was crushed with comparative ease by the Russians.

With the exception of these last rebellions by the Kazakhs and Daghestanis, feudal uprisings had been defeated by the end of the eighteenth century. The native aristocracy had been either co-opted by the Russian Establishment, eliminated or, as in the case of Kazakhstan, stripped of economic power and social standing. The flag of resistance was therefore transferred to the religious leaders and the fight took on the aspect of a *jihad*, a 'Holy War', against the 'Infidel'.

2.1.2 The 'Holy War'. Armed religious resistance began in the late eighteenth century. It was spearheaded by the mystical Sufi brotherhoods (*tariqa*) fighting to establish the reign of God on earth, the first step of the struggle being *jihad*, *ghazawat* − 'Holy War' against the 'Infidel' rulers and the 'Bad Muslims' who served them. Sufi *tariqa* were − and still are − closed societies based on the principle of initiation, iron discipline and total devotion of the adepts (*mürids*) to their masters (*sheikhs, pir, mürshid*). Their fight, which quickly assumed marked puritan and anti-feudal aspects, was certainly more effective than the anarchic, unorganised uprisings of the feudal lords.

The 'Holy War' started in the North-Eastern Caucasus in the late eighteenth century and with short interruptions lasted until 1920-3. It was directed by the Sufi orders — the Naqshbandiya and to a lesser degree the Qadiriya — which at the same time were fighting other 'Infidel' overlords, the Chinese in Sinkiang (the revolt of the Uyghurs and the Dungans in 1860-5), the British in the Punjab and the Dutch in Indonesia.

The first Sufi *sheikh* to engage in a *jihad* against the Russians was a Chechen Naqshbandi, the Imam Mansur Ushurma. In 1785 his warriors encircled a Russian bridge on the banks of the river Sunzha and annihilated it — the worst defeat ever inflicted on the armies of Catherine II. Mansur's movement spread to Chechnia, Northern Daghestan and, in 1790, to the Kuban, but failed in Kabarda. The Imam was captured by the Russians in Anapa in 1791 and died in Schlüsselburg prison in 1793.

The first Sufi resistance movement was thus broken and the Naqshbandiya disappeared from Northern Caucasus for almost thirty years. Activity began again in the 1820s in the province of Shirvan, in the southern part of the country. This time the Sufi missionaries came from the Ottoman Empire.

Sheikh Mohammed Efendi of Yaraglar in Southern Daghestan was the second Naqshbandi *mürshid* to preach the *jihad* against the Russians. He was the master of Ghazi Mohammad and Shamil, the first and third Naqshbandi imams of Daghestan. The 'Holy War', referred to in Russian historical literature as the 'Mürid movement', lasted for 35 years, from 1824 to 1859, when Shamil was finally defeated and captured. It was the longest and fiercest resistance put up by any Muslim population to Russian conquest and long remembered as a model of heroism.

After the occupation of Daghestan-Chechnia by the Russians, the Naqshbandiya went underground and became a clandestine organisation. The leaders were harried and, if caught, deported to Siberia; others emigrated or became 'Robin Hoods', bandits of honour, forming guerrilla groups in the mountains.

The Qadiriya, which appeared in Northern Caucasus after Shamil's defeat, when 'Infidel' domination had become a fact of life, was very different from the militant Naqshbandiya, at least at the outset. Qadiri ideology was inspired by mysticism rather than by 'Holy War', but the mystical detachment of the Order was, as in all other *tariqa*, inseparable from the conviction that Russian authority had to be resisted. So, from purely mystical beginnings, this *tariqa* rapidly became another centre of military resistance to the Russian presence. Outlawed in the 1860s, the Qadiriya, together with the Naqshbandiya, were to play an active part in the anti-Russian revolt of 1877–8 in Daghestan and Chechnia.

The October Revolution and the Civil War in the Caucasus provided the Sufi adepts with another opportunity to shake off Russian rule and to try to expel the hated 'Infidels'. For five years the Naqshbandi adepts, led by two *mürshid*s, the Imam Najmuddin of Götzo and Sheikh Uzun Haji, fought first against the White armies of Denikin and then, in 1920, against the Red Army.

During 1920–1 the revolt covered all Chechnia and Northern Daghestan and the Soviets were forced to engage the entire Eleventh Red Army corps to crush the desperate resistance of the Ghazis. Najmuddin of Götzo managed to fight on until 1925, when he was finally captured and executed. Together with the Basmachis movement, the Chechen-Daghestani uprising of 1920–1 was one of the most dangerous challenges to the Bolsheviks since their advent to power in 1917.

After their defeat, the religious elements in Northern Caucasus were submitted to a long and bloody persecution, but it was not long before Qadiri and Naqshbandi were fighting again, this time in a major revolt which broke out in the Northern Caucasus in 1928, which was followed by similar revolts in 1934 and 1940–2. The last uprising started in the winter of 1940 and was led by nationalists, former members of the Communist Party, but the Qadiris were numerous among the guerrilla fighters.

In Central Asia the Sufi brotherhoods were responsible for the Andizhan uprising in 1898. The leader, *ishan* Madali, was a Naqshbandi *mürshid*, but his attempt to overthrow Russian rule in the Ferghana valley failed and he was later hanged.

In Central Asia the Soviets faced another conservative movement, known in Soviet historial accounts as the 'Basmachi Movement' (derived from the Uzbek *basmach* — 'bandit'). This was a popular guerrilla uprising, the leaders of which came from a variety of backgrounds from village notables and tribal chieftains to authentic 'bandits' (*rahzen*). Many of these men were Sufi adepts and several of the more important ones, such as Khal Hoja, Madamin Beg and Junaid Khan, were Naqshbandi sheikhs. The movement started in 1918 in the Ferghana valley and from there it spread to the eastern part of Bukhara (present-day Southern Uzbekistan and Tajikistan) and to Northern Turkmenistan. The movement was eventually liquidated by the Red

Army around 1928 after a long and difficult struggle, but in some areas (especially in the Lokay country of Souther Uzbekistan and in Turkmenistan), the rebels fought on until the mid-1930s.

As in the case of the Naqshbandi 'Holy War' of 1920-1 in the Caucasus, the Basmachi movement was an attempt by the conservatives to preserve their independence as well as the purity and glory of their faith. Both movements provide striking contrast to the ineffective efforts at warding off the Soviets made by Muslim liberal and right-wing socialist groups at the same time. As far as Muslim conservatives were concerned, Soviet power was simply another variant of Russian encroachment – only worse because the new Russians were not only 'Infidels' (*kafir*) and also irreligious (*bi-din*). They were therefore more deserving of contempt than their Tsarist predecessors.

2.2 *The Struggle to Preserve Islam Under 'Infidel' Rule*

With the failure of armed resistance and the imposition of 'Infidel' rule, the Muslim lands of Central Asia, the Middle Volga and the Caucasus could not, strictly speaking, continue to remain part of *Dar ul-Islam*, even though the fiction of *Dar ul-Islam* was maintained in some areas during the Tsarist period: in Crimea, the Ottoman Sultan-Calif remained, theoretically at least, the supreme religious authority and the *khütbe* (Friday prayers at the mosque) was said in his name. In the same way, in Central Asia, the *khütbe* was said in the name of the Emir of Bukhara. Nevertheless, this fiction could not disguise the fact that Muslims were governed by a technically more advanced, dynamic and aggressive Christian Establishment which threatened to swamp the cultural and social traditions, the way of life and the religion of their Muslim subjects. 'How could we make our Tatar ox-cart compete with the Russian steam-engine?' was typical of the questions raised by the Tatar political thinkers on the eve of the Revolution. The need to preserve Islam, to maintain its purity and finally to adapt it to the realities of the modern world took on various forms of approach, which can conveniently be tagged as: (1) the moderate conservative; (2) the modernist liberal; and (3) the radical conservative.

2.2.1 *The Moderate Conservative Response.*
Like all Islamic communities isolated among foreigners, Russian Muslims were profoundly conscious of a sense of religious solidarity. A man was not just Muslim, as distinct from Christian, he also belonged to Islam rather than to Russia. It is fair to say that until the Revolution – and in spite of the strong modernist and secularist trend which began to develop in

Russian Islam in the middle of the nineteenth century — Russian Muslims were among the most religious of the Muslim world. Being a Muslim was, for aristocrat and peasant alike, a condition of survival.

The feeling of religious brotherhood and the need to erect a common front against the Russians even existed between Sunni, Shia and Ismaili communities of the Pamirs, all of whom considered themselves part of the same Muslim *'Umma*. This conscious solidarity, unique in the Muslim world, was made official at the third Muslim Congress of Russia in 1905, when the Shia Jafarite rite (*Ithna Asharia* — 'Those who recognise twelve imams') was solemnly proclaimed to be the fifth legal school (*mazhab*) of Islam on a par with the four Sunni *mazhab*s, Hanafi, Shafei, Maleki and Hanbali. The feeling of solidarity has survived the October Revolution and sixty years of Soviet rule. For example, in Azerbayjan, where about 70 per cent of the population belongs to the Shia sect, religious quarrels with Sunnis are not only extremely rare but the same mosques serve both rites.

In the eighteenth century and the first half of the nineteenth, when confronted with their new Christian overlords and the threat presented by the more advanced civilisation they brought with them, the first reaction of the Muslims was to retire into their shell and refuse to borrow from the Russians. Only a few of the elite chose to imitate the Russian way of life, some even going as far as becoming Christian, after which they were rapidly assimilated. This, of course, meant breaking with their brethren, who were thus able to preserve the integrity and cohesion of Muslim society.

When entering the modern era (in Russia this corresponds roughly to the reign of Catherine II), the Muslims of Russia had already attained a high level of economic development. The Volga Tatar merchant colonies, who controlled trade between Russia, China and Central Asia, were particular prosperous, but, by a curious paradox, they were from an intellectual point of view also the most traditional and conservative Muslim society in the world. Their attitude was to cut Russian Islam off from the reformist currents which first appeared in the Muslim world in the late eighteenth century, such as the Wahhabi attempt to redisover the pristine purity of the 'Golden Age' of the first four Califs.

In 1783, the year of the conquest of Crimea, Catherine II created an official Islamic administration, the Muftiat, with its seat first in Orenburg, then in Ufa. In 1788, a Muslim Spiritual Board was added to the Muftiat. Until the Revolution, this Central Muslim Administration was dominated by the most conservative elements among the Tatars, loyal to St Petersburg and totally opposed to any modernist or reformist ideology.

During the nineteenth century, traditionalist '*Qadymism*' (from the Arabic *qadym* — 'ancient') dominated the intellectual life of Islamic scholarship that served as the model for the Tatars. The Tatar religious schools were copied on the Turkestani model, with Bukharian professors being brought to the Volga area and young Tatar scholars being sent to Bukhara and Samarkand to complete their intellectual education.

The conservatism of the Tatars in the nineteenth century was a logical natural defence against the encroachment of Russian civilisation and the tempting spirit of liberalism and rationalism that came with it. It was also a direct consequence of hostility towards everything Russian brought on by the religious persecutions of the first half of the eighteenth century. Muslim conservatism was moderately xenophobic but at the same time perfectly obedient to the Russian administration. Its aim was purely negative: to keep the Muslim community as remote as possible from the modern world. It was a defensive attitude, not at all militant and therefore very different from the radical conservatism of the combative Sufi brotherhoods in Northern Caucasus. Nevertheless, examined in its historical perspective, this peaceful and moderate conservatism saved Tatar and Bashkir Islam from Russian and European 'contamination'.

This moderate conservative trend disappeared completely around 1905 and left no legacy. At present, Soviet Islam is divided between the reformist-modernist and the radical 'revolutionary' conservative trends. There is no place in the USSR for 'quiet conservatism'.

2.2.2 The Modernist Liberal Response. The move to modernise Islam began in the second half of the nineteenth century. In contrast to the puritan revival of the late eighteenth and early nineteenth centuries which aimed simply to reassert *purity*, this time the emphasis was on regaining *power*. Besides spiritual and cultural renaissance, liberal reformism also had a political objective: that Muslims should first obtain equality with the encroaching Europeans and then win superiority over them. Without questioning the religious foundation of Muslim society, liberal reformers applied themselves to modernise Islam by imitating the spirit of the West rather than its methods.

The reformist movement manifested itself in all Islamic countries from the Ottoman Empire (Abdul Haq Hamid, 1851-1937; Namik Kemal, 1840-88; Tevfik Fikret, 1870-1915) to the Arab world (Sheikh Muhammed Abduh, 1849-1905; Rashid Ridha and the Manar School),

India (Sir Sayyid Ahmad, 1817-98 and Amir Ali, 1849-1928) and even Indonesia (Haji Agus Salim, 1889-1955). It was a powerful movement, led by an influential and energetic new class of native bourgeoisie, which was to dominate the intellectual and political life of the Muslim world and raise many unfulfilled hopes in the process.

In Russia, the reformist movement took on a different character from elsewhere. Not only were Russian Muslims subject to a particularly wide variety of outside influences, but the problem which faced Tatar, Caucasian or Turkestani reformers was not merely how to regain power but how to survive. The movement began in the middle of the nineteenth century with an attempt by Volga Tatar clerics to break with the conservative traditionalism which dominated the spiritual life of Russian Muslims. The first to challenge the scholars, guardians of the status quo, was Abu Nasr Kursavi (1783-1814), who taught in a Bukharian *madrassah*.

Condemned to death for heresy by the Emir of Bukhara and accused of 'impiety' by the Mufti of Orenburg, Kursavi was obliged to flee to Istanbul, where he later died. He was followed by Shihabeddin Marjani (1818-89), the greatest and the most successful of Tatar *ulema*. Marjani fought all his life to rid Islam of the dogmatism of traditional theology and to prove that religion could be, as it was in the Golden Age of Islam, perfectly compatible with progress and modern science. He condemned *taqlid*, blind obedience to traditional authority, and advocated the recognition of *ijtihad* – the right of every believer to find his own interpretation of religious, and therefore of cultural, social, economic and political, questions – in the Quran and the Hadith.

Marjani, like his Wahhabi predecessors, believed that the salvation of the Muslim world lay in its return to purity. But, unlike the Wahhabis who felt that Islam would regain its cultural and political vigour simply by turning the clock back, Marjani advocated cautious imitation of the West on condition that its influence was limited and the integrity of the Muslim faith preserved. Marjani's influence on Russian Islam was profound. He opened the way to vigorous modernist reform, hitherto hampered by fear of accusations of impiety or heresy. He was followed by a pleiad of Tatar, Crimean and Caucasian thinkers who applied themselves to the problem of the scientific, technical and political backwardness of Islam and tried to find a solution in religious reform. In the process these thinkers, Rizaeddin Fahretdin oğlu (1859-1936), Abdul Qayyum Nasyri (1825-1902), Ismail bey Gaspraly (Gasprinsky) (1851-1914), Musa Jarullah Bigi (1875-1949), Abdullah Bubi and many others succeeded in restoring vigour to the Muslim religion in

Russia.

In 1905 Russian Islam was endowed with a powerful religious establishment, consisting of some 25,000 mosques, over 50,000 clerics, thousands of schools (both *mektep* and *madrassah*) using the *jadid* system of teaching introduced by Ismail Gaspraly, a brilliant new Muslim literature inspired by the challenge of the modern world and committed to religious and political reforms, and a rich, diverse and sophisticated periodical press producing material in all Muslim languages of the Russian Empire.

This powerful reformist movement led by the Volga Tatars produced a deep split among Muslim clerics. The liberal, younger elements — the so-called *jadid* (modernist) — campaigned for reform and even took sides with the revolutionary bourgeoisie in opposing the Tsarist monarchy, while the traditionalists (*qadymist*) remained conservative in religion and politics and loyal to the regime. By 1905, the *jadid* movement was dominant, except for Central Asia and the Northern Caucasus, which remained the bastions of conservatism.

The Revolution and the Civil War dramatically changed the religious scene. The first victims were the 'moderate conservative' *qadymists*, loyal to the Romanov monarchy, who disappeared completely. The *jadid* liberals, the majority of whom sympathised with the right-wing socialists (Mensheviks, Socialist Revolutionaries), were bewildered by the suddenness and brutality of the Revolution. A few of them took sides, either with the White counter-revolutionaries or with the Bolsheviks (the so-called 'Red Mollahs'), but most of them refused to take an active part in the events and preferred to remain neutral. Those that joined the Bolsheviks believed, with Musa Jarulla Bigi, that the godless Bolshevik regime, though evil and hostile, would be preferable to the militant Christian counter-revolution, but they were to be the losers in the end. While the radical conservatives fought back or went underground, the *jadid*s were unable to organise their position and subsequently were the main targets of the long and bloody anti-Islamic campaign which began around 1928 and lasted until the war.

Abdurrahman Rasulaev, Mufti of Ufa, one of the few Muslim *jadid* clerics to survive the fearful religious persecutions of 1932–8 when Muslim clerics were harried as 'spies', 'counter-revolutionaries' and 'saboteurs', approached Stalin in 1942 with the project of normalising relations between the Soviet government and Islam. Stalin accepted Rasulaev's proposal, and a concordat was signed along the lines of the concordat which the Metropolitan (later the Patriarch) Sergius had managed to obtain for the Russian Orthodox Church. Persecution and anti-religious propaganda were stopped and Islam was granted legal status, with the creation of an official Islamic Adminstration. It follows the tradition of Imperial Russia and is modelled on the Central Spiritual Muslim Directorate (Tsentral'noe Musul'manskoe Dukhovnoe Upravlenie) for European Russia and Siberia created in 1783 in Orenburg.

At present the Official Islamic Administration is divided into four Muslim Spiritual Boards (Musul'manskie Dukhovnye Upravleniya) in:

(1) Tashkent, Central Asia and Kazakhstan;
(2) Ufa, European Russia and Siberia;
(3) Makhach-Qala, Northern Caucasus and Daghestan;
(4) Baku, Transcaucasia.

The first three are Sunni and the last mixed Shia and Sunni.

Each board is autonomous in both administrative and canonical matters. Until recently there was a marked difference between Tashkent, dominated by progressive *jadid*s, and the Ufa, Makhach-Qala and Baku boards, which were more conservative. But during 1979–80 the muftis of Ufa and Makhach-Qala, as well as the Shia Shiekh ul-Islam of Baku, were dismissed and replaced by very young *ulema* who seem more amenable to government authority, and more 'progressive' in their religious attitude. At present the small circle of 'registered' clerics, composed of the executives of the four directorates and of the staff of the 'working' mosques (probably two to three thousand clerics) represent a homogeneous group. As a rule, they are young (the Mufti of Ufa, Talgat Taziiev, was born in 1948, the Sheikh ul-Islam of Baku, Alla-Shukur Pasha Zade, in 1949 and Mahmud Gekkiev, the Mufti of Makhach-Kala, in 1935) and of excellent, sometimes outstanding, intellectual ability. In Central Asia the professional standard is certainly higher now that it was in pre-revolutionary Russia, and is probably equal to that of any other Muslim country.

'Official' Islam in the USSR represents the last legacy of the brilliant pre-revolutionary *jadid* reformism. The young Soviet *ulema* of today are heirs to the prestigious constellation of modernist and liberal theologians from Shihabeddin Marjani to Rizaeddin Fahretdin oğlu. Like their great predecessors, they reject the *taqlid* and advocate the restoration of the *ijtihad*. They are endeavouring to reconcile Islam with science and progress and to guarantee its survival in a socialist environment.

It is impossible to evaluate precisely the contribution of 'Official

Islam' to the preservation of religion among the Muslims of the Soviet Union. Undoubtedly 'Official Islam' is served by an extremely able 'General Staff' of well trained *ulema,* which at least guarantees the purity and integrity of Islam and prevents the Muslim religion from relapsing into shamanism and ignorance. On the other hand, it is difficult to imagine that with a mere 400-500 'working' mosques — one for every 90,000 Muslims, two *madrassah*s with less than sixty students and one religious periodical which cannot be read by the majority of believers (*Muslims of the Soviet East* is published in Arabic, Persian, French, English and Uzbek — Arabic script), 'Official Islam' can meet even the minimum spiritual needs of Muslims. Clearly another dimension is needed if the religion of the Prophet is to be preserved in the USSR.

2.2.3 The Radical Conservative Response. It is necessary to distinguish between the 'moderate conservatives' and the 'radical conservatives'. The former were dreamers who wanted to be left in peace, and to follow the prescriptions of their religion away from politics and the ruling 'Infidels'. The latter were and still are xenophobic militants who believe that in order to live their religion, they must first drive the 'Infidel' invaders from their land and then build a theocratic state sanctified by sacred law (*Shariyat*).

As early as the twelfth and thirteenth centuries the fundamentalist Sufi orders had provided the only effective Muslim response to the 'Infidels' — Qara-Khitay and Mongols. The same orders fought the Russian conqueror in the eighteenth and nineteenth centuries and the Soviet regime in the 1920s. Since the victory of the Bolsheviks up to the present day, the only serious, organised resistance encountered by the Soviets in the Muslim territories has come from the Sufi *tariqa,* what Soviet sources call the 'Parallel', 'Non-official' or 'Sectarian' Islam.

'Parallel Islam' is more powerful and more deeply rooted than Official Islam. The Sufi brotherhoods are closed, but not wholly secret, societies; they are well structured, hierarchic organisations bound by an absolute dedication to a religious ideal. Their historical role has been to oppose foreign rulers and to preserve the purity of Islam. It is as a result of their constant activity that Islam has survived as a religion and as a way of life in the USSR.

Sufi orders are officially outlawed, and therefore operate completely outside the control of the Soviet authorities and of the official Muslim administration. Where Official Islam is inadequate, it is supplemented and often replaced by Sufi Islam. It is the adepts of the brotherhoods who perform the necessary religious rites, circumcision, *nikah* (religious marriage) and religious burial. They also run numerous religious schools and clandestine houses of prayer.

The activities of the *tariqa* are generally centred around the 'holy places', often tombs (*mazar*) of Muslim saints both mythical and real. These holy places serve as substitutes for the impossible pilgrimage to Mecca and as meeting places for adepts and lay believers. There are prayers for the believers and *zikr* for the adepts so that the holy places have essentially replaced the closed mosques. They are also used by the Sufis as a forum where they can teach Arabic, prayers, a little elementary theology, and where they indulge in a very active counter-propaganda directed against the official atheism of the regime. Soviet sources present Sufi brotherhoods as 'dangerous, fanatical, anti-Soviet, anti-Socialist, anti-Russian reactionary forces', but they recognise their efficiency and dynamism.

Sufi brotherhoods are not small chapels but, according to recent Soviet sources, mass organisations numbering hundreds of thousands of adepts. The figures are certainly higher today than before the 1917 revolution. New branches have been founded since the Second World War, despite the violent anti-religious campaign aimed principally at Sufism. The adepts of Sufi orders are not drawn merely from North Caucasian mountain peasants or poor craftsmen of Central Asian cities; nowadays, a significant and growing proportion are industrial workers and intellectuals (or semi-intellectuals). In 1975, a Soviet sociologist, V.G. Pivovarov (*Sotsiologicheskie issledovaniya problem byta, kul'tury, natsional 'nykh traditsii i verovanii v Checheno-Ingushskoi ASSR*, Voprosy Nauchnogo Ateizma, Moscow Vol XVII, 1975, p.316) established that more than half the believers in Northern Caucasus belong to a Sufi brotherhood. This means that in Northern Caucasus alone the number of Sufi adepts could be around quarter of a million, an incredible figure for an underground society.

Sufi orders exist in all the Muslim areas of the Soviet Union, but their main bastion remains the Northern Caucasus (especially Daghestan and the Chechen-Ingush Republic), where the Naqshbandiya for the last two centuries has been the standard bearer of the resistance to the Tsarists and their Soviet successors. In Central Asia, the home of several important brotherhoods, Sufism remains particularly active in the former nomadic areas where native society has more or less preserved its clan structure, such as Turkmenistan, Kazakhstan, Kirghizia and the southern part of Uzbekistan. In the Volga region, where the Sufi orders played a major role in the Tatar intellectual and cultural revival of the late nineteenth century, they seem to have largely disappeared since the war.

Several *tariqa* dominate Soviet Islam. The most important is the Naqshbandiya, an ancient order founded in Bukhara in the fourteenth century, which has been diffused throughout the Muslim world, arriving in the Volga area and the Northern Caucasus at the end of the eighteenth century. The Naqshbandiya adepts have a long tradition of 'Holy War' against the Russians and more recently participated in several anti-Soviet movements in Northern Caucasus, including the 1941-2 troubles in Chechnia. The order remains possibly the most popular of the Sufi brotherhoods, very conservative in religious matters yet managing to avoid some of the excesses of other *tariqa*. It is an 'aristocratic' order, more 'intellectual' than the popular Qadiriya and probably better fitted for an open 'Holy War' than for underground subversive activity.

The Qadiriya is probably today the second largest order. Founded in Baghdad in the twelfth century, it also has branches throughout the Muslim world from Maghreb to India. It was introduced into the Caucasus relatively late, around 1850, by a Daghestani, Kunta Haji Kishiev. After his death in a Russian prison in 1867, the *tariqa* (also known in the Caucasus as the 'Kunta Haji' brotherhood) was divided into three principal orders:

(1) *the* tariqa *of Bammat Giray* operating in the Chechen country. The most moderate one of the three (its founder, Ali Mitaev, even co-operated for a short time with the Soviet regime before his execution in 1927).

(2) *the* tariqa *of Batal Haji* operating in the Ingush country. It is the most anti-Russian of all Sufi orders operating in the USSR (its adepts have been accused by the Soviets of terrorism). The leadership of the *tariqa* is hereditary in the Belhoroev family. The *tariqa* remains very conservative in religious matters, refusing innovations and observing endogamic taboos towards other Muslims.

(3) *the Chim Mirza* tariqa, the most 'modernist' of the Qadiri branches. Its adepts practice the loud *zikr* with drums and ecstatic dances, After the war, this order gave birth to a fourth brotherhood, the *tariqa* of *Vis* (*Uweis*) *Haji*, founded in Kazakhstan by Chechen exiles. It is the most puritan of all Soviet Sufi orders, but at the same time its adepts have introduced many innovations, such as the use of transistors for propaganda and musical instruments

during the *zikr*, and granted an important place to women in the life of the *tariqa*. The Vis Haji adepts practice rigorous endogamy within their brotherhood. Soviet sources accuse them of terrorism and subversion.

All the four branches of the Qadiriya formerly limited to Northern Caucasus — Chechen-Ingush Republic, Northern Ossetia and Northern Daghestan — have spread to Kazakhstan and Kirghizia since the deportation of the Mountaineers to Central Asia in 1943.

Less 'intellectual' than the Naqshbandis, the Qadiris have a long tradition of underground 'subversive' activity in the Soviet Union. The Qadiri orders are all highly independent and open to more innovations than the conservative Naqshbandis. Because of their radical xenophobia, the Vis Haji and the Batal Haji *tariqa* seem to be especially popular.

Two other local *tariqa*, the Yasawiya and the Kubrawiya, play a part in the religious life of Central Asia (though somewhat modest when compared to the Naqshbandiya and the Qadiriya). The Yasawiya is an old Sufi order founded in Southern Kazakhstan in the twelfth century. Until the October Revolution, the adepts of this highly mystical order practising the loud *zikr* were totally uninterested in mundane affairs. In the late 1920s, probably as a consequence of the repression following the defeat of the Basmachis, the Yasawiya gave birth to a new order, the *tariqa* of the 'Hairy Ishans' (Chachtuu Eshander), a highly political organisation whose adepts believe that the 'Holy War' is the first and necessary step on the path leading to God. Soviet sources accuse this *tariqa* of terrorism, subversion and political agitation. Since the war, several have been tried in Kirghizia for opposing Soviet laws, organsing clandestine Quranic schools and underground houses of prayer and in general for 'sabotaging the Soviet regime and preparing the foundations of an Islamic theocratic state' — *Musulmanabād*.

The Kubrawiya is another ancient mystical brotherhood founded in the twelfth century in the Khwarezm (south-east of the Aral Sea in present-day Turkmenistan). This *tariqa* practises the loud *zikr*. It is limited to Turkmenistan, the Karakalpak ASSR and the north-eastern part of the Uzbek SSR.

Finally, there are numerous 'wandering' mystics, especially in Central Asia. Some of them are loosely connected to a brotherhood such as the Kalendariya, with its spiritual centre in Samarkand, others, with no particular affiliation, being part Muslim clerics (*ruhani*), part Turco-Mongol *shaman* ('witch-doctor').

For the last ten years, anti-religious agitprop in Central Asia and Northern Caucasus has been directed against Sufi Islam, a fact which testifies to its power and hold on the population. Soviet sources recognise that it is as a result of the combined efforts of 'Official' and 'Parallel' Islam that religion has survived among the Muslim population of the USSR. A measure of their success is the fact that 80 per cent of the population are 'believers', whilst only 20 per cent are declared atheists, whereas the percentage is exactly the reverse among the Christians, so called.

The role of radically conservative Muslims in the USSR is not limited just to the preservation of religious beliefs, and the *tariqa* are not concerned merely with cult observance. In Islam, the religious, national and political spheres are tightly interwoven, and consequently the Sufi brotherhoods have become the focal point of traditional opposition to the Russian presence. The militant ideology of the Sufi *tariqa* has also helped to maintain within the full spectrum of society the notion of belonging to a pan-Islamic brotherhood. For the present, the Sufi orders remain traditionalist, closed societies believing that only religion can constitute the proper basis of the unity of the Muslim *'Umma* – 'the community of the believers'. However, since the war some orders have became more and more infused with nationalism, with the result that any nationalist movement – even progressive – which is bound to emerge will be strongly influenced by the traditionalist conservative ideas of Sufism. That such a movement will emerge is beyond doubt.

2.3 Co-operation with the 'Infidel' Ruler

Colonial powers have always found among the colonised elites individuals who for various reasons (more often than not selfish) were ready to co-operate with the conquerors, and Russians were no less successful in this respect than the British, the Dutch or the French. Even before the conquest of Kazan, the Great Princes of Moscow had in their vassal khanate of Kasimov a store of Chingisside princes who served them loyally as distinguished military commanders.

Later on, during the eighteenth and nineteenth centuries, the Russian government managed to co-opt the Tatar merchants and use them as middlemen in their dealings with the as yet unconquered Muslim regions. It also obtained the full and loyal co-operation of the moderate conservative clerics who dominated the Spiritual Muslim Directorate of Orenburg.

When the *jadid*s served Russian interests, it was for personal rather than for 'ideological' reasons. A Crimean Tatar nobleman serving Ivan the Terrible or a Kazan Tatar merchant representing Russian trading interests in Central Asia did not attempt to explain his behaviour, still less justify his co-operation with the *kafir* rulers. Likewise, the first Muslim *prosvetiteli* ('enlighteners') — Chokan Valikhanov of the Kazakh Steppes, Abbas Kuli Bakikhanly (1794–1847) and Fath Ali Shah Akhundov (1812–78) in the Cascasus, or Shihabeddin Marjani (1818–99) in Kazan — never tried to present a philosophical or political explanation of their 'Westernism'. They sincerely believed that Islam was hopelessly backward and that it was of benefit for Muslims to draw on Western culture.

Before Gasprinsky no one imagined that the relationship between the Muslims and their Russian rulers could evolve into an association between two equal partners of mutual benefit to both sides.

Ismail Gaspraly (Gasprinsky) (1851–1914), the son of an impoverished Crimean Tatar nobleman, was one of the most distinguished Muslim thinkers of the later nineteenth and early twentieth centuries. After graduating from a Quranic school in Baghchesaray and the Cadet Corps in Moscow, Gaspraly lived for some time in France and the Ottoman Empire before returning to Crimea in 1877 and being elected mayor of Baghchesaray. In 1882, he launched a political programme aimed at the unification of the Turkic world of the Russian Empire which was to last until his death, on the eve of the First World War. Gaspraly had been influenced by many foreign ideologies, among them Russian populism in its Slavophile form, French liberalism and Young Turk and German romanticism, which he then blended to produce a doctrine of liberal pan-Turkism. He was the greatest educator, linguist, historian and political leader of his time. His influence on the intellectual life of Russian Islam and on the Muslim world in general was tremendous.

Unlike his predecessors, Gaspraly was deeply conscious of the potential might of *Dar ul-Islam*. He was convinced that the decline was only temporary and that the future of humanity belonged to Islam — especially to Turkic Islam. It was this immense area extending from the Bosphorus to the Chinese border that Gaspraly tried to gather in and unify around his slogan 'Dilde, fikirde, işte birlik', 'Union in language, in thought and in action'.

Gaspraly was the first to expound pan-Turkism among Russian Muslims, although he rejected its more violent, anti-Western manifestations. He also refused to accept the radicalism of al-Afghani (who preached rebellion of the Muslim world against the encroaching West) on the basis that an assault on a powerful adversary — Russia — was ill-conceived and bound to fail. But he also condemned the submissive attitude of some of his predecessors, the 'Westernisers' who considered that the salvation of Islam lay in the imitation of European civilisation. Gaspraly thought that Islam was strong enough to vie with the West and still retain its soul.

What Gaspraly was offering to the Russian Empire was nothing less than partnership on equal terms for the conquest of the world. Gaspraly expanded this idea, first in a pamphlet called *Russian Islam* (*Russkoe Musul'manstvo*, Simferopol', 1881) then in many articles of his newspaper, *Terjüman* (*Interpreter*, Bagtchesaray, 1883–1914) and more thoroughly in his *Russian Muslim Agreement* (*Russko-Musul'manskoe Soglashenie*, Bagtchesaray, 1895).

Gaspraly thought that of all European nations, Russia was closest to Islam. Eight centuries of contacts, some of them unfortunate but others positive, had resulted in a certain symbiosis between the Russians and the Muslim Turks. Therefore, if the Muslim world had to choose a European partner, it was preferable that this partner should be Russian.

In exchange for total religious and cultural freedom and absolute equality for Russian Muslims, Gaspraly offered Russia the full support of the Muslim world in the fight against British, German and French colonialism.

Thus, a real Russian-Muslim-Turkic alliance was to be established for the mutual benefit of both partners. Gaspraly was a monarchist and his offer was addressed to the Romanov monarchy, but no one in St Petersburg paid the slightest attention to this obscure Tatar pamphleteer. The Tsarist Establishment was unwilling or unable to respond to this appeal.

Around 1905 other liberal Muslim political leaders, discouraged by the lack of Tsarist response, thought of offering Gaspraly's Russian-Muslim alliance to Russian liberals, more precisely to the 'Constitutional Democrats' (KD). Some of them even joined the KD Party and tried to make use of its prestige and influence at the Duma. One such was the Tatar Yusuf Akchura oğlu (Akchurin, 1876–1933). Akchura oğlu, a member of a rich family of industrialists from Simbirsk, went on from a brilliant academic career at Istanbul and Paris universities to play a prominent part in the political life of Russian Islam. He was one of the founders of the great Muslim political party, Ittifaq al-Muslimin. In 1905, he joined the Constitutional Democrat Party and became a member of its Central Committee. Akchura oğlu pinned his hopes on the political evolution of Russia along liberal democratic lines. He believed that Muslim demands could be satisfied by legal action and was elected a Deputy together with 24 other Muslims at the First Duma; at the second 34 were elected, most of whom were liberal democrats.

Akchura oğlu's dreams of Russian-Muslim partnership were quickly shattered when not a single demand presented by Muslim delegates at the Duma was satisfied by Russian liberals of the KD Party, who proved to be either perfectly indifferent to the national aspirations of their Muslim fellow citizens or, like the Tsarist government, were unable to cope with them. Disenchantment followed with the result that there were 10 Muslim Deputies in the Third Duma and only 7 in the Fourth. Yusuf Akchura himself, convinced that co-operation with Russian liberals was impossible, decided in 1908 to emigrate to Turkey, which became his second homeland.

Even after the failure of the Romanov monarchy and the Russian liberal bourgeoisie to satisfy Muslims' demands, some Muslim leaders still refused to abandon the dream of a Russian-Muslim partnership. In spring 1906, the most radical revolutionary elements among them — Ayyaz Iskhaki, Fuad Tuktar and Abdullah Davletschin — founded the Tangchylar ('Those of the Morning Star') which went along with the political programme and the populist ideology of the Russian Socialist Revolutionaries. This last pre-revolutionary attempt to link the destiny of Russian Muslims to the right wing of Russian social-ism met with the same fate as the previous attempts. As soon as the right-wing socialists (Socialist Revolutionaries and Mensheviks) ob-tained power in February 1917, they behaved towards the Muslim minorities with traditional Great Russian chauvinism. There remained, however, one alternative of finding a Russian partner willing to co-operate with the Muslims — the Bolsheviks.

2.3.1 Co-operation with the Bolsheviks – Muslim National Communists (1918–28). Muslim National Communism was the last endeavour of Soviet Muslim intellectuals to find a solution for their collective national problems in co-operation with the Russians and within the framework of a Russian or a Russian-dominated state. It was a unique experiment which lasted from 1918 until 1928 and was to leave its particular, highly volatile mark on the further develpoment of all Muslim national movements. It was the synthesis of various, often contradictory, ideologies and practical ideas thrown up by a group of highly sophisticated young nationalists, members of the upper strata of society who before the Revolution belonged to various right-wing as well as left-wing political groups. They joined the Russian Bolshevik Communist Party between 1917 and 1920, some of them working as Stalin's assistants at the Narkomnatz ('People's Commissariate for the Affairs of Nationalities') and remained in power for the first ten crucial, formative years of the Soviet Union.

Apart from Azerbayjan, there were no Muslim Bolsheviks before 1917 but, between February 1917 and the end of the Civil War in 1920, they were accepted in their thousands into the Party. There were those who joined individually like many Tatar *jadid*s, but many transferred their allegiance *en masse* such as the Azeri Hümmet, the Kazakh Alash Orda, the left wing of Milli Firka in Crimea and the Young Bukharians and Young Khivians in Central Asia.

Their main reasons for joining the Communist Party were:

(1) the political incompetence of the White Armies' leaders and their total lack of understanding of Muslim national aspirations;
(2) Stalin's personal influence in attracting the radical elements of the national movements;
(3) the vague and ambiguous promise made by Lenin in his 'April thesis' to give Muslims the right of secession;
(4) finally, the hope that the October Revolution would be the first step towards the liberation of the entire Muslim world, and that Communism, better than any other political movement, could serve as a weapon for revenge on the European oppressors, including the Russians.

Ideological basis. In 1918, while the Russian Empire was plunged in civil war, the Bolsheviks, who were in control of the Russian centre, were anxious to establish their authority over newly conquered territory, but were not yet sure how they would implant Marxist theory among the non-Russian population. Most of the non-Russians who joined the Bolsheviks saw in the Revolution and in the ensuing Civil War the seeds of victory over Russian hegemony. They believed that the new socialist order could rid them of colonial domination at one blow and lay the foundation for Muslim emancipation.

Their contacts with the Bolsheviks, who were careful not to alienate the minorities while the outcome of the Civil War was still in doubt, had convinced many non-Russian Communists or fellow travellers that Marxism was an ideology which could be adapted to their own national needs. Faced with the problem of carrying out a Marxist revolution in societies with practically no proletarian elements and of operating within revolutionary organisations overwhelmingly dominated by Russians, the National Communists set about shaping the new ideology to their specific aims. Although there was no common doctrine and National Communism did not present a united front, certain ideas were central to most of the theories formulated at the time and these conferred a measure of ideological unity on the movement. These ideas were first formulated by the Tatar Sultan Galiev, the most brilliantly daring and influential National Communist.

The first was based on the notion that non-proletarian nations could bypass the capitalist stage of development and leap directly from feudalism to socialism. The world, according to Sultan Galiev, was divided into the oppressors and the oppressed. He went on to argue that all Muslims, of whatever class of society, who had been subjected to colonialist oppression had the right to be called 'proletarians'. It was therefore legitimate to conclude that national liberation movements in Muslim countries were in essence socialist revolutions. As for class struggle, that could be postponed indefinitely, since class distinctions in native societies were not strong enough to justify it. National Communists supported their argument by pointing out that social and economic conditions were not ripe for engaging simultaneously in social revolution against indigenous capitalists and feudal lords and in a revolution of national liberation. A revolution of national liberation was thus considered more important as far as the interests of the native population were concerned.

The second idea explicitly rejected orthodox Marxist dogma according to which socialism would solve the national question by destroying nations and replacing them with socio-economic classes. With long experience of Russian domination, the National Communists dismissed the notion that the Revolution had changed the inherently aggressive nature of Russian imperialism. In doing so, they rejected the theory that national aggression was the product of capitalist imperialism and that the establishment of a socialist order would automatically remove the source of oppression. They claimed that the proletariat of an imperialist nation which inherited power from the bourgeoisie was not intrinsically different from its forebears and that it was bound to retain the old system of colonial oppression while giving lip-service to the rights of colonised people. The necessity or attractiveness of imperialist gains would, they felt, not be lost on the proletarian Russian dictatorship and colonial exploitation would continue — if not expand — after the Socialist Revolution.

As to the problem of religion, the Muslim National Communists felt that if they were going to avoid a disastrous collision and implant Marxism successfully in their society, they had to reconcile Marxist teaching with that of Islam. Imitating the *jadidists* who had insisted upon the right to interpret the Quran according to their own lights, the Muslim National Communists claimed a similar right to interpret Marx, implying that socialism could assume the character of the nation which adopted it. They were therefore eager to preserve Islamic culture and the Muslim way of life. They argued that Islam should be secularised, not destroyed, and while the most outdated, 'reactionary' and objectionable aspects should gradually be purged, Islam's strong moral, social and political influence should be retained. It was thus that the *'Umma*, the community of believers, would be preserved.

Eastern Strategy. In the 1920s, the Muslim National Communist theoreticians, both intellectuals and men of action, were above all realists. Having concluded that the prospect of socialist Revolution in the West was highly unlikely (on the basis that the proletariat was too weak to overthrow the bourgeoisie) and suspecting their own Russian masters of wishing to perpetuate the imperialist policies of their Tsarist predecessors, the Muslim Communists adopted a strategy which, if successful, would enable them to neutralise Great Russian imperialism and might even offer them supremacy.

The aim of this new strategy was to establish alliances and coalitions against the Russians by exporting the Revolution beyond the borders of the former Tsarist Empire so as to scoop up millions of oppressed Asians, mostly Muslims, into the Communist world. To justify their position, they argued that the Communist movement was from the start aimed in the wrong direction: revolution in Europe was dead, whereas Asia was a powder keg ready to explode. For an international socialist revolution to be successful, the participation of the East was essential, but to achieve it, the grass-roots support and leadership of the movement would have to be altered. Workers' organisations were weak and insignificant in the East, so it was up to the peasantry to ally itself with the indigenous revolutionary bourgeoisie and clergy and be led by them along the path to national liberation.

For Sultan Galiev and his comrades, the 'sovietisation' of non-Russian territories of the Union did not mean acceptance of Great Russian domination: on the contrary, it meant freedom from Russian domination and control. Russian Communists were not qualified to lead the Revolution beyond purely Russian confines, as they were 'ignorant and afraid of the East'. Contacts between Russian and native Communist parties were therefore not encouraged in the belief that such associations would jeopardise the chances of carrying the Revolution beyond the Soviet borders towards the East.

Whether all National Communists shared Sultan Galiev's theories is arguable, but they all chose to support the movement energetically in an attempt to create an arena of political cohesion outside Russian control, if only to ensure their political survival.

By 1923, Sultan Galiev had already completely rejected any hope of co-operation with the Russians. Russia, Tsarist or Soviet, he pointed out, would always belong to industrial Europe, to the oppressors in other words. Sultan Galiev felt that a Colonial International should be created independent of — if not opposed to — all European Communist parties, including the Russian. To quote Sultan Galiev:

> We think that the plan to replace one class of European society by world dictatorship by its adversary — that is by another class belonging to this same society — will bring no significant change to the oppressed section of humanity. Should there be a change, it would be for the worse, not for the better.

It was between 1919 and 1923 that he elaborated the concept of the Republic of Turan, embodying all the Muslim revolutionaries' pan-Islamic and pan-Turkic aspirations.

Russian reply. Russian Communists answered these unorthodox arguments almost from the start, stating that a native proletariat did indeed exist, but that it was 'too weak and morally unstable to become the leading class'. They insisted that it was impossible to postpone the class struggle because it was more important than national liberation and rejected outright Sultan Galiev's concept of 'proletarian nations'. To reinforce its political and territorial gains, the Party admitted massive numbers of new Russian recruits in 1920. This influx was made up of tough, primitive Russian peasants and violently aggressive workers who had been hardened by the Civil War campaigns, a far cry from the intellectual westernised Old Bolsheviks of the earlier days. They regarded the native Communists as a hostile, chauvinistic element which should be kept in its place.

Open conflicts between the Muslim National Communists on the one hand and Lenin and Stalin on the other broke out in 1919 concerning the autonomy of the Muslim Communist Party and unification of the Tatar-Bashkir Republic. The Muslims defended their position — in vain — at the Second Congress of Communist Organisations of the Peoples of the East (Moscow, November-December 1919), at the First Congress of the Peoples of the East (Baku, September 1920) and at the First Conference of the Turkic People's Communists of the RSFSR (Moscow, January 1921) when Stalin attacked local nationalism as the 'obstacle to the development of Communism in the East'. The first serious attacks on pan-Islamism and pan-Turkism were voiced at the Tenth Congress of the Bolshevik Party in April 1921. The Bolshevik leaders were determined that Communist revolution in the West should have precedence and that revolution in the East should conform strictly to the Russian model. There could be only one Communist Party in the Soviet Union – the Russian one.

The crisis came to a head with the purge of the Communist Party of Turkestan in December 1922 and the arrest of Sultan Galiev in early 1923. Then followed a period of uneasy truce, during which the Muslim National Communists tried to strengthen their position by organising clandestine groups whose purpose was to raise the anti-Russian consciousness of the native masses and oppose cultural, administrative and biological assimilation as well as the forced linguistic division of the Turkic territories.

According to Soviet sources, between 1923 and 1929 Sultan Galiev had created a network of underground secret organisations, based in Moscow and Kazan, but with offshoots stretching as far as Alma Ata and Tashkent. Many Muslim National Communist leaders seem to have been connected with these organisations, but the extent of their involvement has not been revealed by Soviet official sources, who remain reluctant to go into the subject in detail. The accusation levelled against one such organisation, Ittihad ve Tarakki ('Union and Progress'), was that it tried to infiltrate National Communist Turks into the Communist Party and the Soviet government apparatus, to gain control over the educational system in Muslim Republics in order to inculcate pan-Islamic and pan-Turkic ideals and finally to establish contacts with counter-revolutionary organisations abroad and in the Soviet Union, especially the Basmachis.

The great purge in the Muslim republics, which was to destroy the brilliant pre-revolutionary Muslim intelligentsia, began in 1928. It started in Crimea with the execution of Veli Ibrahimov, First Secretary of the Tatar Communist Party, and the liquidation of Milli Firka. Tatarstan and Bashkiria followed: the leaders of the Tatar-Bashkir *obkom*, of the Communist Party, the Union of Writers, government publishing houses, universities of Kazan and Ufa and even the Tatar Union of the Godless were all killed. In Azerbayjan the repression started after the death of Narimanov in 1933, and by 1937–8 all the Azeris, leading Communists and old members of Hümmet, were murdered. In Kazakhstan, the elimination of Alash Orda coincided with the forced sedentarisation of the nomads, which was to ruin the country and cost thousands of lives. In Central Asia, all the Young

Bukharians and nearly all the pre-Revolutionary intellectuals were eliminated from local Communist parties between 1922 and 1938.

The Muslim National Communists were liquidated by Stalin in the 1930s. With their demise also went the attempt at partnership with the Russians, which was seen by the Muslims as the least painful means of throwing off foreign domination. One final attempt, however, was made to shake off the 'Infidel' yoke, when during the war the conservative North Caucasian Mountaineers rose in armed revolt. But this attempt too was crushed.

What remains today of the lengthy and multifaceted struggle against the Russian conqueror?

(1) It seems that the hope of achieving a partnership on equal terms with the Russians has been abandoned by the Muslim elite. The Russians retain an absolute superiority in the USSR and there is no evidence at all that they would abandon even a small part of it.

(2) Armed uprising, for the time being at least, is not considered as a possible way to liberation except maybe by some hard-core 'fanatics' in the North Caucasus.

(3) The new Soviet Muslim intelligentsia appears thoroughly modern, Western, and even Russian in outlook. Central Asian, Tatar and Caucasian intellectuals are authentic and probably sincere Communists, but at the same time they remain deeply nationalist and conscious of their past. Their nationalism is not a mere survival of capitalist mentality or of pre-revolutionary bourgeois traditions as the Soviet authorities claim, but an expression of a political and cultural individuality which distinguishes them from the Russians and which, far from losing its strength, is growing steadily.

(4) As before the *jadid* revival of the late nineteenth century, the Muslim community of the USSR protects itself from 'contamination' and assimilation by isolating itself from the alien Russians. Today mixed marriages between Muslims and 'Europeans' in the Muslim republics are as exceptional as they were fifty years ago. In all Muslim territories the two communities coexist side by side, but they do not mix. The persistence of religious traditions, rites and customs among Muslims, including those who do not practise their religion, is part of this defence. Even if some Muslims fall victim to unrelenting Russian anti-religious pressure and become — outwardly at least — atheists, the differences dividing the two groups will still be enormous. Consequently, so long as Islam remains, Muslims will continue to be members of an *'Umma*, a community of believers

hostile to Russian intentions.

(5) Having refused assimilation while accepting Marxism-Leninism merely as a technique of bureaucratic management (or mismanagement?), not as a quasi-religious philosophy, the Muslim community of the USSR is prepared for the inevitable showdown with its Russian rulers.

It is obviously too early to speculate on the form and timing of this showdown. It might be a major armed confrontation or a steady 'prise de pouvoir' by the Muslim cadres submerging their Russian comrades and pushing them out of their national territories, and finally achieving an authentic autonomy or even full independence and sovereignty. As the Turks say: 'Allah bilir'.

3 SOVIET MUSLIMS AND THE MUSLIM WORLD ABROAD

1 The 'Forgotten Muslims' — Muslims under Tsarist Rule (1552–1883)

The discovery of the sea route to the Far East by the Portuguese marked the beginning of the economic decline of the caravan trade between China, India and Europe. All the territories situated along the Silk and Spice roads — Turkestan, the Caucasus, Kazan — were affected. But the decline was a slow process. Until the seventeenth century, the Muslim states of Central Asia continued to mount an impressive façade of power and prosperity and to constitute an integral part of the Muslim world. Later on, in the eighteenth century, economic decline was followed by loss of political power and intellectual stagnation. The Caucasus and Central Asia, formerly the very heart of the Muslim world, had become unimportant, marginal areas. The decline reached its nadir on the eve of the Russian conquest.

Russian occupation brought a dramatic change in all Muslim territories. Prior to the conquest, Central Asia and the Caucasus, though decadent and backward, still belonged to the *Dar ul-Islam*, the 'Abode of Islam' ruled by Muslim sovereigns, in which Islamic law was supreme and the non-Muslim inhabitants were subject to Muslim control.

From the point of view of Islamic law, Muslim territory conquered by 'Infidels' which is forced to accept an alien legal system ceases to be part of the *Dar ul-Islam*. The territory in such a situation becomes part of the *Dar ul-Harb*, the 'House of War', from which it is the duty of all Muslims to withdraw.

This legal position should be kept in mind when analysing the attitude of the rest of the Muslim world towards Islamic countries of the Middle Volga, the Caucasus and Central Asia under Russian domination. Legally, they ceased to exist, and their Muslim inhabitants who could not or did not wish to emigrate to the *Dar ul-Islam* were dismissed as 'non-persons' and disappeared completely from the Muslim horizon.

Such was the fate of Kazan after 1552, of Crimea after 1783 and of the Caucasus after the final defeat of Shamil. In Central Asia only, the survival of the emirate of Bukhara and of the khanate of Khiva allowed Muslims to claim this area as still legally part of the Muslim world, though governed by the 'accursed Infidels'.

The immediate consequence of this psychological 'iron curtain' drawn by the Muslim world around the Islamic territories of the Tsarist Empire was the almost total cessation of intellectual and cultural contacts between these territories and the Muslims abroad. Muslims of Russia were abandoned by their brethren, 'left to themselves', and their survival became their own private business.

However, in spite of the indifference and ignorance of the Muslim rulers and elites beyond the frontiers, all relations could not be completely severed. Pilgrimage to the holy places of Arabia, though expensive and difficult because of the immense distances involved and the severe control exercised by the Russian authorities, was never definitely suspended.

In the eighteenth century and in the first half of the nineteenth, another channel was opened, and this time, curiously enough, the intellectual influence was directed from North to South. Daghestan was then the only Muslim territory in the world where classical Quranic Arabic was not only used as the official literary language, but also as a spoken *lingua franca* — the only means of communication betweeen some two dozen ethnic groups speaking languages which differed widely from one valley to another and were not understood outside their specific territory. As a matter of fact, this position remained unchanged until the 1917 Revolution. Daghestani scholars (called the 'Arabists') came to be regarded as some of the most distinguished *ulema* of the entire Muslim world. Students from every part of the Middle East flocked to the remote *aüls* of the Northern Caucasus which acquired fame as one of the most distinguished centres of conservative Muslim learning of the world. At the same time, learned Daghestani 'Arabists' were invited to teach Arabic and theology abroad. The vigour of this movement is attested by the names of the descendants of these learned men: 'al-Daghestani' (in Arabic), 'Daghistanly' (in Turkish) are very numerous in all Middle Eastern countries.

Yet another channel was opened up in the second half of the nineteenth century, when Russian Muslims, especially the Volga Tatars and the Turkestanis, began to send their children — as yet in small numbers — to finish their education in the schools of the Ottoman Empire. At the same time, Ottoman teachers appeared in the Volga and Central Asia *madrassah*s, bringing with them Turkish school books and periodicals. It is through this last channel that the modernistic ideas of the *Tanzimat* began to penetrate Russian Islam.

2 Russian *Jadidist* Influence in the Muslim World Abroad (1883-1917)

The turning-point in relations between Russian Islam and the Muslim world abroad was the publication in the Crimean city of Baghchesaray of the daily newspaper *Terjüman* (*The Interpreter*), edited by the great reformer Ismail bey Gaspraly.

This periodical first appeared in the most tragic period of the history of Islam. The Ottoman Empire had suffered a severe defeat in the war of 1877-8. Russian armies were camping in Erzurum, in the heart of Anatolia, and their vanguard was close to Istanbul, the imperial city, considered by all Russian Turks as their true capital. The discovery of the tragic weakness of Turkey, hence of the entire Muslim world, was the shock that awakened political awareness amongst Russian Muslims and gave birth to 'pan-Turkism', whose most energetic exponent was Ismail bey Gaspraly.

The role of Gaspraly in bridging the gap of ignorance and indifference between Russian Islam and the Muslim world abroad was immense. The instrument that served this purpose was his *Terjüman*, written in 'pan-Turkic' language: a simplified Turkish purged of arabisms and farsisms and understandable 'from the Bosphorus to Sinkiang'. It was one of the most popular periodicals of the Muslim world and had subscribers in the Ottoman Empire, in the Maghreb, in Iran, in India and China. The first issue of *Terjüman* appeared in 1883 and it continued to be published until the death of Gaspraly in 1914. Together with other periodicals he published (*Alem-i Niswan* (*The World of the Women*, Bagchesaray, 1906-14); *Alem-i Sibiyan* (*The World of the Children*, Baghchesaray, 1906-14); *An-Nahda* (*Renaissance*, in Arabic, Cairo, 1908))), *Terjüman* was for a quarter of a century the flag-bearer of liberal *jadidism* and the link between Russian Islam and the rest of *Dar ul-Islam*. In the same way, the small *madrassah* founded by Ismail bey Gaspraly in Baghchesaray became a model for all reformed establishments throughout the Muslim world. Through these two channels, Gaspraly's ideas on the social, economic, religious and cultural rejuvenation of the Islamic world were transmitted to the Muslim countries abroad, where they were on the whole received sympathetically.

Ismail Gaspraly, who spent his life travelling in the Middle East, was not the only Russian Turk to visit the Muslim world outside. He was preceded, accompanied and followed by a great number of brilliant intellectuals representing the best elements of Russian Islam, who used to visit the Ottoman Empire, especially its capital, Istanbul. After 1908, some of them settled in Turkey for good and became Turkish citizens.

Volga and Crimean Tatars were the first and most numerous of such visitors to Turkey. They were followed by the Turkestanis and the Caucasians. Long before 1905, it became a habit among Russian Muslims, conservatives as well as liberals, to send their children to finish their education in the *madrassah*s of Istanbul, Cairo and Medina in Arabia and in the University of Istanbul. The majority of the theologians, writers and political leaders who later played an outstanding part in the intellectual and political revival of Russian Islam had studied in the Ottoman Empire, in Egypt and in Arabia, and were deeply marked by this experience. Turkish influence was especially strong in Central Asia. In 1910, Turkestani *émigrés* in Istanbul founded the Association for the Development of Knowledge Useful for Bukhara, which soon became the meeting place of all radical elements, including many of the future leaders of the secret society Young Bukharians, such as Abdurrauf Fitrat, Osman Khoja and Ata Khoja.

The same year, former Istanbul students founded two societies in Bukhara: Barakat and Maarifat, to import from abroad — especially from Turkey — radical periodicals such as *Sirat-i Mustaqim* from Istanbul, *Habl ul-Matin* from Calcutta and *Siraj ul-Akhbar* from Kabul. It is through this channel that the revolutionary influence of the Young Turks penetrated into Bukhara and, from there, into the whole of Central Asia.

In 1908, when it became evident that the moderate liberal Russian 'bourgeoisie' which dominated the Duma was unable and unwilling to satisfy their demands, the Muslim intellectual elite began to emigrate. The largest *émigré* colony was in Istanbul. The most distinguished Tatar and Azeri leaders were among those who settled permanently in Turkey: Yusuf Akchura oğlu, the Tatar member of the Central Committee of the Russian KD Party and one of the founders of the Ittifaq al-Muslim, the Azeri politicians Ali Husein Zade and Ahmed Aga oğlu, the Siberian Tatar Abdurrashid Ibrahimov, disciple of the Jemaleddin al-Afghani and leader of the most radical wing of the Muslim national movement in Russia, and many others. Giving up any hope of return to Russia, they became Turkish citizens and took a very active part in the intense political life of the Ottoman Empire: Husein Zade, since 1910 Professor at the Military Faculty of Medicine of Haydar Pasha, became member of the Central Committee of the Turkish party Ittifaq ve Tarakki; Aga oğlu was one of the leaders of the Kemalist movement in the 1920s, while Yusuf Akchura oğlu became the leading theoretician of the new pan-Turkic movement.

It is certain that the influence exercised by this remarkable group of highly cultured and politically liberal immigrants on the Turkish elite was exceptionally important and lasting. It was thanks to their activity that shortly before the First World War the two traditional ideologies of the Ottoman Empire, the 'Ottomanism' and the 'Pan-Islamism' were replaced by 'Turkism' (*Türklük*).

The part played by the immigrants is demonstrated by the great number and extraordinary prestige of the periodicals which they published. The most important was the famous *Türk Yurdu* (*The Turkish Fatherland*), first published in Istanbul in 1911 by Yusuf Akchura oğlu, Ahmed Aga oğlu, Abdurrashid Ibrahimov and Galimjan Idrisi (a Siberian Tatar). Russian Turks also actively contributed to several other Istanbul periodicals:

Islam Dünyası (*The World of Islam*), 1911–13, chief editor Abdurrashid Ibrahimov;

Islam Mejmuası (*Islamic Review*), 1911–17. The director was a Turk and several Tatar theologians and writers were among the contributors, including Rizzaeddin Fahreddin oğlu, Musa Jarullah Bigi and Fatyh Emirkhan;

Khalqa Doğru (*Toward the People*), 1911–14, published by Türk Yurdu, to which all pan-Turkic leaders, Turks and Russians contributed — Ziya Gökalp, Fuad Köprülü, Yusuf Akchura oğlu, Ahmed Aga oğlu, Ali Husein Zade, etc.;

Türk Sözu (*Turkish Voice*), 1912–14, also published by the Türk Yurdu and involing pan-Turkic contributors.

Whilst the liberal leaders emigrated to the Ottoman Empire, the socialist elements, mainly Caucasians, went to Iran, which at that time was the scene of violent social and political upheavals (the Tabriz Revolution and the Constitutional Movement). The most famous of these Caucasian revolutionaries was Mehmet Emin Rasul Zade (1884–1954), an Azerbayjani socialist, one of the founders of the social democrat Hümmet party. In 1908, Rasul Zade emigrated to Tehran. There he played an active part in the Constitutional Movement and from 1908 to 1910 published the radical newspaper *Iran-i Now* (*The New Iran*). Banished from Iran, Rasul Zade went to Turkey, where he changed his political *Weltanschauung* and joined the Türk Yurdu group. In 1913, he returned to Russia and in 1917 became the leader of the nationalist party, Musawat. In 1919 he was elected President of the independent Republic of Azerbayjan and after the Revolution emigrated once again to Turkey.

Between 1917 and 1920 a new wave of Russian Muslims, fleeing the Revolution, settled abroad, mainly in Turkey. Among them were many distinguished intellectuals, writers and political leaders, mainly Tatars and Bashkirs. Some of them later worked at the unversities of Istanbul and Ankara. Amongst these *émigrés* were Ahmed Zeki Velidi Togan, former President of the Bashkir government, Akdes Nimet Kurat, Rashid Rahmati Arat, Saadet Chagatay, Musa Jarullah Bigi, Ayaz Iskhaki, Fuad Tuktur and many more.

Thus, between 1883 and 1920 Russian Muslims exercised a deep and lasting cultural influence on their coreligionists abroad — Turks, Iranians and Arabs. They were in many cases the channel through which Western 'progressive' ideas and 'know-how' reached the Muslim East. Included in their ranks were schoolteachers, religious leaders, journalists and university professors. They brought with them some Western *political models*, in particular Russian populism, but as a general rule it was from the Muslim world abroad that *political theories* were brought to Russian Islam. Young Turks, Iranian Constitutional Democrats and the revolutionaries of Tabriz were until the 1917 Revolution the real master-minds and models of action in so far as the Tatar, Azeri and Turkestani nationalists were concerned. The situation underwent a sudden change in February 1917.

3 Muslim National Communists and the Muslim World Abroad (1918–28)

From 1918 until 1923, for the first and only time in its history, Moscow became the revolutionary forum of the Third World, the meeting place of all revolutionary elements from Asia, Africa and Latin America. Turkish prisoners of war, Iranian democrats, Indian revolutionaries, Indonesian freedom fighters, Indian Muslim militants of the Califat movement and Arab radicals all flocked to Moscow. This was the new Mecca for those — and there were many of them — who believed that the October Revolution was only the first step on the road towards the liberation of *Dar ul-Islam* from the colonialist rule of the hated West.

The leaders of the Bolshevik party were confident of the triumph of the proletarian revolution in the West, but some were well aware that, without the help of the Orient, their victory would be much less certain. As early as 1918, the Bolsheviks were appealing to the colonised and semi-colonised peoples to rebel and achieve liberation. Hoping for a huge response to their call for revolution throughout the Muslim East, the Bolsheviks found themselves forced to adopt a policy of the utmost indulgence towards the revolutionaries of the colonised world, even towards those whose radicalism had a strong flavour of nationalism and whose background was bourgeois or aristocratic. Thus the Russian Bolshevik hosts were not too punctilious at this stage about the ideological purity of the newcomers. This atmosphere of intellectual freedom encouraged contacts among non-Russian revolutionaries; foreign Muslims of the radical camp freely met and exchanged ideas not only with the Russian or West European Communists but also — and this was crucial — with the numerous Muslims (Tatars, Caucasians, Turkestanis) belonging to the same ideological camp, but whose Marxism was strongly tainted with pan-Islamic aspirations.

A number of important gatherings took place during this time, including three Komintern congresses (the second in 1920, the third in 1921 and the fourth in 1922), the Congress of the Toilers of the East in Baku (September 1920) and the Twelfth Congress of the RCP(b) (April 1923). Both Muslim National Communists and foreign revolutionaries attended these congresses and their ideas were openly discussed. An even more important centre for the diffusion of National Communist ideas abroad was the Communist University of the Workers of the East (KUTVA), which opened in September 1921 and was an extremely active and influential organisation until 1924, when its staff was purged. Almost all the important Muslim Communist leaders, including Sultan Galiev, Turar Ryskulov, Nariman Narimanov and Ahmed Baytursun lectured there full-time. Foreign Communists, such as the Indian Manabendra-Nath Roy, the Dutchman H.J.M.F. Snevliet and the Iranian Sultan Zade, were invited to teach there: they were eventually to formulate the same ideas as Sultan Galiev. The list of KUTVA's students was no less impressive and included the Japanese Sen Katayama, the Indonesian Tan Malaka, the Chinese Liu Shao-Chi and the Vietnamese Ho Chi Minh.

Several foreign revolutionary organisations had appeared in Russia even before the October Revolution: an Indian Muslim political group in Tashkent, an Iranian socialist party in Baku, a Turkish revolutionary centre in the Crimea. They were destined to play an important part in the development of Communism in the neighbouring countries, especially in Turkey and Iran, which both the Bolsheviks and the Muslim National Communists considered the ideal base for the propagation of Communism throughout the Middle East and Africa.

The conditions in Iran and Turkey were somewhat similar to those of Russia in 1917. In 1918, Turkey appeared ripe for a social revolution: she had suffered a military defeat which had destroyed the Ottoman dynasty, foreign occupation, economic ruin and unemployment; finally, she was engaged in a national liberation movement which, according to the Bolshevik thesis, was capable of being transformed into a socialist movement.

In Iran, conditions seemed equally favourable (from the Bolshevik point of view): double foreign occupation (by British and Russian troops), the small merchant class economically ruined, poverty amongst the peasants, a long revolutionary tradition among the 'Westernised' intellectual class and finally a religious, anti-imperialist, anti-monarchist, radical revolutionary guerrilla force in the northern province of Ghilan, the 'Jengeli' movement.

The Soviet reconquest of Azerbayjan in April 1920 gave a fresh impulse to the Jengeli revolution. The same month a Soviet flotilla occupied Enzeli, a port in Ghilan. The Jengelis took advantage of this development to occupy the entire province of Ghilan and, supported by the commander of the Soviet fleet, Raskolnikov, proclaimed the 'Soviet Socialist Republic of Ghilan' in June 1920. The leader of the Jengelis, Mirza Kuchek Khan, was elected President. The government of the new Soviet socialist state was formed by a coalition of the religious nationalists of the Jengeli camp and the Communists. A speedy victory over the crumbling Qajar monarchy appeared fairly certain.

In both Turkey and Iran, Communist organisations (closely related to the Turkish and Iranian Communist groups in Soviet Russia) flourished during 1918–19. Almost at the same time the first Communist and socialist cells made their appearance in other parts of the Muslim world, notably in Egypt (the Egyptian Socialist Party was founded in Alexandria in 1920) and in Indonesia (the Indonesian Communist Party was founded in the same year).

In the spring of 1918, a socialist refugee from Turkey, Mustafa Subhi, with the help of the Muslim Section of the People's Commissariat of Nationalities, recruited the first Turkish Communist group amongst the prisoners of war in the Crimea. In April 1918 this group published the first Communist Turkish newspaper, *Yeni Dünya* (*The New World*), which was later moved to Moscow.

In July 1918, Sultan Galiev and Mustafa Subhi convened the Conference of Turkish Socialists in Moscow and began to form Turkish military units recruited from amongst prisoners of war. Two such Turkish battalions were formed which were destined to become the training-ground of the cadres of the future Turkish Communist Party. In the spring of 1920 Mustafa Subhi settled in Baku and from there directed Communist activity in Turkey, In September 1920 a congress of Turkish Communists held in Baku decided to amalgamate all the Turkish socialist and Communist organisations in Turkey and Russia into a single Turkish Communist Party.

In Iran, the foundation of the first Persian Communist group goes back to 1917, when the Iranian socialists of Baku, members of the Hümmet Party, formed the Adalet (Justice) society. In the spring of 1920, the leader of Adalet, Haidar Khan Amu, and other prominent members of the party, left Baku for Ghilan and in June 1920 held a congress in Resht which adopted the new name of the Persian Communist (Bolshevik) Party.

In 1920, hopes for a successful Communist revolution both in Turkey and Iran appeared reasonable. This was especially true of Turkey, where several local Communist and socialist groups were engaged in mobilising both the masses and the intellectuals. One of the oldest established groups was the Türk Ishtirakiyun Firkası (Turkish Socialist Party), founded in Istanbul in 1919. It was followed in September 1919 by the more radical Socialist Party of the Workers and Peasants of Turkey, formed mainly of former prisoners of war and Turks who had been influenced by the Spartakus Bund whilst in Germany. In June 1920, the underground Leninist Turkish Communist Party was founded in Ankara, followed in December 1920 by the Socialist Party (Ishtirakiyun Firkasi). Finally, there appeared a curious Communist-nationalist party, drawn from the peasantry, the Green Apple (Yeşil Elma) which during the war against the Greeks controlled large guerrilla detachments known as the 'Green Army' ('Yeşil Ordu').

Thus for a short period after the October Revolution the hetero-dox ideas, programmes and theories of the Russian Muslim National Communists (rather than the orthodox theories of Russian Bolsheviks) began to penetrate the Muslim world abroad.

These ideas contrasted strongly with the classical attitude of the Russian and West European Communist leaders (as affirmed at the Baku Congress of the Toilers of the East in September 1920) towards revolution in the colonial world. While the Bolsheviks reduced the colonial revolution to the rank of a positive but marginal pheno-menon, Muslim revolutionaries, both Russian and foreign, stressed the prime importance of anti-imperialist movements in Asia. Sultan Galiev wrote in-1919:

The East with its population of one and half billion enslaved by the West European bourgeoisie was forgotten by the Bolshevik leaders. The development of the international class struggle continued by-passing the East . . . Because of ignorance concerning the East and of the fear which it inspired, the idea of the participation of Eastern revolutionaries in the world revolution was systematically rejected ('The Social Revolution and the East', *Zhizn' Natsional'nostey*, 39 (47), 1919).

Sultan Galiev tried to remind his Russian comrades that 'the East is the principal source of nourishment of international capitalism . . . deprived of the East and cut off from India, Afghanistan, Persia and other Asian and African colonies, Western European imperialism will wither away and die by itself' ('The Social Revolution and the East', *Zhizn' Natsional'nostey*, 42 (50), 1919).

The second guiding principle which Muslim National Communists exported abroad, where it was received enthusiastically, concerned the unity of the Muslim world. Its corollary was that the 'artificial' frontiers created by the imperialist powers (Tsarist Russia or Great Britain) in the nineteenth century, separating Russian Islam from the Muslim world abroad, were to be abolished and the Soviet Muslim republics to become revolutionary spingboards for the liberation of the entire colonial world.

The sovietisation of Azerbayjan [writes Sultan Galiev] is a highly important step in the evolution of Communism in the Near East. Just as Red Turkestan is acting as a revolutionary beacon for Chinese Turkestan, Tibet, Afghanistan, India, Bukhara and Khiva, so Soviet Azerbayjan, with its ancient and experienced proletariat and its already united Communist party, will become the Red beacon for Persia, Arabia and Turkey . . . From Azerbayjan we could hurt the British in Persia, reach out to Arabia and lead the revolutionary movement in Turkey (*Zhizn' Natsional'nostey*, 18 (70), 1920).

Sultan Galiev wanted his Tatar countrymen to play a similar role in Asia ('Tatar Autonomous Republic', *Zhizn' Natsional'nostey*, 1923, p. 25): 'Living in an immense territory extending from the Middle Volga to Siberia and Central Asia, the Tatar workers are the best conductors of revolutionary energy in the territory they inhabit and onwards, to the entire East.'

Other National Communist leaders expressed the same hope. For example, the Caucasian Communist leader, Najmuddin Efendiev Samur-skiy, wrote about his native Daghestan:

> Daghestan is an oriental country that has preserved contacts with all neighbouring oriental countries . . . It can and should serve as a bond between the Soviet Union and the East and it should become, more than any other region of the Soviet Union, the channel for Communist ideas directed towards the Near East (*Daghestan*, Moscow, 1924, pp. 117-18).

Sultan Galiev insisted that 'the people of the East must play an active part in the liberation [of the East] and Muslim Communists must be at the heart of this struggle'. In other words, revolution in the East must be led by the Muslims themselves, in accordance with their pro-grammes, and not by Russian or European Communists. That is why the Bolshevik leadership from the very beginning refused to endorse such a heretical strategy. The first warnings against any revolutionary activity in the Muslim East undertaken independently of the directives of the Komintern were addressed to the Soviet and foreign Muslim Communists at the Congress of the Toilers of the East in Baku (September 1920) by a number of Komintern leaders:

> We must never forget this simple truth: the people of the East can not obtain their freedom without the help of the Western prole-tariat (*Premier Congrès des Peuples d'Orient*, Baku, 1920, Petro-grad, 1921, report of Pavlovich, p. 146).

> The salvation of the East can only come through the victory of the Western proletariat (ibid., report of Mustushev, p. 154).

> Liberation from foreign rulers will not of itself bring true freedom to the Eastern masses. They must also free themselves from their national oppressors. (ibid., report of Bela Kun, pp. 172-3).

After Baku, and against the wishes of Muslim leaders, contacts with the revolutionary movements in Turkey and Iran were entrusted to the Russian Communists and not to the Muslims. The Red Army division which had been sent to Ghilan to assist the Jengelis was an ethnically Russian unit. No Tatar Communists were allowed to join the Turkish Communist Party. In sum, Muslim revolutionaries were not permitted to export world revolution to the Muslim world abroad.

After the Baku Congress, Communism suffered a major and long-lasting reverse in all the Muslim countries of the Middle East.

In Iran, the common front of nationalists and Communists, a front which had been achieved for the first time in history and which held so much promise in terms of revolutionary potential, dramatically collapsed in 1921: the Jengeli leader, Mirza Kuchek Khan, clashing with his Communist allies on the question of leadership of the revolutionary movement, decided to break with them and proceeded to slaughter the entire Central Committee of the Iranian Communist Party. He was abandoned by the Soviets, and in September 1931 his army was defeated and destroyed by the Iranian Army.

In January 1921, Mustafa Subhi and his comrades of the Turkish Communist Party of Baku travelled from the Soviet Caucasus to Turkey, believing that they were influential and powerful enough to force Kemal Ataturk to transform his national democratic revolution into a socialist one.

On their arrival in Trabzon, Subhi and his comrades were trapped and murdered. In 1922, Communism was declared illegal in Turkey and subsequently disappeared for many years from the Turkish political scene.

Thus in contrast to the earlier period (1883–1917), Soviet Muslims during the first ten years of the Bolshevik regime were deprived of the chance to act as 'middlemen for the world revolution'. However, personal contacts between the brilliant theoreticians of National Communism and the foreign revolutionary leaders were numerous and had far-reaching consequences. It was due to these contacts that the bold theories of Muslim National Communism penetrated the Muslim world abroad. It is not difficult to understand why the cause of National Communism had a direct appeal for the colonised world. It touched the native leaders profoundly and showed them an escape from Western domination, whilst orthodox Marxism with its stress on class struggle, internationalism (as seen through European eyes), destruction of traditional society, industrialisation, etc. simply appeared as a new facet of the old domineering imperialist West. Many Asiatic members of the Komintern, which had its headquarters in Moscow, had heard the Muslim National Communist leader's warnings that Russian Communism was not intrinsically different from Russian Tsarism and that eventually it would become an instrument of Great Russian imperialism. The Russians, who dominated the Komintern, denied the legitimacy of the aspiration of any nationalist-cum-socialist party to lead a Communist revolution in colonised countries because of the absence of an industrial proletariat. The alternative, as advocated by the Komintern, was to establish, with Soviet help and management, a Communist Party which would automatically become the representative of the non-existent working class. After eventual victory, imposed if necessary by force, an industrial proletariat would be created. A present-day example of the application of this theory can be seen in Afghanistan, and one can easily understand why it lacks attraction for national leaders. It typifies the orthodox Marxist failure to come to grips with non-Western conditions, whereas the main principles of Muslim National Communism as put forward by Sultan Galiev and his companions in the 1920s have been adopted by virtually every present-day national liberation movement that claims Marxism as its source of inspiration.

4 The Period of the Iron Curtain (1928–68)

This was the most tragic period in the history of Soviet Islam: the era of the first Five Year Plans, Stalin's purges, brutal sovietisation and the breakdown of local society. It was in those years that Communism acquired a Russian identity. This started in 1928 and was finally completed during the war. Stalin's theory of 'Socialism in One Country' was victorious over Trotsky's internationalism and permanent revolution. A complete fusion took place between the Soviet Union, 'Fatherland of Socialism', and Mother Russia. Finally, it was during that period that the Komintern ceased to be an autonomous institution and became a mere appendage of the Commissariat of Foreign Affairs, an instrument of the Russian Communist Party.

There were weighty reasons for this change of task. The Communist parties controlled by the Komintern had suffered heavy defeats in foreign Muslim countries. The nationalist governments of Turkey and Iran, led by Kemal Atatürk and Reza Shah respectively, governments which Moscow had favoured and, in the case of Turkey assisted militarily and financially, moved closer to the capitalist West and adopted an openly hostile attitude towards their former friend. In both countries, the local Communist parties were outlawed, hunted down and quickly liquidated. From 1928 on, they ceased to be a political force and even today they play no significant part in the life of their respective countries.

In 1928, the effects of the 'treason' of Kemal Atatürk and Reza Shah and the subsequent set-back to Communism in Turkey and Iran were further aggravated by the downfall of the last Eastern 'neutral' government favourable to the USSR: that of the King Amanullah of Afghanistan. This put an end to Soviet hopes of using Eastern democratic national bourgeois governments against the West. At the same time, the Egyptian Communist movement, the most powerful of Arab Communist parties, was destroyed by its stronger rival, the Wafd, and eliminated from the Egyptian political scene.

This collapse in the Middle East was preceded in 1927 by an even greater disaster in China, where the Communist Party was crushed in Shanghai by the Kuomintang. The following year an attempt by the Communists (in which the Russians were directly involved) to seize power in Canton ended in a worse catastrophe.

The tragic lessons of China, Turkey, Egypt and Iran were accepted at the Sixth Congress of the Komintern and its strategy towards the colonial world was modified dramatically. The Russian Communist Party, and therefore the Soviet government, followed suit. The earlier strategy of co-operation between the local Communist parties and the national bourgeois democratic movements (of the Kemalist, Wafdist or Kuomintang type) against the common enemy, British imperialism, was replaced by the direct opposite, a strategy of 'class against class': the proletariat and the peasantry versus the bourgeoisie (whether conservative or progressive). Consequently, Communists in the Muslim world were ordered to break their connections with the bourgeois parties, their former allies, especially with the radical religious groups, and to embark upon a two-fronted campaign: against Western (British and French) imperialism; against local feudalism, bourgeoisie and clericalism.

This strategy was, of course, highly unrealistic: it overestimated the revolutionary potential of the Muslim peasant or proletarian 'masses' and disastrously underestimated the dynamism of the nationalist bourgeois movements endowed with a powerful repressive military and police apparatus. The result was complete isolation for the already weakened local Communist Parties. In consequence, two of the most distinguished leaders of Asian Communism, the Indian Manabendra-Nath Roy and the Indonesian Tan Malaka, broke with the Komintern.

The 'class against class' strategy was followed by a period, from 1928 to 1935, during which Soviet influence in the Muslim world abroad fell to its lowest level. The USSR had nothing to offer to the independent and semi-independent Middle Eastern states, either in terms of economic assistance or of political ideology. Throughout the colonial world the national bourgeois democratic movements promised (and were believed to be able) to solve all the problems — the economic situation, national liberation and social change through modernisation and secularisation — and all on a non-socialist model. In the face of their powerful rivals, the local Communist parties, often controlled by representatives of the minorities (Kurds in Syria, Jews in Egypt), appeared weak and useless.

In 1935, at the Seventh Congress of the Komintern, the absurd 'class against class' strategy was discarded, to be replaced by the 'Popular Front' policy. Indeed, around 1933 it became evident that it was not British or French imperialism that was the main danger for the USSR but Germany and Fascism, which were making spectacular progress in the colonial world and being accepted by a number of young Muslim radicals who were disappointed with both Marxism and liberal nationalism. At the same time, the economic and political influence of Germany and Italy were growing in the Muslim world.

The Soviet Union was thus threatened by a new Fascist menace more dangerous than the old capitalist threat of the revolutionary period. To counter it, the surviving local Communist parties were ordered once again to modify radically their general line. Forsaking the 'class struggle', they were invited to collaborate tactically with such bourgeois parties as were anti-Fascist, though they were to refuse any form of merger with these parties and were supposed to denounce, whenever possible, the vicious bourgeois philosophy of their new allies.

This new strategy was even less realistic than the previous ones and as a consequence Communism practically disappeared from Middle Eastern countries.

During this thirteen-year period (1928–41) chances of a revolution in the East seemed nil and, as a corollary, Muslim republics of Central Asia and the Caucasus were no longer seen as springboards for the conquest of Asia.

This period was marked by the collectivisation of agriculture and the settlement of nomads (leading to over a million deaths from famine), the destruction of the pre-revolutionary elites, a massive anti-religious drive and a ten-year campaign against the 'National Communists'. The Iron Curtain was brought down hard, completely isolating the Soviet Muslim territories from the Muslim world abroad. All contacts between Soviet Muslims and their brethren over the border were stopped. Pilgrimages to Mecca and to the Shia holy places in Iran and Iraq were forbidden.

There was virtually no Soviet involvement in the Middle East, and the few Soviet officials who did visit Muslim countries were, by and large, Russians or foreign agents of the Komintern. As far as we know, only one Muslim played a certain part abroad during these years: a Volga Tatar, Hakimov, who, in 1928, headed a short-lived Soviet mission in Sana'a in Yemen, at the court of Imam Yahya.

After the war and the 'normalisation' of Soviet government relations with the Muslim religious establishment, pilgrimage to Mecca was cautiously re-established for the benefit of some chosen members of the Ufa Spiritual Board, and in 1945–6 a few Shia dignitaries from Baku visited the holy places of Mashhad and Qum in Iran. But contacts between Soviet Muslims and the Muslim world abroad remained limited and intermittent until the later 1960s. Moscow still distrusted her Muslims and when the Soviet Union spectacularly reappeared on the Middle Eastern scene, it was once again with a Russian profile. The numerous pro-Soviet periodicals which appeared in several Arab countries during and immediately after the war, as well as the Soviet-sponsored 'friendship societies' and 'houses of culture', stressed Russian-Arab friendship and traditional 'Russian' culture — not socialism, and even less Islam. In 1946, Mgr. Alexis, Patriarch of Moscow, was the first non-Communist dignitary to visit the Middle East from the USSR, acting as an emissary of 'Eternal Russia'.

Till the later 1960s, Soviet Muslims lived behind an impenetrable Iron Curtain.

5 Soviet Muslim Religious Leaders and the Muslim World Abroad (1968–80)

In the post-Khrushchev era, the Moscow authorities gradually raised the Iron Curtain which had for decades isolated Central Asia and Caucasus from the world of the *Dar ul-Islam*. In 1968, the Soviet Union reappeared on the political scene of the Middle East with a new 'Muslim face', and from then on the Kremlin, at first cautiously, used its Muslim leaders as 'roving ambassadors' and spokesmen to the Muslim world at large. Since these cautious beginnings the trend developed dramatically. The objective was threefold:

(1) to demonstrate to the outside world and the Third World in particular, by using Central Asia and Caucasus as a showcase of Communist economic achievements, that the Soviet experiment is more successful and rewarding than Western capitalism;

(2) to testify to the freedom, welfare and general prosperity of Islam in the Soviet Union;

(3) and thus to demonstrate that the Soviet Union is the best friend and partner of the Islamic world.

At first sight it seems a paradox that Soviet Islam should further the aims of the atheist state which had dominated it for decades, but Islam has had to adapt itself to the new situation under the Soviet regime. Muslim official leaders have co-operated, apparently willingly, with the Soviet authorities in certain fields, particularly regarding relations with the Muslim world abroad. This can be understood if one remembers that to the Soviet Muslims there is little difference between their 'Infidel' master in Moscow now and in Tsarist times — the same Russians, formerly Christian, now atheists. If anything, they may appear less dangerous than the proselytising Russian Christians of the past.

Unlike Tsarist Russia, the Soviet Union has devised a deliberate, if cautious, policy, aimed at using Islam for Soviet ends. In this the Muslim religious establishment, represented by the four Muslim Spiritual Boards, has proved to be the most effective instrument for advertising the freedom of Islam in the Soviet Union and for establishing contacts with conservative pro-Western Muslim states such as Saudi Arabia, Jordan, Tunisia, Morocco and Sudan, which are still closed to Soviet diplomats.

The co-operation of the Muslim religious establishment in promoting foreign policy is manifest in three ways: visits and conferences in the Soviet Union; visits abroad by Soviet muftis; propaganda broadcasts by Soviet Muslim authorities.

5.1 Visits and Conferences in the Soviet Union

Foreign Muslim delegations coming for 'friendly visits' or international conferences are received by Soviet Muslims. The pattern of such visits is unvarying. An invitation is issued by the Grand Mufti of Tashkent, Ziautdin Babakhanov. The visit begins in Tashkent with a reception given by the officials of the Board and often, though not always, by the representative of Uzbekistan's Communist Party and government. The reception is followed by a trip to the two Soviet *madrassah*s of Mir-i Arab in Bukhara and Imam Ismail al-Bukhari in Tashkent and to some of the most famous 'working' mosques in Tashkent, Bukhara and Samarkand. After the visit to Central Asia, the foreign delegation is generally taken to Baku to meet the *Sheikh ul-Islam* at the 'Taze Pir' mosque. Finally, the delegation goes to Leningrad and Moscow, where the delegates are received by the imam-khatibs of the local mosques and also, in Moscow, by representatives of the Soviet government, in particular the Abdullah Nurullayev — an Uzbek — Deputy Chairman of the Council for Religious Affairs of the Council of Ministers of the USSR. Sometimes they also visit Ufa, where they are greeted by the mufti of European Russia and Siberia.

Here are examples of delegations which have visited the Soviet Union in recent years: Jama'at-i Ulema-i Islam of Pakistan, the 'Young Muslim Society' of Egypt and a delegation of Muslims from Singapore in 1974; Abdul Razzak Mohammed, Deputy Prime Minister of Mauritius, and a delegation of Somali *ulema* in 1975; an Afghan *ulema* delegation headed by the Minister of Religious Affairs in 1976; and in 1978 a delegation of Turkish *ulema*, a Pakistan delegation headed by the Secretary General of the World Islamic Conference as well as a Jordanian delegation.

These visits are intended to produce the impression not only that Islam is free and prosperous, but also that Soviet Islamic leaders are treated by Soviet authorities as equal 'partners' and not as 'tools' of the government.

The various international congresses organised by the Spiritual Board of Tashkent are another way of demonstrating the unconditional support of Soviet Islamic leaders for Moscow's foreign policy. The following are some of the main events:

- 1970, a conference organised in Tashkent on the theme 'Unity and co-operation of Muslim peoples in the struggle for peace', chaired by Ziautdin Babakhanov and attended by a hundred Soviet *ulema* and representatives of 24 Muslim countries. Violent attacks were made against American, Israeli and South African 'imperialism'.
- 1973, a conference in Tashkent on the theme 'Soviet Muslims support the just struggle of the Arab people against Israeli imperialist aggression'.
- August 1974, an important international congress in Samarkand to commemorate the 1200th anniversary of Imam Ismaïl al-Bukhari. High-ranking representatives from 25 Muslim countries attended the congress, including representatives from Saudi Arabia, Egypt, Morocco and Jordan. On this occasion, however, there were no attacks against the US or Israel.
- October 1976, a congress convened in Tashkent by Babakhanov to celebrate the thirtieth anniversary of the Central Asian Board.

Representatives from Syria, North Yemen, Morocco, Jordan, Tunisia, India and Pakistan were present.

— 3 July 1979, an international conference held in Tashkent to celebrate the tenth anniversary of the journal *Muslims of the Soviet East*, chaired by Grand Mufti Babakhanov and attended by representatives from Jordan, Iraq, India, Turkey, Tunisia, Pakistan, Kuwait, Iran, Lebanon, Japan, Bulgaria and Ethiopia. The final communiqué signed by all the delegates contained violent attacks against 'Israeli, USA, South African and Chinese imperialism'.

— September 1979, a symposium convened in Düshanbe by the Central Asian Board on the 'contribution to the Muslims of Central Asia, the Volga and the Caucasus, to the development of Islamic thought and to the cause of peace and social progress'. Delegates from 30 Muslim countries were present, and the Grand Mufti Babakhanov once again took the opportunity to denounce 'US, Israeli and South African imperialism'.

5.2 Visits Abroad by Soviet Muslim Leaders

Between 1968 and 1979, Soviet religious leaders also visited Muslim countries frequently, especially those with conservative pro-Western governments. The delegations were usually headed by Ziautdin Babakhanov or one of his two assistants: the deputy muftis Abdulgani Abdullayev and Yusuf-Khan Shakirov. The members of such delegations speak perfect Arabic and have a thorough knowledge of all aspects of Islam and are thus the best ambassadors that the Soviet Union could send to the Muslim world. Some of their recent trips include:

— 1972, a delegation led by Babakhanov to Morocco.
— 1974, a delegation headed by Babakhanov to North Yemen.
— summer 1975, an important delegation including Babakhanov to Iraq, Jordan (where it was received by King Husein) and Egypt (including a visit to the University of al-Azhar).
— September 1975, a delegation to a conference in Mecca on the 'Mission of the Mosques' (on this occasion Babakhanov was received by King Khalid of Saudi Arabia).
— October 1975, a delegation to the International Symposium on Islamic Education, in Lucknow, India.
— October–November 1975, a delegation headed by Yusuf-Khan Shakirov — the Deputy Mufti of Central Asia — to Somalia and Mauritius.

- 1976, a delegation led by the Deputy Mufti Abdullayev to a Muslim-Christian conference in Tripoli (where they were received by Muamar Qadhafi).
- winter 1977, a delegation conducted by Abdullayev to the International Conference on 'Islamic Thought' in Wargla, Algeria.
- March 1977, a delegation led by *Imam-Khatib* of the 'Tilla Sheikh' mosque of Tashkent, Yunus Abu Turab, to an international symposium in Bangladesh on Muslim preaching.
- July 1978, a delegation headed by Babakhanov to an international conference in Karachi on the propagation of Islam.
- summer 1978, a delegation led by Abdullayev to Niger, Mali and Senegal.
- September 1978, a delegation headed by Babakhanov to an international conference in Istanbul on the Hegira calendar.
- winter 1978, a delegation headed by Abdullayev to the Twelfth International Conference on 'Islamic Thought' in Batna, Algeria.

5.3 Propaganda Broadcasting

Finally, an important factor in Muslim co-operation in Soviet foreign policy is propaganda broadcasting by Soviet muftis and other representatives of the Soviet Islamic establishment. These broadcasts, in Arabic, Persian, Pashtu, Urdu and Turkish, have increased since 1978. Their themes do not vary much from standard Soviet propaganda, but have a much greater impact on foreign Muslim audiences, as they are broadcast by the highest religious authorities. Here too Israeli, Chinese, American and South African imperialism are condemned, political harmony between Islam and the Soviet government is advocated and numerous 'enemies' are denounced, including Soviet Muslim *émigrés*. Recently the Afghan people have been exhorted to resist 'wicked fanatics'.

So far this co-operation has been fruitful and advantageous for the Soviet government. For some years now, respected religious leaders have praised the Soviet government and denounced the 'imperialists' at every Islamic conference throughout the world, including those held in the holy cities of Saudi Arabia. Furthermore, not a single word has ever been said at these conferences in defence of the United States or the West in general. These Muslim religious leaders, acting as special ambassadors, the avant-garde of Soviet foreign policy in Islamic countries where they were immediately accepted as fellow Muslims, have been a tremendous asset to the Soviet government in establishing their image of the Soviet Union as Islam's 'best friend'. However, everything has to be paid for, and the Soviet government has had to make important concessions to the religious establishment, in particular toning down anti-religious propaganda and permitting the opening of new mosques.

The period of co-operation between the Soviet Islamic establishment and Moscow, notwithstanding the advantages to both parties, seems to have come to an end with the invasion of Afghanistan.

6 The 'Backlash' — Soviet Islam and the Destabilised Middle East (1980–   )

Though the change is as yet hardly noticeable, a turning point in the history of Soviet Islam came in 1978, with two major external events: the downfall of the Shah of Iran followed by the triumph of the Islamic Revolution in Iran and the April (*Saur*) Communist revolution in Afghanistan which led inevitably to the invasion of the country by Soviet forces in December 1979.

Before 1978, as far as the USSR was concerned, the Middle East was a relatively stable area, ruled by conservative monarchies or moderate democracies. These governments were admittedly hostile to Marxism and harried the few local Communists that there were. Several states refused to enter into diplomatic relations with Moscow, though the majority were on friendly terms with the USSR. All were absolutely indifferent to the fate of Soviet Muslims. The area presented no danger whatsoever to the stability of the Soviet Union: Soviet Muslims could not be reached by any alien ideology, any models of subversion or any appeal to resist the Russians. For the Muslim population of the Caucasus and Central Asia, well protected by a complete Iron Curtain from any outside contamination, the Muslim world abroad was very remote, almost on another planet, despised rather than envied.

The revolutions in Iran and in Afghanistan, followed by the Soviet invasion of Afghanistan, changed dramatically this peaceful picture. They destabilised not only their own countries but the entire Middle East, transforming this relatively quiet territory into a boiling revolutionary cauldron, whose upheavals may have unpredictable consequences all round, and first and foremost for the Soviet Union. The first direct consequence was the destabilisation of the entire southern frontier of the USSR. By force of circumstances, the Iron Curtain along the Afghan frontier had to be raised, whilst on the Iranian frontier it became more breachable.

Today, in contrast with the stable pre-1978 Muslim world, the

Middle East appears a potential source of trouble for the USSR, an area from which various subversive and radical ideologies may penetrate and contaminate Soviet Islam.

To understand the present relationship between Islam inside and outside the USSR and to evaluate the likelihood of a backlash in the Soviet territories as a result of the Iranian and Afghan tragedies, we must bear in mind the fact that despite sixty years' isolation, Soviet Islam is still part of the *Dar ul-Islam* and that Central Asian and Caucasian Turks and Iranians have the same ethnic, cultural and religious background as the populations on the other side of the border. Among the various factors linking the Muslim peoples of the USSR with foreign Muslims, the religious and ethno-linguistic ties are the strongest.

Islam in the Soviet Union sixty years ago came under the domination of an atheist state whose avowed aim was, and still is, the eradication of all religious creeds. As a result of half a century of anti-religious campaigns, Islam in the USSR lost a percentage of its believers and became a 'personal matter'. Its administrative structure was modified, the better to fit into the Soviet system. Islam adjusted itself to these new circumstances. However, though forced to adapt, it has not in any way been contaminated by Marxism. From the point of view of Islamic law and theology, Islam in the USSR is the same untainted religion it was before 1917, and its leaders, though submissive to the godless state, have never been accused of indidelity (*kufr*), heresy (*shirq*), or even innovation (*bida'*), even by their enemies. Paradoxically, Soviet Islam today appears more conservative and more traditionalist than the religion practised in many Muslim countries of Asia and Africa and the very progressive *jadid* Islam of pre-revolutionary Russia. Also Soviet Muslims and those from abroad feel completely at home with each other in whatever country they meet. They belong to the same Muslim *Millet* and share the same spiritual background that rules their everyday life. They observe the same religious rites and social customs. They have the same dietary traditions, wear almost the same clothes and display the same attitude of deep-rooted distrust towards the non-Muslim West, as represented by Europeans and Americans in the Middle East and by Russians in Central Asia and the Caucasus. In short, they are brethren facing a hostile world together.

Religious kinship is felt between members of the three main branches of Islam currently represented in the USSR, and they have more or less succeeded in preserving their contacts with their co-religionists abroad. The Sunnis, who constitute the vast majority of the Turkic, Iranian and

Caucasian Muslims, have maintained their links with foreign religious centres — the holy places of Saudi Arabia and the Islamic universities of Al-Azhar (Cairo) and Qarawiyin (Fez). The great Sufi orders (especially the Naqshbandiya and the Qadiriya) which exist in the USSR and throughout the Muslim world are highly decentralised, but their spiritual doctrine and rituals (especially the *zikr*) are strictly uniform everywhere.

Shia Islam (the *Ithna Ashariya* or 'Twelvers') has some 4 million followers in the USSR (70 per cent of the Azeris and some small groups in Central Asia). Unlike Sunni Islam, this branch has a centralised hierarchy of clerics, who constitute what can be termed a 'church'. Their spiritual centres are outside the USSR: An-Najaf and Karbala in Iraq, Mashhad and Qum in Iran. The Shia 'Church' of Soviet Azerbayjan is cut off from these spiritual centres, and contacts are absolutely minimal. However, the fame of the Shia holy places in Iraq and Iran and therefore the prestige of their ayattolahs remain high among the Soviet Shia Muslims.

The third branch is represented by some 60,000 to 100,000 Ismailis of the Nizarite sect ('Followers of the Aga Khan') in the Pamirs (autonomous region of Gorno-Badakhshan of the Tajik Republic). It is a highly centralised sect, and according to recent Soviet sources, Soviet Ismailis succeeded, at least until the 1950s, in maintaining illegal contacts with the Ismaili spiritual centres in India.

Soviet Muslims also identify themselves with their Muslim brethren abroad through ethnic and linguistic kinship. The southern frontiers of the USSR are purely 'political' and do not reflect any national division. As a result, almost every Soviet Muslin nationality has a corresponding 'brother' group abroad. Some large nationalities are distributed in practically equal numbers between the Soviet Union and one or several foreign states. These include the Azeris (5.5 million in the USSR and probably around 5 million in Iran), the Turkmens (2 million in the USSR and probably over 1 million in Afghanistan, Iran, Turkey and Iraq) and the Tajiks (3 million in the USSR, 3 to 4 million in Afghanistan). Other large USSR nationalities have corresponding minorities beyond the Soviet border: the Uzbeks (12.5 million in the USSR and about 1.5 million in Afghanistan), the Kazakhs (6.5 million in the USSR, small groups in Afghanistan and an important minority — about 800,000 — in Sinkiang), the Kirghiz (2 million in the USSR, around 100,000 in China and a small group of less than 10,000 formerly in Afghanistan, now living in Pakistan).

The third category consists of the immigrant nationalities in the

USSR with majorities abroad. These include the Uyghurs (210,000 in the USSR in 1979 and over 6 million in China), the Dungans (50,000 in the USSR and over 5 million in China), the Baluchis (13,000 in the USSR and an indeterminate number in Pakistan, Iran and Afghanistan) and the Kurds (over 150,000 in the USSR, 1 million in Iran, 4 to 6 million in Turkey and 1 million in Iraq).

Finally, there are Soviet Muslim nationalities that have established colonies of varying sizes abroad. These colonies have not lost their original national identity or their language, and in some cases they maintain contacts (official or clandestine) with their original homeland and their brethren in the USSR. This is the case with the so-called Circassians (Cherkess) in Turkey, Jordan, Israel and the United States.

The bonds of religious, ethnic and sometimes tribal kinship (tribal in the case of the Turkmens and the Kazakhs) between the 45 million Soviet Muslims and the Turko-Iranian world of over 100 million beyond the Soviet border make for a complex relationship between the Soviet Muslims and the Muslim world abroad.

One crucial question arises: what and where is the real national centre of these populations? Is it in the USSR, where Muslims enjoy a measure of cultural and linguistic freedom and are formally endowed with an autonomous administrative status, but where they continue to be subjected to unrelenting anti-religious pressure and where their cultural and political development is placed under the control of the Russian 'Big Brother'? Or is it abroad, where their communities often have no national existence at all (in Iran and Afghanistan local Turkic languages, such as Azeri, Turkmen and Uzbek, are not recognised as literary languages), but where they are granted full religious freedom and where, as individuals, they have access to political power?

It is significant that the Soviet government has never formulated any irredentist claim in connection with the Azeris, Turkmens, Uzbeks or Tajiks living in Iran or Afghanistan (they did raise claims to the former Armenian and Georgian territories of Eastern Anatolia). Soviet propaganda ignores them. Their ethnic or religious kinship with elements of Muslim population in the USSR is never mentioned. According to the Moscow line, Soviet Muslims look upon their Russian 'Big Brother' as 'their nearest and dearest', much closer than any 'bourgeois', 'feudal' or 'clerical' brethren living abroad. Soviet Muslims are allowed to express their solidarity only with those who are engaged in the struggle against imperialism and colonialism, regardless of their creed. Thus, an Angolan Marxist fighting South African 'imperialism' is deemed closer to a Soviet Turkmen than his cousins across the border in Iran.

This official attitude does not correspond to the passionate interest of the Central Asian and Caucasian elites for their coreligionists abroad, nor to their complete indifference for the struggling Angolans or Salvadorians. They are generally well informed about the political and spiritual evolution of the Muslim world at large (while, with a few exceptions, the Middle Eastern elites know little of Soviet Islam) and their attitude is a complex and paradoxical blend — sympathy, disdain, an ardent desire to help and a deep-rooted feeling that this foreign *Dar ul-Islam* is the source of models of national liberation.

As to Soviet policy in the Middle East, Soviet Muslim elites have been traditionally more radical and adventurous than the Russian leadership of the Communist Party. *Vis-à-vis* the Ghilan Republic in 1920 and Iranian Azerbayjan and Kurdistan in 1946, these elites had endorsed the most drastic policy: the annexation of the whole of Northern Iran. It is very likely that the present-day Muslim elites favour Soviet annexation, if not of the whole of Afghanistan, then at least of Afghan Turkestan north of the Hindu Kush. Such an annexation would considerably strengthen the Soviet Muslims' demographic and political position *vis-à-vis* the Russians.

With this background in mind, let us examine the reaction of Soviet Muslims — the elites as well as the masses, to the dramatic events just beyond the border.

6.1 Soviet Islam and Afghanistan

The direct involvement of Central Asian Muslims in Afghan affairs started in April 1979 with the attack on Mohammed Daud. Intent at first on helping a friendly Marxist regime and then moved by the urgent need to prevent the total collapse of the state administration in Afghanistan, wrecked as it was by successive purges, the Soviets were forced to send large numbers of Central Asians, mainly Uzbeks and Tajiks, to act as administrative and technical cadres, because Russians lacked sufficient knowledge of local conditions and languages. Late in 1979, several hundred Soviet Muslims held positions in all levels of the Afghan administration, from the lowest jobs (the most numerous) up to the post of Deputy Minister. These Soviet Muslim cadres were able to establish contacts with the native Muslim population practically without any Russian control, which was a completely new experience in the history of the Soviet Union. It is quite likely that some of these Central Asian cadres realised the dream of the Muslim National Communists of the 1920s, namely to export Communism to a neighbouring Muslim country, with whose population they practically share a common ethnic and linguistic background. Moreover, in December 1979, Central Asian soldiers formed a fair percentage, possibly 30 to 40 per cent, of the invading Soviet forces. It would seem that the Soviet military command was obliged to draw on reserves available in Central Asia to complete the divisions stationed along the Afghan border which were not yet combat ready.

Other Central Asians were mobilised and sent to make camp along the border of Afghanistan. Still others went to Afghanistan in construction units to repair airfields and to build camps. In the winter of 1980, an estimated 30,000 to 40,000 Central Asian soldiers went into Afghanistan. It may have been the intention that the Central Asians were to engage in occupation duties and not to fight the *mujahideen*s. Whatever the position, by late February 1980 the Soviet military authorities had started removing units with Central Asian soldiers and replacing them with entirely Russian (or 'European') divisions. At the same time, the Soviet Muslims manning the Afghan administration were systematically replaced by Russians.

What reason or reasons forced the Soviet authorities to sacrifice the benefits of using their Muslim citizens in Afghanistan? There were many important benefits both before and after the invasion. Central Asians served as interpreters for the Soviet armed forces. They helped the Afghan administration to function during the occupation. Furthermore, their presence tended to give to this Soviet intervention in a foreign country the appearance of an inter-Islamic affair. This may have been the original intention of the Soviet leadership, when Uzbek and Tajik soldiers paraded spectacularly in Kabul. But friendly contacts were established far too fast with the local population, without the Russians being able to prevent it. Widespread fraternisation took place between the Central Asians and the local populations and even with the Afghan resistance. In some places, including Kabul, an active 'black market' in Qurans was organised. Soviet Muslims underwent religious and political 'intoxication' at the hands of the Afghans. When it became necessary to send Central Asian soldiers into combat against the *mujahideen*s they did not 'perform' well. Eventually, in January and February 1980, some Central Asian soldiers deserted and went over to the rebels. Furthermore, it is possible that the flood of wounded and dead Muslims brought back to Central Asia and the unpleasant incidents which followed had a direct bearing on the withdrawal of Muslim soldiers from Afghanistan. Indeed, in March 1980 rumours circulated in Moscow of a riot in Alma Ata where the Kazakh population violently opposed the Russian military authorities' plan to give Muslim troops killed in Afghanistan a military burial in a non-Muslim cemetary and not according to Muslim tradition.

After two years of guerrilla warfare in Afghanistan, it is possible to draw two preliminary conclusions.

Although the majority of Soviet Muslims engaged in one way or another in the Afghanistan operation remained obedient to Soviet orders, the authorities in Moscow came to question their reliability as a fighting force and their commitment to the Soviet homeland.

As suggested above, the Iron Curtain between Muslim brethren residing on either side of the border is crumbling as a result of the uncensored exchange of information and ideas that is taking place. One of the key sets of ideas which could strike responsive chords in Central Asia is a fundamentalist, religious revivalism which would reinforce the already existing trend in Central Asian republics. The Sufi brotherhoods hidden away in the Soviet republics would probably welcome even a temporary success of the religion-inspired resistance in Afghanistan, with its strong flavour of a Holy War. If armed resistance continues in this region, it might well become a model of heroism for contemporary Muslim nationalists — the same way as Shamil and his Naqshbandi *mürid*s inspired all the nationalist anti-Russian movements in the Tsarist Empire.

The Soviets' room for manoeuvre in Afghanistan is therefore very limited. Their victory must be rapid, complete and spectacular. Failure or even a limited success could provide a dramatic signal to Central Asian Muslims, in the same way as the defeat of the Tsarist armies in Manchuria in 1905 hastened the birth of a Muslim national movement.

There is plenty of evidence to suggest that the Soviet authorities are taking very seriously the danger of a backlash in Central Asia as a result of the Afghan war. In 1980, there was a significant change in the style of the Central Asian press. The emphasis switched from the theme of the 'friendship' between the local Muslims and their 'Elder Brother' to that of the ability of the same 'Elder Brother' to maintain law and order and to eliminate various 'traitors'. Two themes were specially popular in 1980 and 1981: the Basmachis and the KGB.

The Basmachi movement has been more or less taboo as a topic for the last forty years. Now it is once again in the headlines. Memoirs, historical surveys, television series and novels are appearing in all languages, with two new angles: the movement is linked to 'foreign imperialism' and is connected to the reactionary Muslim clerics and the Sufi brotherhoods. The message is clear: 'We beat you before; if necessary, we will beat you again.'

A mass of publications glorifying the KGB, the Border Guards and the whole Red Army is also significant. Never before has literature devoted to our 'brave *Chekisty*' and to the legacy of 'Iron Felix' (Dzerzhinski) been so abundant. The message here is also crystal clear.

6.2 *Soviet Islam and the Iranian Revolution*

The influence on Soviet Islam of the events in Iran may be deeper and, in the long run, more dangerous than the guerrilla war in Afghanistan.

Viewed from the Soviet Muslim borderlands, Iran is undergoing an Islamic fundamentalist and anti-imperialist revolution not very different in character from certain radical religious movements in Russia, such as the 'theocratic state' or Uzun Haji in 1919–20 which has left an indelible impression on North Caucasian Muslims. Iran has always enjoyed — and continues to enjoy — immense prestige in the entire Turco-Iranian world not only because of its unique and advanced culture, but also because of its long tradition of statesmanship. This is especially true of Caucasian Muslims, for whom Iran remains — despite the present uncertainty — an inspiring model.

Several aspects of the Iranian Revolution arouse particularly strong sympathy in the younger generation of Muslim intellectuals and in the numerous 'religious fanatics' of the Caucasian region (i.e. members of the Sufi orders).

The 'anti-imperialist' aspect of the Iranian Revolution is one of them. It is easy to draw a parallel between the 'foreign imperialism' of the Americans in Iran and the 'imperialism' of the Russians in the Caucasus and in Central Asia. As the Iranian Shia religious leader Ayatollah Sayyed Kazem Shariyat Madari put it in a broadcast from Tehran (22 February 1979 in Persian), 'The Iranian Muslim people's triumphant struggle constitutes a turning point in the history of world struggles and the best model to follow by the oppressed Muslim peoples of the world.' Ayatollah Shariyat Madari — an Azeri Turk from Tabriz — was probably thinking of his brethren of Northern Soviet Azerbayjan.

The 'populist' character of 'Khomeiniism', with its promise to replace the old corrupt bureaucracy and to bring to power a new category of younger leaders of more popular origin, is also highly popular with the younger Muslim intellectuals.

The exaltation of the cultural, moral and political values of Islam flatters the innate sense of superiority of the Caucasian Muslims with regard to their non-Muslim (Russian or Armenian) neighbours.

The fact that 'Khomeiniism' is a purely Shia phenomenon and has 'reactivated' Shia minorities in Iraq, Syria and Yemen, making them more conscious of the differences separating them from Sunni Islam, would probably not be a great obstacle to Muslim religious unity in the Caucasus where differences of dogma between Sunnis and Shias have become less marked over the sixty years of Soviet rule.

Religious fundamentalism is not the only ideology that Iran can export to its northern neighbours. Radicalism in a variety of guises — always spiced with a time-honoured religious flavour — is another possibility. One such is the wildly romantic philosophy of Ali Shariyati which attempts to reconcile Marxism with Shia Islam. 'Islamic Marxism' (or 'Marxist Islam'), with its tremendous pathos, constant references to the glories of the past and promise of a happy and mighty future, constitutes a powerful and dynamic revolutionary ideal much more inspiring than the emasculated, bureaucratic Russian model.

All these factors help to explain a dramatic reversal in the flow of influence between the Soviet Union and Iran since the fall of the Shah in January 1979. Where once Iranians listened to propaganda broadcasts from Radio Baku, today it is the Soviet Azeris and Turkmens who follow with interest the broadcasts from Tabriz, Tehran and Gorgan. In June 1979, Allah Shukur Pacha Zade, then *akhund* of the Baku *jami* mosque and Shia deputy chairman of the Muslim Spiritual board for Transcaucasia (at present he is the Shia *Sheikh ul-Islam*), told a group of foreign journalists in Baku that 'events in Iran do not mean that Islam will make new inroads in the Soviet Union'. Whether this official statement represents a sincere and realistic assessment of the situation is open to some doubt. Once more, as in 1908, Iran presents the picture of a 'revolutionary' country where 'something is on the move'. Even if the Muslims of the USSR prudently express the view that developments in Iran cannot affect their life and ideology, their Shia brethren's success in humiliating United States 'imperialism' must raise their own hopes that its rival and counterpart, Soviet 'imperialism', will also be defeated one day in the Caucasus.

Soviet concern over developments in Iran is clearly illustrated by several recent official statements. Reference to 'subversive activity' by Sufi brotherhoods and to the possibility of Muslim fundamentalism along Iranian lines spilling over into the Soviet Union became more numerous in 1980, coupled with appeals for vigilance by the KGB and border guards. Of particular significance was an article by General Yusif Zade, Chairman of the Azerbayjan KGB, in the *Bakinskii Rabochii* of 19 December 1980, entitled 'Foreign Espionage and

Diversion', in which the General denounced the 'infiltration of foreign agents through our borders' and the anti-social activity of the 'sectarians' and of the 'reactionary Muslim clergy' (both terms denoting the Sufis).

6.3 Soviet Islam and Other Middle Eastern Countries

Increased contacts with revolutionary Arab countries and organisations such as Syria, Libya, Algeria and the PLO, which claim to follow a 'Muslim way to socialism' could bring to the USSR ideologies and theories comparable to those of the Soviet Muslim Communists of the 1920s. In spite of their obvious lack of sophistication, these ideologies have a powerful appeal. Then there is Turkey, a country which holds a special significance for all Turks from the Balkans to the Pacific Ocean. Given the present political set-up in Turkey, the country is unable to exercise any influence on the Soviet Turks. A change in the political leadership in Ankara could, however, find an immediate echo in the Caucasus and Central Asia. A switch to the left, bringing to power radical socialist — but also nationalist — elements could give birth in Turkey to a 'Turkish Marxism' closer to the subversive ideas of Sultan Galiev than to the Russian variety. A switch to the right would, inevitably, be followed by the victory of the Islamic fundamentalists whose pan-Islamic theories might have an even more profound effect on Soviet Islam.

In spite of impressive technical and intellectual achievements, Soviet Islam, stultified by decades of enforced conformity to stale Russian Marxism, has nothing to offer Muslims abroad at the political level. On the contrary, it is the Soviet Muslims who are likely to be influenced by the ideas (perhaps even by the political terrorism and guerrilla methods) adopted by the newly radicalised Middle East. These ideas, ranging from the most conservative religious fundamentalism to the wildest revolutionary radicalism, share one common characteristic: the potential for destabilising Soviet Islam, thereby undermining the stability of the USSR itself.

6.4 Soviet Islam and China

China's strategy towards Islam, and her own Muslim population in particular, could become a major factor in destabilising Soviet Islam.

The Sino-Soviet frontier in Inner Asia is an artificial barrier separating ethnic groups closely related by common bonds of language, religion, culture and historical tradition. The total population of Sinkiang was estimated in 1978 at 11 to 12 million, of which 60 per

Table 3.1: Muslim Population of China, 1978

Chinese Muslims (in Chinese 'Hwei', in Russian 'Dungans')	6,500,000
Uyghurs	5,500,000
Kazakhs	800,000
Dongxiang (Muslim Mongols)	90,000
Tajiks	22,000
Salars	50,000
Uzbeks	7,000
Tatars	3,000

cent were Muslim Turks, whereas Muslims represented around 70 per cent of the total population of Central Asia at this time. Unlike the population in Sinkiang which can easily be submerged by Han Chinese immigrants, the proportion of Russians and other Europeans in Central Asia can only decrease. In 1978, the total Muslim population of China was estimated at nearly 13 million, as can be seen in Table 3.1. Muslims therefore represent less than 1.3 per cent of the population of China compared with 17 to 18 per cent in the USSR. This is the most ominous difference between China and the USSR.

In the USSR, non-Russian nationalities (including Ukrainians and Belorussians) account for half the population. In China non-Han nationalities total between 55 and 65 million, or less than 6 per cent of the total population. It follows that the nationality problem in the USSR is potentially much more serious than in China.

The presence in the heart of Inner Asia of 45 to 50 million Muslims distributed between the two Asian superpowers has forced them to devise 'Muslim strategies', both defensive and offensive in character.

Initially, the Chinese perceived their position as being weaker than that of the Russians, and for that reason adopted a purely defensive stance. To the Muslims the Chinese are pre-eminently a race of 'Infidel', *bot parast*, idolators, with whom compromise is legally impossible. The Russians are more fortunate, for in spite of their atheism, they are considered as belonging to the *Ahl al-Kitab* ('People of the Book'), spiritual descendants of a common ancestor, the Prophet Ibrahim (Abraham). Legally, a Muslim may marry an *'Ahl al-Kitab'* woman and 'People of the Book' may remain citizens of a Muslim state, but this right is denied to 'Infidels'.

In the tradition of the epic songs and folklore of Central Asian Turks the 'Chinese' represent the symbol of the arch-enemy, the pitiless invader, threatening the very existence of the Muslim *Millet*. More recent tragedies have increased the inherent hostility of Muslims toward the Chinese. In 1862 a major Muslim revolt against Chinese rule broke out which eventually spread throughout the Chinese North-West. In 1865, taking advantage of the rebellion, a Uyghur, Yaqub Beg, set up an independent Uyghur state with the tacit support of the Russians. When the state was finally overthrown by the Chinese, many thousands of Uyghurs and Dungans fled to Russia and settled in Kazakhstan and Northern Kirghizia, where their descendants now form an important colony (211,000 Uyghurs and 52,000 Dungans according to the 1979 Soviet census).

After the collapse of the Ching dynasty, Sinkiang, although nominally remaining under Chinese rule, arrogated autonomy to itself. After the Second World War an Uyghur 'East Turkestan Republic' was created with the open support of the Soviets. The Republic was liquidated after the reconquest of Sinkiang by the Communists in 1949, and by 1951 most of the pro-Soviet local leaders had been removed. In 1956 the Chinese authorities started shifting large numbers of Han Chinese settlers to Sinkiang and two years later the 'Great Leap Forward' was initiated, modelled on Stalin's big anti-Muslim offensive of the 1930s. The relative tolerance enjoyed by the minorities was at an end. Property was confiscated and Sinkiang Muslims were asked, among other things, to learn Han Chinese and to give up various outdated customs — including their religion. The brutality of the Cultural Revolution provoked intense resentment among all minorities, especially the Muslims. In 1962, in the province of Ili, an anti-Chinese demonstration was brutally repressed and dozens of Uyghurs and Kazakhs were killed. News of the massacre spread rapidly, and rioting ensued throughout Sinkiang followed by a massive exodus of Kazakhs and Uyghurs. According to the Soviets, over a hundred thousand Muslim Turks crossed the Russian border while the Chinese admit to 60,000 people having emigrated.

At the time of the break between China and the USSR, the prestige of China among Muslim Turks of Inner Asia was at its lowest. A priori, the Soviets appeared in a much more favourable light. Since Mao's death, however, the Chinese have been steadily improving their image. The first real change in strategy took place as late as 1980, with the announcement in the official *Jenmin Ribao* (Peking, 15 July 1980) that 'the old Maoist line has been discarded in favour of a more realistic pragmatic approach to the problem of nationalities'. The Chinese admit that their position in Sinkiang has been weakened by the anti-religious drive of the last ten years. To make up for lost ground, all atheistic activities against Islam have ceased and the observance of religious rites is no longer impeded. The Chinese, probably for the first time in history, are set to compete with the Russians for the psychological conquest of Islam in Inner Asia. In their struggle, as yet limited to propaganda, the two rivals have certain points in their favour, but both also face drawbacks.

Until 1980, the odds were stacked heavily in favour of the Soviet Union. Soviet Muslims undoubtedly enjoy a higher standard of living and Soviet Central Asia could, at least in theory, prove attractive to Muslims from across the border. June Teufel-Dreyer, the leading expert on China's minorities ('Ethnic Minorities in the Sino-Soviet Conflict' in McCagg (ed.), *Soviet-Asian Ethnic Frontiers*, New York, 1979, p. 219), wrote in 1978:

> Given the higher degree of ideological orthodoxy demanded and the lower living standard prevailing on the Chinese side, the Soviet Union would probably enjoy an advantage in any contest between the two states for the loyalties of the Central Asian peoples.

Until now, the Muslim population of Sinkiang provided an excellent target for subversion by well organised Soviet anti-Chinese propaganda. Broadcasts in almost all the Turkic languages, spoken in Sinkiang, Uyghur, Kazakh, Kirghiz and Uzbek as well as in Chinese, are beamed from stations in Tashkent, Alma-Ata and Frunze. The Soviets promote themselves as champions of the cause of Chinese Muslims by harping not only on the material well-being of Soviet Turks, but also on the anti-Chinese tradition: the revolt of 1862–5, the East Turkestan Republic, the 1962 massacre and so on. The propaganda message is carried also by two newspapers specially published in Alma-Ata in Uyghur and Kazakh (Arabic script) for the benefit of Sinkiang Muslims. Both bear the name *Our Fatherland* (*Bezning Vatän*). In addition, there is a special edition in Arabic script of the Uyghur newspaper *Yeni Hayat* (*New Life*) aimed at those who fled Sinkiang in 1962. Finally, it is probable that spies and agitators drawn from local Turkic nationalities are being sent to China.

Soviet propaganda has a twofold aim: to win popularity among Chinese Turks by projecting a rosy image of the Soviet Union, 'friend of Islam and of the Turks', and to maintain the image of 'China — enemy of Islam'. This second aspect of Soviet propaganda is played cautiously and in a minor key, lest their attempt to exploit the religious and ethnic differences between Han Chinese and the Turks of Sinkiang provokes a dangerous backlash in the Soviet's Central Asian backyard, especially among the Kazakhs, who remain the most anti-Russian of all the Soviet Muslims.

Soviet propaganda carefully avoids any allusion to the possibility of independence for Chinese Muslims and no irredentist claims are presented on behalf of Soviet Kazakhs or Uyghurs to the territory of Sinkiang. Such appeals are clearly too dangerous for the Soviets to countenance.

It is difficult to measure the impact of Soviet propaganda on Chinese Islam, because, as June Teufel-Dreyer writes (ibid., p. 218):

the exact nature of Kazakh and Uyghur demands on the Chinese government has never been made clear. There are references to separatism, implying an independent Sinkiang, to joining together with other Turkic Muslims . . . in a larger, separate state; to demands for the greater autonomy of Sinkiang within the Chinese state, some of them including demands for the Han Chinese to leave Sinkiang and others simply asking that they relinquish their commanding positions in the province's economic and administrative infrastructure.

Chinese propaganda seems cruder, but it may nevertheless be effective. It insists on the 'colonialist' character of the Russian presence in Central Asia and on 'Soviet Union — prison of nations'. Unlike the Soviets, the Chinese present irredentist claims to large parts of Kazakhstan (south-eastern and eastern regions, including the capital city of Alma-Ata), substantiated by the fact that the Kazakhs of the Great Kazakh Horde (*Ulu Zhuz*) had solicited and were granted the status of Chinese 'protected persons' between 1723 and 1725, when the threat from the Oïrots was at its greatest.

In spite of the fact that neither the Chinese nor the Russians can be certain of the loyalties of their respective Turks, by virtue of the small size of her Turkic population China's manoeuvring possibilities in Central Asia seem more favourable than those of the Soviet Union. Recent developments go to prove that the Chinese are aware of this and are willing to go much further than the Russians in terms of concessions to the Muslims. Chinese efforts have three objectives:

(1) to restore peace in Sinkiang and to raise the standard of living there;
(2) to co-opt Muslims into the elite of the province;
(3) to win over the religious leaders.

As we have already noted, important concessions were granted to the minorities in 1980 by the Chinese, including the suspension of anti-religious pressure and the reopening of old mosques and the building of new ones. The Russians are unwilling or unable to adopt the same policy in Soviet Central Asia. A recent American visitor to China found over a hundred 'working' mosques in Turfan while Bukhara, one of the great capitals of Islamic culture, has two. The Chinese have clearly recognised that an entirely new policy towards the Islamic religion is a high priority. In 1980, the Arabic alphabet was officially introduced for the Kazakh and the Uyghur languages, a measure greatly appreciated by the native intellectuals, who once again have access to their prestigious patrimony. Moscow, on the other hand, still controls the access by Soviet Turks to their cultural heritage by having transliterated their languages into Cyrillic. Thus, in the long run, the Chinese may be better equipped than the Russians to play the part of the 'Best Friend of Islam'. It should also be remembered that half the Muslims of China, the 'Hwei', are ethnic Chinese, so that Islam in China is almost a national religion, while Islam in Russia has always been a hostile, alien body.

The attitude of the Chinese towards Soviet Islam remains essentially cautious and defensive. For the time being, Chinese interest in Soviet Muslims appears to spring from a need to follow closely moves by the Russians that might have a knock-on effect on their own Muslim minorities. Nevertheless, the Chinese appear to recognise the burden which Islam could pose to Soviet power and to view the Muslim problem as a potential Achilles heel of Moscow. A shift towards a more offensive strategy by the Chinese should not, therefore, be dismissed.

There is plenty of evidence that some Soviet Muslim minorities, in particular the Kazakhs and the Kirghiz, might actually welcome the Chinese: 'Wait till the Chinese come, we will show you . . .' is a statement often heard in Central Asia.

Taking advantage of the Soviet invasion of Afghanistan, the Chinese have been trying to mobilise Muslim world opinion against the Russians. In 1980, the Chinese authorities, imitating Soviet methods, began to use their Muslim clerics as propagandists and overseas ambassadors. In January 1981, Salih An-Shiwei, a Hwei, Imam of the Dongsi mosque of Peking and Chairman of the Islamic Association of Peking, was invited to Islamabad and elected as a member of the Muslim League. His first act upon arriving in Pakistan was a violent attack on Soviet imperialism and an expression of the deep concern of Chinese Muslims for their Afghan brethren slaughtered by the Russian *kafirs*.

It is as yet too early to speculate what impact the Chinese might have on Soviet Islam, but there is plenty of evidence that Chinese pressure will persist and grow in intensity. The 'Yellow Peril' so often stressed by Soviet leaders may well become a reality.

4 SOVIET ISLAM IN PERSPECTIVE — MUSLIMS AND RUSSIANS IN THE YEAR 2000

In view of the rapidly changing political pattern of Soviet Islam, it would be foolhardy to attempt a forecast for the near future — and the year 2000 is but one generation removed from us. Nevertheless, the general lines of the evolution are already clearly drawn and it is possible to formulate some general observations regarding the situation in twenty years' time. Four main factors will dominate the coming twenty years and shape the future Muslim-Russian relationship.

1 The Demographic Factor

The demographic factor is not only the most important, it is also the best known and can be analysed with scientific precision. There is a curious analogy between Soviet Central Asia and Quebec, in that both have passed through the experience of the 'revenge of cradles'.

Like the French Canadians in the nineteenth century, the best defence of Soviet Muslims against their conquerors has been (and will remain for a time yet) their biological dynamism and vigour, which has cancelled out all Russian attempts at biological or cultural assimilation.

This problem has been analysed in detail by several US demographers, and in particular by the leading experts in the field, Murray Feshbach and Stephen Rapawy ('Soviet Population and Manpower Trends and Policies' in *Soviet Economy in a New Perspective, a Compendium of Papers*, submitted to the Joint Economic Committee, Congress of the United States, 94th Congress, 2nd Session, 14 October 1976); also by Godfrey S. Baldwin (*Population Projections by Age and Sex for the Republics and Major Economic Regions of the USSR, 1970 to 2000*, Foreign Demographic Analysis Division, US Bureau of the Census, International Population Report, series P-91, no. 26, September 1979) and Edmund Brunner Jr. (*Soviet Demographic Trends and the Ethnic Composition of Draft Age Males — 1980-1995*, Rand Publications Series, February 1981, N-1654-NA). We have used their findings extensively.

According to the Soviet censuses of 1926 and 1939, the growth of

Table 4.1: Muslim and Russian Populations, 1926 and 1939

	1926 census	1939 census	Increase (per cent)
Total population of USSR	147,000,000	209,000,000	42
Russians	78,000,000	114,000,000	47
Total Muslim population	17,000,000	24,000,000	41

the Muslim population of the USSR was slower than that of the Slav, and indeed below the average for the USSR as a whole. The fertility of the Slavs — especially of the Russians — was still high, while the natural increase of the Muslims was largely compensated by a high mortality rate. This situation was spectacularly reversed during the war. The entire weight of the conflict was borne by the three Slav groups: Russians, Ukrainians and Belorussians, and their losses were tremendous. Their fertility rate fell while that of the relatively protected Muslims soared.

Since the war, the demographic development of the Soviet Union has been a race between the Slavs and the Muslims (mainly Turks), with the Slavs steadily losing out. Between 1959 and 1970 the total population increase of the USSR was 1.33 per cent per year. The increase of the Russians of 1.12 per cent was well below the national average, while that of the Muslims at 3.19 per cent was almost three times that of the Russians and nearly 2.5 times the national rate. Between the 1970 and 1979 censuses the average growth of the Soviet population as a whole slowed to 0.92 per cent per year, but the Muslim peoples collectively still managed the highest growth rate of 2.17 per cent per year as against 0.7 per cent for the Russians. Central Asian Turks and Iranians attained the most notable growth rates. Smaller Muslim nationalities of Northern Caucasus have also displayed spectacular growth rates, including those who were victims of attempted genocide during the war (Chechens, Ingushes, Balkars). Only the Volga Tatars, a diaspora nationality, exhibited a growth rate comparable to that of the Russians. This was not, however, the result of a low fertility rate (it is probably only slightly below that of other Muslim Turks of the USSR), but to an advanced process of Russification (and even of total assimilation) of the Tatar's colonies in Siberia and in the Russian area of the RSFSR.

A comparison of the three post-war Soviet censuses (1959, 1970, 1979) has revealed two basic and closely interrelated trends which will almost certainly persist well into the future, strongly influencing the evolution of the next two decades. These are the concentration of

Table 4.2: USSR Populations and Growth Rates, 1959–79

Nationalities	Numbers (millions)			Annual increase (per cent)	
	1959	1970	1979	1959–70	1970–9
Total USSR	209	242	262	1.34	0.90
Russians	114	120	137	1.12	0.70
Ukrainians	37	41	42	0.82	0.48
Muslim peoples (total)	24	35	44	3.19	2.37
Uzbeks	6	9	12	3.93	3.43
Kazakhs	3.8	5.3	6.5	3.53	2.40
Tatars	5	6	6.3	1.62	0.71
Azeris	3	4	5	2.52	1.69
Tajiks	1.4	2.1	2.9	3.93	3.43
Kirghiz	0.9	1.5	1.9	3.72	3.11

Table 4.3: Population Growth Rates in Northern Caucasus, 1959–79

	1959–70 Annual Increase (per cent)	1970–9 Annual Increase (per cent)
Chechens	4.2	2.6
Ingushes	3.46	1.93
Karachays	2.94	1.87
Daghestanis	4.78	2.26

Muslim populations in their national territories and the resulting reduction in immigrant minorities.

The steady concentration of Muslim indigenous nationalities in their own constituent territories, federal republics and autonomous regions is due to several factors: the slowing down of Russian and other European immigration (and in some territories of the Caucasus the beginning of the emigration of Russians), the tremendous natural growth rate of the indigenous groups, the almost total absence of emigration of Muslims (with the exception of the Volga Tatars and to a lesser degree of the Bashkirs) from their natural homelands, and, finally, the assimilation of immigrants by the dominant nationality. With a few minor exceptions, the proportion of Muslims in all Muslim administrative units has been growing rapidly during the last twenty years, whilst that of the Russians and of other Slavs has been steadily falling (the only exceptions being the Tatar Autonomous Republic and the Adyghe Autonomous Region). Muslim territories have been steadily 'going native' and this trend is affecting, albeit more slowly, the capital

Table 4.4: Percentage of Central Asians within Central Asia, 1959–79

	1959	1970	1979
Uzbeks	97.2	99.2	99.3
Kazakhs	87.3	90.8	91.9
Kirghiz	–	99.0	99.0
Tajiks	–	99.0	99.2
Turkmens	–	96.8	97.8

Table 4.5: Percentage of Russians in some Muslim Territories, 1959–79

	1959	1970	1979	Loss 1959–79
Uzbekistan	13.5	12.5	10.8	– 2.7
Kazakhstan	42.7	42.4	40.7	– 2
Kirghizia	30.2	29.2	25.9	– 4.3
Turkmenistan	17.3	14.5	12.6	– 4.7
Azerbayjan	13.5	9.9	7.9	– 5.6
Tajikstan	13.3	11.9	10.4	– 2.9
Bashkiria	42.4	40.5	40.3	– 2.1

cities of the Muslim republics which in the past have been heavily dominated by Russian immigrants, with the result that natives were supposed to be rapidly 'Russified'. The detailed data of the 1979 census has not yet been released, but it is probable that in Baku, Tashkent, Ashhabad and Düshanbe Muslims have now regained absolute majority.

The 'concentration' of Muslims within their native administrative territories during the last twenty years illustrates their refusal to emigrate from what they still consider as *Dar ul-Islam*.

The figures for the Kazakhs shown in Table 4.4 need some explanation: in 1979 8.1 per cent of the Kazakhs lived in the RSFSR, made up of old rural border colonies in Western Siberia, the Southern Urals and Southern Volga.

In comparison with the figures shown in Table 4.4 it is interesting to note the steady decline of Russian and other non-Muslim colonies in practically all the Muslim territories shown in Table 4.5. The same process may be observed in Northern Caucasus, where the percentage of non-Muslims dropped between 1970 and 1979 from 52 per cent to 47.6 per cent in the Karachay-Cherkess Autonomous Region, from 38.9 per cent to 33.5 per cent in the Chechen-Ingush Autonomous Republic, and from 18.8 to 14.7 per cent in Daghestan. In the Kabardo-Balkar Autonomous Republic the percentage of non-Muslims remained stable (45.5 per cent) between 1970 and 1979 and during the same period

only in two territories did the Muslims lose ground: in the Tatar Autonomous Republic, where there was a drop from 49.1 to 47.6 per cent
and in the tiny Adyghe Autonomous Region where there was a fall of
0.6 per cent to 21.4 per cent. In neither of these cases was the relative
decrease of the native population due to emigration of Muslims, but to
a heavy immigration of Russians or, in the case of the Adyghe Autonomous Region, of Armenians.

This 'nativisation' of Muslim republics and autonomous regions is
especially remarkable if we take into account the fact that the immigration of Russians and other 'Europeans' is still continuing, although at a
slower rate than in the early 1950s. The increase of the native population is now so rapid that it cannot be compensated by Russian immigration, even though between 1970 and 1979 the overall rate of growth of
the Russian population was higher in Central Asian republics than elsewhere in the USSR: 14.8 per cent in Tajikistan, 13.1 per cent in
Uzbekistan, 11.5 per cent in Turkmenistan, 8.5 per cent in Kazakhstan
and 6.6 per cent in Kirghizia, as opposed to 6.5 per cent for the rest
of the country.

In the Muslim Caucasus, with the exception of the Kabardo-Balkar
Republic (increase of 7.1 per cent), the growth rate of the Russians has
been lower than average: 1.8 per cent in the Karachay-Cherkess Autonomous Region and 3.3 per cent in the Adyghe Autonomous Region.
In Azerbayjan, Daghestan and the Checheno-Ingush republics, Russian
colonies *decreased* in absolute numbers between 1970 and 1979 by
35,000 individuals in Azerbayjan, 20,000 in Daghestan and 33,000 in
the Checheno-Ingush Republic. Taking into account an average growth
rate of 6.5 per cent for the Russian population as a whole, the loss was
nearer 170,000 in real terms.

The concentration of native Muslims in their national territories
has reduced immigrant colonies to the position of steadily dwindling
minorities, and may well mark the beginning of the Muslim *reconquista*
of their homelands and the end of the dream of 'getting nearer'

Table 4.6: People Claiming their National Language as their Mother Tongue, 1959–79 (per cent)

	1959	1970	1979
Uzbeks	98.4	98.6	98.7
Kazakhs	98.4	98.0	97.5
Azeris	97.6	98.2	97.9
Tatars (in the Tatar Republic)	98.9	98.5	95.9

Table 4.7: People Claiming the National Language as their Mother Tongue, 1959–79 (per cent)

	Inside the National Territory			Outside the National Territority	
	1959	1970	1979	1959	1970
Adyghes	99.0	99.1	98.7	85.9	84.9
Kabardians	99.2	99.1	98.8	78.9	79.2
Balkars	98.9	98.8	?	89.3	86.8
Chechens	99.7	98.9	99.7	97.7	94.5

Table 4.8: Volga Tatars Claiming the National Language as their Mother Tongue, 1959–79 (per cent)

In the Tatar ASSR			Khabarovsk Kray (East Siberia)			Yaroslav Oblast' (North Central Russia)		
1959	1970	1979	1959	1970	1979	1959	1970	1979
98.9	98.5	99.9	59.1	46.7	44.0	77.2	66.4	43.9

(*sblizhenie*), the basis of Soviet ethnic policy. Demographic developments in Central Asia and the Caucasus have also been accompanied by a resurgence of the local culture. As a result, the hoped-for biological symbiosis between the native and immigrant communities, the substitution of local language by Russian and replacement of the local popular culture and way of life by the Soviet (i.e. Russian) model have become unattainable dreams. As a corollary of this trend, Muslim colonies which have been placed in a purely Russian environment and deprived of their national schools and press are rapidly losing their national profile. The first stage in this process is the loss of the mother tongue. In this respect, the comparison between the three post-war census shows some interesting results.

There is no linguistic assimilation of the natives in the Muslim territories, even where the Muslim community has been reduced to the status of a minority (as in the case of the Adyghe Autonomous Region, where Muslims constitute less than 25 per cent of the population). As a rule, the percentage of people who claimed their native language as their 'mother tongue' was high everywhere and has changed little over the last twenty years.

There is a striking difference between the attachment to the native tongue *inside* the national territory and the progressive linguistic Russification of the same ethnic groups *outside* their national territory.

Table 4.9: Percentage Annual Increase of Total Population by Republic

Republics	1970–9	1990–5
RSFSR	0.62	0.23
Uzbekistan	3.00	2.55
Azerbayjan	1.83	1.90
Kirghizia	2.09	2.07
Tajikistan	3.05	2.52
Turkmenistan	2.76	2.43
Kazakhstan	1.36	1.34
By comparison:		
Estonia	0.87	0.13
Latvia	0.73	0.08
Ukraine	0.61	0.24

From the comparison shown in Table 4.8 it is clear that Tatar colonies in purely Russian territories are doomed shortly to complete linguistic Russification, a probable first step to total assimilation.

In twenty years' time, at the turn of the century, the demographic situation of the USSR will present a somewhat different picture. There will be a general slackening of the growth rate of all nationalities, but the Slavs and in particular the Russians will be most affected, while the Muslims will maintain a relatively high rate of increase. According to various demographic surveys (especially Edmund Brunner, *Soviet Demographic Trends*, whom we are following here), in the year 1995 the difference in the growth rates of various Soviet republics will be as shown in Table 4.9.

In the year 2000, the total population of the USSR will be 300–310 million. Various Muslim nationalities will represent 22 to 25 per cent of this total (66 to 75 million). Russians will total about 150 million and the three Slav groups together a little over 200 million.

However, this prognosis does not take into consideration the assimilation of non-Russian nationalities by Russians. This process is already affecting national groups deprived of national territory such as Poles, Germans and Jews, together with various small nationalities lacking authentic national cultures distinct from the Russian like the Christian Turks (Chuvash, Gagauz), Eastern Finns (Mordvinians, Mariis, Udmurts, Komis, etc.) and even Ukrainian, Belorussian, Moldavian and Tatar colonies established outside their national territories. It may be assumed that in twenty years' time an important proportion of these national groups will have been assimilated by Russians and listed as such in future censuses. Thus, the total number of Russians in the year 2000 could be around 175 million, a higher proportion of the total population than at present, i.e. 56 per cent instead of 51 per cent. By the turn of the century the USSR will present a picture of a polarised nation with the Slavic majority confronted by a strong Muslim-Turkic minority, and in between certain national groups impervious to assimilation by either the Russians or the Muslims, such as Armenians, Georgians and Baltic peoples. Thus the Muslim-Turkic minority will be the only minority to increase its proportional share of the total population of the USSR.

In the year 2000 the Muslims will be divided among the following three areas: Central Asia – 50 million; Transcaucasia and Northern Caucasus – 16 million; Middle Volga and the Urals – 9 million. The Uzbeks will be by far the most important Muslim group, numbering some 25 million, followed by the Kazakhs (11 million), the Azeris (9 million), the Tatars (7.5 million), the Tajiks (5.5 million), the Turkmens (4 million), the Kirghiz (3.5 million), the Daghestanis (2.5 million), the Bashkirs (2 million) and the Chechen-Ingush (2 million). The forecast may, however, be modified because of the inter-Muslim assimilation of the smaller groups (Karakalpaks, Uyghurs, Dungans) by the stronger and more dynamic ones (Uzbeks, Kazakhs). Not to be ignored is the fact that certain formerly Christian Turks (Chuvash) and Eastern Finns (Mariis) might be converted to Islam by the Volga Tatars – as happened between 1905 and the Russian Revolution.

Two problems which will be preoccupying the Soviet leadership at the end of the century will be the 'nativisation' of the borderlands and the Soviet armed forces. The implications for the USSR can be examined.

1.1 The 'Nativisation' of the Borderlands

These vitally important strategic territories will steadily lose their Russian and other 'European' immigrants and become more Islamic and more Turkic. This process started in the late 1970s early 1980s (notably in Azerbayjan, North-Eastern Caucasus and to a lesser degree in Central Asia) as a result of a rapid population growth of the Muslims, which we have discussed already, plus a further three demographic trends that also look set to continue for some time.

(1) Muslims living in the RSFSR or in other non-Muslim republics of the USSR are immigrating into Central Asia. This shift is particularly evident among the Tatars and Bashkirs from Siberia and European Russia with the result that, by 1979, over a million Volga Tatars (i.e. one-sixth of the entire Tatar population) and over 70,000

Bashkirs were living in Central Asia. There are good reasons to believe that this movement will gather momentum and by the end of the century there will be of the order of 2 million Tatars and Bashkirs settled in Central Asia.

(2) There is little Muslim emigration to the industrial or rural areas of European Russia and Siberia. A serious shortage of manpower is already evident in these regions and is likely to be further exacerbated by the refusal of the working masses of Central Asia to leave their sunny homeland for dreary Western Siberia or Central Russia. Despite strong official encouragement, the already small number of Caucasians and Central Asians working in the industrial areas of the USSR had actually decreased by 1979. There was a cautious attempt in the 1970s to resettle some Uzbek and Kirghiz *sovkhoz* in the North Central part of European Russia (about Kalinin and Yaroslav), but this was a modest programme involving probably less than 5,000 all told. With Central Asia playing host to an even larger active population by the end of the century and since this territory cannot absorb an unlimited number, it will be the non-Muslims who will have to go.

(3) Russian and other European immigration to the Muslim territories has ended, and a process of non-Muslim emigration back to European Russia has begun. This movement is already evident in the North-Eastern Caucasus and Kirghizia and is likely to affect Turkmenistan, Uzbekistan and Tajikistan before long. The reasons can be summed up as follows: the limited space for rural colonies in the desert-oasis territories (Uzbekistan, Turkmenistan) and the high mountains of Tajikistan and Kirghizia; increasing competition from the native cadres; and, above all, the 'psychological pressure' and the general atmosphere of xenophobia which is plain to see in the countryside and becoming more evident in the cities. As a rule, Russians are not a migratory people and to feel at home they need the reassurance of a strong Russian ambience (*kak u nas*). In Central Asia and Caucasus, the Russians remain an alien body in a hostile environment, but the situation is bearable so long as they are numerous and strong enough to isolate themselves from the natives. For the time being at least, Tashkent, Düshanbe, Alma Ata or Frunze are still acceptably 'Russian' cities, but the same cannot be said for Baku, where the Russians feel a distinct sense of unease.

By the turn of the century, the population of Central Asia will have increased to around 60 to 65 million (from the present 40 million), of of which 50 million will be 'natives', with the balance made up of Russians and other Europeans. In the Caucasus the native population will reach 23 to 25 million, made up of 16 million Muslims, 3.5 million Georgians, 4.2 million Armenians and 1 million various smaller groups (Ossetians, Abkhaz, etc.).

Thus the entire southern 'soft underbelly' of the Soviet Union will became decidedly 'native', a perfectly acceptable situation for the Russian leadership of the Soviet Union so long as the nationalities remain 'trustworthy' and submissive. But will they be twenty years from now? Local nationalism is growing in the Caucasus and (more slowly) in Central Asia: then there is the threat from a hostile China and an unstable and unpredictable Middle East, which could easily create insecurity and unrest in the region.

1.2 The Soviet Armed Forces

By the turn of the century, the number of Muslims eligible for the draft (males over 18) will have increased from about 23.5 per cent of the total in 1980 to about 29 per cent in 2000. Meanwhile Russians, who now represent 49 per cent of those eligible, will have fallen to about 45 per cent and the figure for the three Slav nationalities in total will have dropped to 61 per cent from 67 per cent in 1979.

As a rule Central Asian and Caucasian Muslims are not drafted into fighting units but into construction battalions and special internal security units directed by the Ministry of Internal Affairs (MVD), whose job it it to ensure political order, including riot control and the guarding of the extensive network of Soviet penal institutions. Thus over the next two decades the Soviet Union will experience a growing intake of Muslims at the expense of more reliable (i.e. Slav) recruits. The Russians could grasp the nettle and increase the number of non-Slavs in military positions now reserved for Slavs, but this would raise fears of what the Russians call the 'yellowing of the Red Army' *(ozheltenie Krasnoy Armii)*. The alternative is a reduction in the size of the armed forces, but this solution seems unlikely in the presence of a hostile China and the build-up of US military power.

At the civilian level, the shortage of qualified industrial manpower which now faces the Soviet Union will create further difficulties for the regime. The solutions proposed so far are to engineer (by force if necessary) the transfer of Central Asia's excess manpower to the industrial areas of European Russia and Siberia, bring industry to Central Asia, or simply do nothing and muddle through with the present policies: all involve certain drawbacks. A massive population transfer is probably unrealistic in present circumstances, while a voluntary emigration from Central Asia northward seems highly unlikely; a shift in the industrial axis from Western Russia to Central Asia also seems unlikely given the close proximity of China and the risk of tilting the political balance towards the native elites and providing them with arguments for greater autonomy or even independence.

How would this evolution affect Muslim-Russian relations? Assuming that the next twenty years will be peaceful and devoid of major clashes between Russians and native Muslims — which is far from certain — the picture at the turn of the century will be as follows.

The 'European' community, reduced to the rank of a minority, will still be strong enough to encourage a climate of growing xenophobia, rural colonies will practically disappear (except in Kazakhstan), Muslims will dominate the cities (with the possible exception of Alma-Ata and Frunze), mixed marriages will become — as before 1928 — a rare exception, and the dream of Russian becoming the main language will be abandoned (even if Russian becomes a 'second mother tongue'). Native cadres will gain greater authority in the internal affairs of their republics, while the Russian cadres will be reduced to the status of technical experts instead of policy-makers. The process of rediscovering the past with its glorious cultural patrimony — including Islam — will be accelerated and magnified and a growing feeling of 'us versus them' will prevail in the relationship between natives and immigrants. Finally *sblizhenie* — 'the getting nearer' — leading to the emergence of a 'Soviet man' will appear as an impossible dream.

What will Moscow's response be to the growing pressure of the borderland and the gradual 'closing' of the Muslim territories? Three different policies are possible.

(1) To yield and admit the Muslim republics as equal partners, but this would involve drastic economic, administrative and political reforms. Such a course would also imply decentralisation of the Communist Party and the conceding of real autonomy to the republican branches of the Party. The history of the USSR indicates that fundamental change is impossible within the Soviet political framework.

(2) To exert tight control involving a programme of assimilation through forced emigration of the Central Asian and Caucasian Muslims to European Russia and a corresponding immigration of 'Europeans' to Central Asia and the Caucasus — in other words, through a policy of colonisation. The dangers of this are obvious and there is no evidence that the Soviet leadership would wish to incur the risks

involved.

(3) To continue with present policies, avoiding any drastic change and hoping against hope that the problem of nationalities may be solved by 'sovietisation' of non-Russian nationalities, the promotion of Russian and containing of national unrest with propaganda and force if necessary, encouraging the spirit of 'international friendship' between Soviet peoples, guaranteeing material equality to all ethnic groups and exercising severe control over their cultural life in order to kill any budding nationalism.

There is every reason to believe that the Soviet leadership will choose this last alternative. At best it might result in a measure of improvement, but it will certainly not solve the nationalities problem as a whole.

2 The National Factor — Several Nationalities or One Nation?

One of the most important factors to influence Muslim-Russian relations at the turn of the century will be the question of the national identity of the Soviet Muslims. The Soviet policy of nationalities inaugurated in 1924 with the *razmezhevanie* ('parcelling') of Central Asian republics aimed at dividing the Muslim *'Umma* and raising formidable barriers (economic, administrative and cultural) between the artificially created Muslim nationalities, which sixty years on have acquired a certain economic and political reality. Will the Russians be confronted twenty years from now by thirty small nationalities, divided and opposed to each other, vaguely connected by a remote historical tradition and a fast vanishing common cultural background — or by a closely united federation of kindred nations, or even by one Muslim *Millet*?

At present there are three levels of Muslim consciousness: a subnational, clan or tribal consciousness; a supranational religious (Islamic) or ethnic (Turkic) consciousness, and a national consciousness. The subnational and the supranational are both deeply rooted in the culture of Central Asia and the Caucasus. The national, on the other hand, is a Soviet creation forced upon the population in 1924, with the aim of dividing the Muslim territories and thereby securing Russian control. In spite of all Soviet efforts to eradicate the subnational and supranational consciousness of the people, they remain stronger than ever, cutting across the Soviet-imposed national divisions and contributing to the growth of pan-Muslim unity. In the long term, therefore, Moscow's continued domination of Muslim lands may be challenged.

2.1 The Past and the Present

Before the Revolution there were three basic identities among Russian Muslims: in the case of the sedentary people a purely religious identity — city-dwellers of Central Asia defined themselves as 'Muslims'. Alternatively, they claimed an identity based on the place of residence such as 'Bukharaly' or 'Samarkandî'. In the case of the nomads, or semi-nomads, identity was based on clan or tribal affiliation, 'I am a Qarluq', a 'Lokay', a 'Mangyt', or even 'of the Great Horde'. Some of the great tribal formations of Mongol origin (Nayman, Ktay, Mangyt, Keneges, etc.) which are scattered throughout Central Asia, Northern Caucasus (among the Nogays) and the Urals (among the Bashkirs) have preserved a strong feeling of kinship. Although the tribes and tribal federations lost their political and economic power long before the Revolution, their strong psychological influence survived. In particular the endogamic and exogamic taboos were strictly observed.

Muslim intellectuals had a different kind of awareness, also deeply rooted in the history of Islam. They defined themselves as 'Turks' or 'Turkestani' in Central Asia or as 'Gortsy' (Mountaineers) in Northern Caucasus. Only a few Volga Tatar secularist intellectuals set themselves apart from other Russian Turks by considering themselves 'Tatars'.

Today, after sixty years of administrative effort the national awareness of Soviet Muslims may be described as follows.

The sense of *subnational identity* which has been diminishing among the masses has become more evident among the new Soviet cadres — surprising as this may seem. In many areas, particularly in Turkmenistan but also in Kazakhstan and Kirghizia, the observance of clan-tribal rules has exerted a noticeable influence on the economic, cultural and even political life of the people, such as in the *kolkhozy*, which are often based on clan kinship. In some places, cadres are selected for positions in local Communist Party and government organisations according to clan-tribal structures, which lends a curiously unexpected 'familial', indeed 'Mafia', character to local Communist Party organs. This apparent paradox is easy to explain: to survive the ruthless power struggles which are such a feature of Communist Party hierarchies, a native secretary of a district (*raykom*) or region (*obkom*) committee surrounds himself with his kinsmen, members of his clan, tribe or horde, since the traditional links of kinship are more reliable and more loyally observed than the comradeship of the Communist Party. Soviet sources provide countless examples of this 'obnoxious' phenomenon (*mestnichestvo* — 'localism').

The clan-tribal structure also influences the operation of other social organisations. In Turkmenistan, for example, members of the Tekke tribe have traditionally taken over not only the apparatus of the Communist Party but also the higher education institutions such as the University of Ashhabad and the republican Academy of Science. This clan-tribal consciousness obviously restricts opportunity for contact between natives and Russians and endangers the smooth progress of Soviet economic and cultural life.

In some cases, these survivals of the clan-tribe system provide the basis for illegal religious organisations, for example recruitment of certain Sufi brotherhoods, especially in Turkmenistan and in Northern Caucasus, is often limited to specific clans or tribes. (This is also true of certain particularly militant groups of the Qadiriya Sufi brotherhood.) Thus the Battal Haji *wird* (branch), the most violently anti-Soviet of all North Caucasian *tariqa*, limits the recruitment of its members to some Chechen and Ingush clans and *taipa*s (extended families). Soviet sociological surveys often point to the frequent attempts of the *tariqa* to 'gain control over the extended families and the clans'. These clan-religious groups, attracting a double loyalty to the brotherhood and the clan, are closed societies which can neither be won over nor infiltrated by Soviet police and which thus provide a potential threat to the Soviet Establishment.

The *supranational identity* is more difficult to analyse. The masses and intellectuals of Central Asia still define themselves as 'Muslim', but here the term has a national rather than religious meaning. Furthermore, when, say, a young Uzbek member of the Communist Party declares 'I am an Uzbek and therefore I am a Muslim', this statement does not involve an Islamic confession of faith, it means that he feels that he is both a member of the modern Uzbek nation and of the greater Muslim *'Umma*. It is still believed in Central Asia, as well as in the Caucasus, that a non-Muslim cannot be an Uzbek or a Kirghiz or a Turkmen, which goes to prove that Muslim consciousness continues to enjoy priority in the minds of Central Asians and Caucasians. Among the elite, the supranational identity — the feeling of belonging to a common Turko-Iranian *Millet* — has been cultivated since Stalin's death by the slow but steady rediscovery of the classical culture of the Muslim past. The movement, called '*mirasism*' (from the Arabic *miras* — 'patrimony'), has brought about a more or less complete rehabilitation of the traditional Arab-Iranian-Turkic literature and philosophy shared by all Turkic, Caucasian and Iranian people of Islamic background. It reinforces their feeling of historical and cultural unity and helps to maintain among the new generation of intellectuals a pan-Islamic and pan-Turkic sense of brotherhood. It also provides a feeling of spiritual, ethnic and historical solidarity between Muslims of the USSR and those of the world at large. Lastly, it maintains the insuperable barrier which separates the Muslim republics from the non-Muslim territories of the Soviet Union — the alien *Dar ul-Harb*.

At present, pan-Islamic and pan-Turkic sentiments are for all practical purposes one and the same, and as such represent a potent obstacle to the 'friendship of the Soviet nations'. Moreover, these sentiments have been growing during the last twenty years, helped by the fact that the new Muslim elite of the USSR has been brought up in the same Soviet academic institutions and moulded in a common intellectual frame. The introduction of a uniform political and economic vocabulary has also meant that the linguistic differences between the various Turkic languages are rapidly disappearing.

The purely *national awareness* of belonging to a modern Soviet nation is even more difficult to analyse. Completely artificial in the beginning, these nations have had to become economic and administrative realities. However, a purely Uzbek or purely Karakalpak culture has not yet emerged in spite of half a century of efforts. Neither has a feeling of local Uzbek patriotism been created, and it is doubtful whether it will emerge in the near future. The general trend is towards a greater unity and not towards the cultural division of Soviet Islam. However, the increasing participation of native cadres in the economy, state and educational apparatus has produced competition between various Muslim nationalities, especially in Central Asia, and this in turn has created friction among them. This process may eventually accentuate the differences already existing between Turks (Uzbeks) and Iranians (Tajiks), sedentaries (Uzbeks) and former nomads (Kazakhs), and between Sunnis and Shiites. Nevertheless all Soviet sources attest to the fact that up to now such friction is manifest chiefly between Europeans and Muslims, and not among Muslims themselves.

2.2 The Future

Let us consider the possible evolution of these trends.

(1) So long as native cadres have to compete with Russians and other Europeans, in the Communist Party organisation, the subnational identity, clan and tribal, far from disappearing, will increase, since it

provides them with a unique guarantee of loyal support against their Russian comrades. Paradoxically, therefore, it is the Communist Party which preserves tribalism and clannishness among Muslim political cadres.

(2) The supranational identities: 'Pan-Turkism', 'Pan-Turkestanism' or 'Pan-Islamism' will grow in parallel with the development of higher education, with the rediscovery of cultural and historical patrimony, and possibly also with a religious revival which could follow the gradual crumbling of the 'Iron Curtain', isolating Soviet Islam from the rest of the Muslim world.

'Pan-Turkism', 'Pan-Turkestanism' and even 'Pan-Islamism' are by no means exclusive and together they represent the most clearly formulated cultural expression of Central Asian dissent. This trend, first noticeable after the death of Stalin, has a long way to go before it spills over into open political dissent, but the foundation for such action in the future is there.

(3) As to national identity, development here will depend on the size and historical background of each Muslim nationality. Undoubtedly the next twenty years will witness a rapid 'consolidation' of the most important Muslim groups, while the smaller and the weaker ones, without a clearly definable character and owing their survival to the protection of Moscow, will be assimilated by their stronger brethren. Certain small Daghestani groups already look set to be assimilated by the Avars as well as the Karakalpaks (who in turn may well be assimilated by the Uzbeks).

It is ironic that the most artificial of all Central Asian nations — the Uzbeks — should be emerging as a real 'nation' with strong 'imperialistic' tendencies. Before the Revolution, the term 'Uzbek' was applied exclusively to Turkic nomadic or semi-nomadic tribes. The expression 'Sarts' was used to describe Turcophone or Iranophone sedentaries and 'Sart-Uzbek' for the Turkic-speaking sedentary groups of various origins which preserved their clan-tribal structure. At present, the Uzbeks are by far the largest and most developed group among Central Asians and their position has been further strengthened by the settling of former nomadic groups, such as the Lokays. The Uzbek Republic contains all the cultural and historical capitals of Central Asia — Bukhara, Samarkand, Kokand, Urgench, Shahrisabz and Khiva. The best Central Asian universities (Tashkent and Samarkand) and scientific institutions (the Uzbek Academy of Science in Tashkent) are in Uzbekistan, and so is the seat of the Muslim Spiritual Directorate and the only working *madrassah*s (Tashkent and Bukhara). The Uzbeks, not surprisingly, also have the largest and most sophisticated native intelligentsia of Central Asia to act as guardians of the national culture and the traditions of Central Asia.

Uzbek communities outside Uzbekistan (260,000 Uzbeks in Kazakhstan, 880,000 in Tajikistan, 450,000 in Kirghizia and 230,000 in Turkmenistan) enjoy an extraterritorial cultural autonomy (Uzbek press and Uzbek schools), while the numerous 'foreign' colonies in Uzbekistan (600,000 Tajiks, 650,000 Tatars, 620,000 Kazakhs and 140,000 Kirghiz) are denied this privilege. These advantages have allowed the Uzbeks to claim the Muslim culture of Turkestan between the ninth and nineteenth centuries as their own. Avicenna, Timur, Ulugh-beg, Ali-Shir Navai and the Emperor Babur are all claimed as Uzbeks, with the result that the Uzbeks are promoting the merger of 'Uzbek' and 'Turkestani' consciousness. The Uzbeks are now recognised as the leaders of Central Asia by most other Central Asians, and while this role is more psychological than economic or political, it is nevertheless certain that the importance of the Uzbeks as the leaders of Central Asia — and eventually maybe of all Soviet Islam — is growing.

It is probable that by the turn of the century the Uzbek nation, some 25 million strong, will act as the pole around which other nationalities of Central Asia will federate. If Turkestan is to be united again, as in the time of Timur, it will be around the great cities of Tashkent, Samarkand and Bukhara once more, and under Uzbek leadership.

3 The Religious Factor — Islam in the Year 2000

What will the position of Muslim religion be in the USSR at the turn of the century? Will the children of today's Muslims still belong to the world of Islam or will they have been transformed into Soviets — totally liberated from the *perezhitki* (vestiges) of the past and indistinguishable from their Russian comrades? It is important to analyse these two alternatives.

A brave new world where all the peoples of the USSR share a common way of life, culture and aspirations fits the vision of the Soviet leaders. According to their forecasts, Islam in the year 2000 (like all other religions of the USSR) will at last have died out. With a few exceptions among the older generation, all Soviet citizens will be atheists. Soviet religious specialists are optimistic on this score — at least in their official declarations — an optimism which, they claim, is based on the results of recent sociological surveys. According to these surveys, the Muslim population can be divided into eight categories, as follows. (We are following one of the best Soviet specialists, Zhumanazar Bazarbaev, *Opyt sotsiologicheskogo Izucheniya Ateizma i Religii (Experience of Sociological Research on Atheism and Religion*, Nukhus, 1979).)

(1) firm believers — those 'militant and intolerant fanatics' who refuse to participate in the collective social life and who force their views and ideals upon their neighbours and relatives;

(2) belivers by tradition — those who believe in God and strictly observe all religious rites and customs but who are not fanatics and do not try to force their views on others;

(3) hesitants — those who believe in God and observe some religious rites and customs;

(4) non-believers — those who do not pray and do not fast during the month of Ramadan but who observe some rites of Islam: circumcision, religious marriage, religious burial, payment of *sadaqa*, celebration of the great Muslim festivals, etc.;

(5) non-believers — those who observe religious rites under pressure from their social or family environment and through respect for their elders;

(6) indifferent atheists — those who consider that the 'fight against religion is no concern of theirs';

(7) emotional atheists — those who are firm, fanatical adversaries of religion and who advocate the use of 'exceptional measures';

(8) convinced atheists — those who believe that religion must be fought and destroyed by education and who represent the 'right attitude'.

In another of his works, devoted to the religious life of the Karakalpak Republic — *Sekularizatsiya Naseleniya Sotsialisticheskoi Karakalpakii (Secularisation of the Population of Socialist Karakalpakistan*, Nukhus, 1973), Zhumanazar Bazarbaev gives the following percentages of these eight categories:

firm believers	11.4
believers by tradition	14.4
hesitants	13.6
non-believers (group 4)	18.5
non-believers (group 5)	20.6
atheists (groups 6, 7, 8)	21.5

Table 4.10: Religious Belief by Age Group in the Karakalpak Republic, Early 1970s

	Age Groups			
	18 to 20 (per cent)	30 to 42 (per cent)	42 to 54 (per cent)	Above 54 (per cent)
Firm believers	–	–	5.9	31.6
Believers by tradition	–	1.2	14.0	36.0
Hesitants	1.4	13.0	28.7	9.4
Non-believers (group 4)	18.6	21.0	24.4	12.7
Non-believers (group 5)	32.2	30.0	17.1	3.5
Atheists (groups 6, 7, 8)	47.8	34.8	13.2	6.8

While these figures may be accepted as holding good for the USSR as a whole, the proportion of believers (both categories) and hesitants is higher in Northern Caucasus, but lower among the Volga Tatars. The incidence of believers is also greater among women than men and among peasants than industrial workers. But if we consider the figures according to age groups, using Bazarbaev's findings, the picture shown in Table 4.10 emerges.

Bazarbaev believes that in the youngest age group (below 18 years) religion is already completely and totally destroyed, and if the age group of 12 to 17 years were to be included in the statistics, the proportion of believers in the total population of the Karakalpak Republic would be dramatically reduced to 5 per cent for the firm believers, 5 per cent for the believers by tradition and 6 per cent for the hesitants.

Certain agitprop specialists automatically transfer the 1970s figures to the end of the century. They believe that if anti-religious education is maintained at the present level, or possibly improved, the young atheists of today will still be atheists at the turn of the century when they are forty to fifty years old. Other even more optimistic Soviet specialists go so far as to proclaim that in twenty years' time the 'Fatherland of advanced socialism' will reach the happy era when all physical, economic and social evils will be finally eradicated. They conclude: 'when a Paradise is built on this earth, who will care about the other world?' thus religion will die out. In order to hasten this state of affairs, an intense anti-religious campaign was launched in all Muslim republics in 1980. It is more massive, more brutal and quite different from the 'scientific' and relatively moderate propaganda which marked the post-Khrushchev period. All Communists and all 'honest Soviet citizens' are ceaselessly reminded that it is their duty to engage in a 'merciless struggle against religion which poisons the minds of people'. To the old classical themes of anti-Islamic propaganda (incompatibility between science and religion, superiority of Communist morals, the distasteful character of religious customs, etc.) two new themes have recently been added: 'the anti-socialist character of Islam' and the 'danger of counter-propaganda by religious activists'. One may reasonably conclude that the year 1980 marked a change in the relationship between the Soviet government and Islam and that the era of relative religious liberalism and partnership has come to an end and will be gradually replaced by a new period of conflict comparable to that which characterised the leadership of Khrushchev. The anti-religious drive gained vigour in 1981.

Not all Soviet specialists, however, are quite as optimistic; some suggest, on the contrary, that by the turn of the century Islam will not only have survived but will be in stronger shape than it is now. They point out that belief and disbelief are more a question of age and social environment than of education and propaganda. At a critical age — between 40 and 45 — non-believers and even atheists revert to religion. The Central Asian and Caucasian press is full of stories of former anti-clerical militants who have become pious at the age of 45. There are several reasons for this change of attitude, among which social pressure and the spiritual void of Marxism-Leninism seem to be the most important. Soviet sources also reveal that there are no absolute atheists among Soviet Muslims. Even the most intolerant militant Communists observe the three essential Muslim rites, circumcision, religious marriage and religious burial in Muslim cemetaries.

There are three reasons which favour the survival of the Islamic religion at the turn of the century:

(1) The growing confusion between the notions of 'national' and 'religious'. A new sense of Muslim consciousness is emerging among the intelligentsia, tightly linked to the social and political, rather than to the strictly religious, aspects of Islam. Some of these intellectuals may indeed be atheists and Soviet sources themselves suggest that it is hard to draw a line between believers and atheists in Central Asia, even among officially atheist intellectuals, including the graduates of various higher educational institutions and the officials of the Party and state apparatus. An atheist intellectual or a Party member will nevertheless comply with certain religious rules and customs for 'national' reasons, since to spurn the religious traditions of the nation would be tantamount to betrayal of the nation. A

true atheist would be rejected by his community and condemned to assimilation by the Russians. It is doubtful whether this confusion between nation and religion, so characteristic of a Muslim milieu, will disappear during the coming twenty years.

(2) The confusion between faith (*iman*) and morality, honest, conscience (*khujdan*) still persists in spite of the efforts of official agitprop to implant a new, Communist, Marxist-Leninist moral code. The expression *imanly*, 'faithful', 'believers', is still used to designate an honest moral person, whilst *imansiz* ('non-believer') is synonymous with an immoral scoundrel.

(3) The evident contrast between the spiritual, aesthetic and cultural wealth of Islam, recently rediscovered, and the intellectual and spiritual misery of an alien Marxist-Leninist doctrine.

It is probable that Islamic religion will survive, although over the next twenty years it will undoubtedly lose believers (firm believers or believers by tradition) as a consequence of hard anti-religious pressure. Some of them, especially among the less developed rural and urban masses, may become hesitant or non-believers, others — a minority — could even become official atheists. But at the same time, for the reasons mentioned above, a number of intellectuals will return to the religion of their ancestors. Islam will thus undergo the same elitist evolution that is evident among certain Christian creeds: a loss of the less developed and demanding of the popular masses but an increase of new adepts from the upper intellectual strata of society.

What tradition will predominate at the turn of the century in Soviet Islam? As already noted, since the latter part of the nineteenth century two trends have been active in Russian Islam: the modernistic, liberal, highly intellectual trend of the Tatar *jadidism*, and the conservative, fundamentalist trend of the Caucasian *müridism*, both of which are still alive in present-day Soviet Islam. Each has its positive points and its drawbacks, but both can work towards the final victory with optimism.

The liberal *jadid* tradition is represented by the Official Muslim Establishment, headed by the four Muslim Spiritual Boards. Politically, the official hierarchy is conspicuous by its loyalty to the Soviet regime. It never protests against anti-religious pressure and fulfils the task with which it is entrusted — to demonstrate to the Muslim world at large the happiness and prosperity of the faithful in the Soviet Union. Like the Orthodox Church of Moscow, it is integrated within the fold of the regime and constitutes a precious ally and a valuable ambassador for Moscow.

It must, however, be remembered that Sunni Islam admits faith without religious practice and has neither a 'clergy' nor an established 'church'. Anyone with a certain knowledge of Arabic who is able to read the Quran and recite prayers can perform the rites. Such characteristics make Islam more flexible and less susceptible to external pressure than other creeds. The closing of a mosque or of a *madrassah* does not have the same significance for the Muslim faithful as the destruction of a church or the prohibition of formal religious instruction for Christians. The Soviet Muftis are members of an adminstration, not 'bishops', their political declarations and their professions of loyalty towards the Soviet regime constitute no commitment on the part of the flock, but simply for themselves. What is more, in the legal pronouncements of Muslim officials (*fetwas*), in certain articles published in *Muslims of the Soviet East*, and also in what may be gleaned between the lines of Soviet anti-religious propaganda, we find evidence of the existence of a small authentic Muslim religious elite. This elite is responsible for what may be called a 'religious-intellectual' revival among the Muslims of the USSR. It has engaged in cautious but demonstrably effective propaganda in support of Islam. Among the most important themes advanced by this religious group is that Islam is the most liberal, humanist and 'advanced' of all religions, that it is endowed with the highest and most progressive culture, is the best fitted to prepare the faithful for the construction of real socialism and that Muslims are the best — even the *only* people capable of building socialism. Finally, they propound the theory that there is no contradiction whatsoever between Marxism and Islam, since socialism in its ideal form is but a fulfilment of Islamic promises.

This ideology is the direct legacy of the old pre-revolutionary Tatar *jadidism*. The great Tatar theologians and philosophers, Shihabeddin Marjani, Musa Jarullah Bigi, Rizaeddin Fahretdin oğlu, Abdullah Bubi and Qayyum Nasyri are still its intellectual guides. Thus, from the historical point of view, Soviet 'official' Islam appears as the last incarnation of the old nineteenth-century Muslim liberalism. It enjoys increasing prestige among the young intellectuals who have detected that it is true to the national heritage, unlike the official 'Soviet culture' which has been shaped by Russian thinking. Its chances of survival until the year 2000 are reasonably high and enhanced by the fact that official Islam remains a useful ally of Moscow while being afforded a measure of protection by 'parallel' Sufi Islam. Should Soviet pressure on official Islam become unbearable or should the attitude of the official Muslim hierarchy become too submissive, believers would not be forced into atheism, but would instead turn to the violently anti-Soviet militant Sufi brotherhoods. Commenting on the failure of the anti-religious drive launched by Nikita Khrushchev, *Komsomolskaya Pravda* wrote on 15 August 1965:

> Insults, violence and forced closing of churches [mosques] not only fail to reduce the number of believers but increase it. They promote the proliferation of clandestine religious groups and antagonise the believers against the Soviet State.

The second tradition of Russian Islam is represented by the clandestine and semi-clandestine Sufi brotherhoods (*tariqa*). From the religious standpoint Sufism is neither a heresy nor a schism. It is perfectly legitimate and, like 'official' Islam, it belongs to the mainstream of Muslim religion. It differs from official Islam in its attitude towards the Soviet regime: the Sufi *tariqa* represent the popular, militant, 'Holy War' (*jihad*) aspect of Islam, totally hostile to the *kafir* establishment.

The existence of this second trend has certainly saved Islam in the USSR (as it saved Central Asian Islam under the Mongols in the thirteenth century) by protecting it against the two main dangers which threaten all religions there — official atheism among the intellectuals and relapse into superstitution by the masses. The combination of 'official' and 'unofficial' Islam has promoted a revival of interest in and a sympathy for Islamic religious and cultural traditions among the intellectuals, while helping to maintain religious life among the Muslim masses.

What is the future of Sufism in the Soviet Union? To answer this question we must first examine the position of Sufi *tariqa* abroad. In countries where Islam is the ruling faith and is safe from external or internal danger, the brotherhoods tend to become a kind of club or meeting place for pious, religious-minded notables of the middle and lower middle classes. In these countries, Sufism is losing its hold on the intellectuals and its ability to incite the masses into action. But where Islam is threatened by persecution, excessive secularisation or open attack from anti-religious regimes (as was the case in Yugoslavia, Sinkiang, Turkey, Indonesia and, since 1979, Afghanistan), the Sufi orders revert to their initial mission, that of the defence of Islam, and become bastions behind which resistance is organised. In the Soviet Union, where Islam is threatened both by the alien 'Infidel' oppressor and by the internal danger of atheism, Sufi *tariqa* represent the only organised opposition to the Communist power. They have thus become the rallying points for the growing number of people who radically reject the Soviet order. To them, Sufi brotherhoods offer superior organisation, fighting spirit and discipline, while also appealing to the emotions through the aesthetic qualities of their *zikr*.

Thus, at the turn of the century, Soviet Islam will probably appear as a dynamic establishment exhibiting two facets: an intellectual, 'elitist', liberal, even progressive one, as represented by the official clerics, and a deeply popular, conservative, intolerant and aggressive 'Holy War' one, with an ideology incorporating various fundamentalist currents, as represented by the Sufi brotherhoods. This combination allows the best possible division of tasks between the liberals and the radical mystics and it will help guarantee not merely the survival but the revival of Islam. Also, so long as the Muslim religion survives, the hope of symbiosis between the Muslims and Russians in a happy, brave new Soviet world will remain wishful thinking.

4 The Political Factor

The Muslim elites already have access to the administrative, economic and technical sectors of their national republics, but not so far to real decision-making — the privilege of the Communist Party whose top echelons are still entirely controlled by Russians. This situation will not change to a significant degree in the next two decades and so the already difficult relations between Russians and Muslims will be exacerbated, with the spawning of an active Muslim nationalism one of the possible outcomes.

At present, for lack of a clear-cut nationalist movement in the Muslim republics, we find a violent and growing popular xenophobia, born of fear and disdain of the Russian masters. The Muslim masses continue to live in a world moulded by Islam, and this situation will certainly last for several more decades. Members of the Muslim political elite, intellectuals and Party members tend not to sever the links with their environment and in many aspects their present position may be likened to that of the nineteenth-century Russian *narodniki*, whose intellectual attitudes were necessarily influenced by a populism which required them to pay the utmost attention to the demands, expressions of sympathy or hatred coming from below. (Only an isolated minority have separated themselves from their people and act as agents of the Russian power; in doing so they have completely betrayed their origins, often marrying Russian wives and as a rule living in an entirely Russian milieu.) It is this same 'populist' attitude which prevents them from becoming completely loyal allies of the rulers in Moscow. They therefore act partly as agents of their people and at best — so long as they can manoeuvre successfully between the conflicting demands of the native masses and those of the Russian centre — their relations with the Russians reflect a split loyalty. This is an uncomfortable and dangerous position to be in, as demonstrated by the number of purges for 'nationalism' of high-ranking Caucasian and Central Asian Communists since the end of the Second World War. At present, Central Asian politicians may be simultaneously Communists and Muslims as well as 'Soviet patriots' and Russian haters. Loyalty to the USSR does not preclude a strong devotion to their Turkic or Muslim *'Umma* and *Millet* and their superficial internationalism barely hides a deeply rooted nationalism.

Independence, full sovereignty and liberation from Russian control is the final dream of the overwhelming majority of the Muslim intellectuals and political cadres, including members of the Communist Party. How could it be otherwise? They know that Southern Yemen, Libya, Uganda and Angola are sovereign states while glorious Bukhara is not.

It is doubtful whether Soviet leaders can harbour any illusion about the ultimate loyalty of their Muslim comrades. The Soviet leadership is aware that in one or two generations the Muslim nations, by sheer weight of numbers, will obtain a more or less complete *de facto* autonomy. Muslim political leaders also know that 'time is on their side' and that it would be useless to endanger this secure future by foolhardy or premature action against their Russian masters. The Caucasian Sufi 'Holy War' resistance does not appeal to them. Why should it? They are heirs to the imperial Turkic *ulu*s, their ancestors ruled over world empires. They know that the future belongs to them — unless a major catastrophe occurs. The spiritual world of the Muslim Turkic elite in the Soviet Union, by contrast to that of the Russian intellectual elite, is marked by a sense of optimism — probably the only community of the USSR to feel this way.

How does the Muslim elite of today see the situation of Soviet Islam in twenty years' time? How do they see future relations with the Russians and the Muslim world abroad? What are their expectations, their hopes and their dreams? These are difficult questions and our answers are necessarily speculative.

For the time being, there is no organised Muslim nationalist movement in the USSR, no expression of dissent (except in two extreme cases, the Crimean Tatars and the Meshketian Turks), no Muslim *samizdat*. Our knowledge of the *Weltanschauung* of the Muslim intelligentsia and political elite is based on literary works in all languages of Central Asia and of the Caucasus, on the countless articles, reports and official statements denouncing various forms of rampant nationalism and, above all, on personal contacts with Soviet Muslims. It is all this, derived from over thirty years of observation, that we try to summarise below.

(1) Notwithstanding its weak points and the fact that it does not promise Muslims full independence, the Soviet regime is achieving the essential dreams of the *jadid* reformers of the last century — a modern Muslim secular society. It has helped the Muslims, especially those of Central Asia, to overcome their centuries-long decline. Therefore, for the foreseeable future, the economic prosperity of the Muslim *Millet* remains linked to the wealth and might of the Soviet Union as a whole. If the USSR is to be preserved in its present form, Muslims must help Russians in their struggle against the Chinese and even in their adventures in the Muslim Middle East. In exchange, Muslims need to be treated as partners with access to decision-making positions in their own republics and a larger share of capital investment. Protected by Russian power, Muslims will have time to develop their national cultures and economies without which Muslim republics would not be self-sufficient. Those who advocate this moderate strategy will certainly remain loyal to Moscow until the turn of the century, assuming that no crisis disrupts the situation. Their position may be compared to that of the pre-revolutionary 'Westernisers', like Chokan Valikhanov, the Kakazh descendant of Chingiz Khan, who wanted to thank the Russians for their help, without which 'the Kazakhs would remain savage *Asiates*'.

(2) Muslim Turks are better Communists than the Russians. History, culture and religion have prepared them to become the true heirs of the October Revolution and to achieve what the Russians have failed to do: the creation of a powerful world empire, which would be both Communist and Muslim. Muslim Turks have a greater sense of national cohesion, of discipline and of devotion to an ideal than the anarchic Slavs could ever possess. They must therefore not only be

entirely responsible for the administration of their own republics, they must also become equal partners with the Russians in the central government of the USSR.

Supporters of this approach are the ideological heirs to the Muslim National Communists of the 1920s. Like their predecessors, they believe that the Soviet Union must undertake the conquest of the Muslim world and become the leader of the Third World. They welcome any new Soviet political or military engagement in Muslim countries abroad and so, far from opposing the occupation of Afghanistan, they welcome the adventure. It is conceivable that they sincerely believed they were helping to liberate their Uzbek and Tajik brothers from the 'imperialists' and from 'feudal domination'. Moreover their involvement in, and voiced support for, the Afghan operation strengthened their bargaining power with the Russians, who might eventually be obliged to make important concessions, such as increasing industrial investment in Central Asia rather than trying to siphon off Muslim manpower to Western Siberia and Northern Russia. The final stages of the conquest of the entire Muslim world would be the achievement of Sultan Galiev's dream of the 'Colonial International' dominated by the Soviet Muslims.

For the advocates of this strategy, the Soviet Union should be preserved, but Russians should be subordinated to the rank of technical experts. 'We will re-establish the Golden Horde,' we were told once by a Central Asian Communist.

(3) Muslim republics must become independent and sovereign. Russians and other Europeans will be expelled and native cadres will assume full responsibility for the administration of the new Muslim states which may be tied to the Soviet Union by some special agreement. As to the regime and the political ideology which will inspire it, opinions differ greatly: it may be a modified form of Marxism-Leninism, a new version of Sultan Galiev's National Communism, a Western-type democracy (the least likely of all solutions) or, more probably, a conservative Islamic radicalism comparable to that of the present-day 'Islamic Revolution' in Iran.

Such are the three possible paths for the future evolution of the Muslim lands of the Soviet Union, as seen by the Muslims themselves. They vary with the character — optimistic or pessimistic — of the informers, with their age (as a rule, the younger generation is more anti-Russian) and with their national, ethnic origin (the Caucasians are generally more adventurous than the Turkestanis, the Tatars more cautious). All three solutions suppose a peaceful evolution, without any major crisis threatening the existence of the Soviet Union. What would happen to the Muslim lands of the USSR in case of a major clash? Or, more particularly, in case of a war with the use of conventional or nuclear weapons?

In the case of nuclear war the main targets would be in the industrial regions of European Russia, Ukraine or Siberia, making the chances of survival better in Muslim territories. Were there to be a conventional war along the southern border of the Soviet Union or in the Middle East, the position of Muslims would be strengthened. It is doubtful that Muslim forces would be engaged in military operations against their fellow coreligionists (their poor performance in Afghanistan has seen to that), but Muslim neutrality would almost certainly involve a price being paid by the Russians. If a conventional war were fought in Europe, the Muslims would undoubtedly be used as cannon fodder by the Russians. In the event, however, of a war with the Chinese, immensely difficult decisions for both the Soviet leadership and the Muslims would be involved. The Soviet government has certainly not forgotten what happened when Muslims came into contact with the Germans in the last war, while the Muslims know full well the price of treason — real or imagined. One thing is certain, however — the Chinese would adopt a much more subtle and intelligent approach than the Germans did in 1942.

Muslim Turks and Russians have been in contact for a thousand years, during which time relations have been mostly hostile. Fifty years ago, the new rulers of Russia believed (or pretended they believed) that their political ideology — a universal panacea for all social, economic and political evils — would solve peacefully, and once and for all, the eternal problem of the conquered versus the conquerors. Half a century of failure has demonstrated beyond any possible doubt that Marxism-Leninism is no more capable of solving the problem than any other political doctrine. No *homo sovieticus* has emerged and it is doubtful whether this species will ever see the light of day. If relations between Muslims and Russians remain more or less peaceful for the moment it is for no other reason than that the Russians are still overwhelmingly strong compared to their Muslim comrades. Any attempt to find yet another solution, whether based on Marxism or not, is feared by both sides.

The most reasonable solution would be to follow Solzhenitsyn's advice and grant the Muslim borderlands the right to secede 'before it is too late', thus reducing the USSR to the size of the Moscow Tsardom at the time of Basil III, the father of Ivan the Terrible. But such a solution would be both 'un-Russian' and 'un-Soviet'. It is not in the Russian tradition to give up what has been acquired by conquest and for a nation to leave the 'worker's paradise' would be proof that the Soviet experiment had failed.

Barring a major crisis — such as a foreign war — the present status quo in the Soviet Union will be uncompromisingly preserved as long as possible. The final, inescapable, violent crisis will be delayed, but for how long?*

---

* It is certain that the rulers of the Soviet Union have never heard the wise advice of a *hadith*, quoted by my friend Yuri Bregel in his lecture at the Centre for Middle Eastern Studies at Harvard University on 15 April 1978: 'Leave the Turks in peace, so long as they leave you in peace' ('Utruku't-Turka má tárakūtum').

APPENDICES

I Muslim Population of the Soviet Union

Nationalities	Numbers in 1979	Ethnic Groups	Area	Religious Rite	Official Written Language
Uzbeks	12,456,000	Turks	Central Asia	Sunni Hanafi (small Shia minority)	Uzbek
Kazakhs	6,556,000	Turks	Central Asia	Sunni Hanafi	Uzbek
Tatars	6,317,000	Turks	Mid. Volga and diaspora	Sunni Hanafi (200,000? Christian)	Tatar
Azeris	5,477,000	Turks	Trans Caucasus	70% Shia Ja'farite, 30% Sunni Hanafi; small groups (50,000?) of Ali Illahi & Bahai	Azeri
Tajiks	2,237,000	Iranians	Central Asia	Sunni Hanafi; some 100,000 Pamirian Tajiks are Isma'ilis Nizari	Tajik
Turkmens	2,028,000	Turks	Central Asia	Sunni Hanafi	Turkmen
Kirghiz	1,906,000	Turks	Central Asia	Sunni Hanafi	Kirghiz
Bashkirs	1,371,000	Turks	Mid. Volga-Urals	Sunni Hanafi	Bashkir
Chechens	756,000	Ibero-Caucasians	North Caucasus	Sunni Hanafi	Chechen
Ossetians	542,000	Iranians	North Caucasus	70% Christian, 30% Sunni Hanafi	Ossetian
Avars	483,000	Ibero-Caucasians	Daghestan	Sunni Shafei	Avar
Lezghins	383,000	Ibero-Caucasians	Daghestan	Sunni Shafei	Lezghin
Kabardians	322,000	Ibero-Caucasians	North Caucasus	Sunni Hanafi	Kabardian
Karakalpaks	303,000	Turks	Central Asia	Sunni Hanafi	Karakalpak
Darghins	287,000	Ibero-Caucasians	Daghestan	Sunni Shafei	Darghin
Kumyks	228,000	Turks	Daghestan	Sunni Shafei	Kumyk
Uyghurs	211,000	Turks	Central Asia	Sunni Hanafi	Uyghur
Ingush	186,000	Ibero-Caucasians	North Caucasus	Sunni Hanafi	Ingush

I Muslim Population of the Soviet Union (*contd*)

Nationalities	Numbers in 1979	Ethnic Groups	Area	Religious Rite	Official Written Language
Karachays	131,000	Turks	North Caucasus	Sunni Hanafi	Karachay-Balkar
Kurds	116,000	Iranians	Transcaucasus	Sunni Hanafi, Shia Ja'fari, Ali-Illali and Yezidis (50%?)	Kurdish
Adyghes	109,000	Ibero-Caucasians	North Caucasus	Sunni Hanafi	Adyghe
Laks	100,000	Ibero-Caucasians	Daghestan	Sunni Shafei	Lak
Ajars (Georgian Muslims)	100,000 to 150,000	Ibero-Caucasians	Trans-Caucasus	Sunni Hanafi	Georgian
Tsiganes	Around 100,000?	Indians	Central Asia & Trans-Caucasus	Superficially Muslims	Language of the area
Talyshis	Around 100,000?	Iranians	Trans-Caucasus	Shia Ja'farite	Azeri
Turcs	93,000	Turks	Central Asia & Trans-Caucasus	Sunni Hanafi	Uzbek, Azeri
Abkhaz	91,000	Ibero-Caucasians	Trans-Caucasus	40% Sunni Muslims, 60% Christian	Abkhaz
Tabasarans	75,000	Ibero-Caucasians	Daghestan	Sunni Shafei	Tabasaran
Balkars	66,000	Turks	North Caucasus	Sunni Hanafi	Karachay-Balkar
Nogays	60,000	Turks	Daghestan and North Caucasus	Sunni Hanafi	Nogay
Dungans	52,000	Chinese	Central Asia	Sunni Hanafi	Dungan (Chinese in Cyrillic script)
Cherkesses	46,000	Ibero-Caucasians	North Caucasus	Sunni Hanafi	Kabardian
Ironis	31,000	Iranians	Central Asia	Shia Ja'farite	Uzbek, Tajik
Abazas	29,000	Ibero-Caucasians	North Caucasus	Sunni Hanafi	Abaza
Tates	22,000	Iranians	Daghestan and Trans-Caucasus	Shia Ja'farite, Jews, Christian (Armeno-Gregorian)	Azeri
Rutuls	15,000	Ibero-Caucasians	Daghestan	Sunni Shafei	Lezghin, Azeri & Russian
Tsakhurs	14,000	Ibero-Caucasians	Daghestan	Sunni Shafei	Lezghin, Azeri & Russian

I Muslim Population of the Soviet Union (contd)

Nationalities	Numbers in 1979	Ethnic Groups	Area	Religious Rite	Official Written Language
Baluchis	13,000	Iranians	Central Asia	Shia Ja'farite	Turkmen
Aguls	12,000	Ibero-Caucasians	Daghestan	Sunni Shafei	Lezghin, Azeri & Russian
Arabs	Around 10,000	Semites	Central Asia	Sunni Hanafi, some Shia Ja'fari	Uzbek, Tajik
Laz	1,000 to 2,000	Ibero-Caucasians	Trans-Caucasus	Sunni Hanafi	Georgian
Khemshins (Muslim Armenians)	1,000 (?)	Armenians (Indo-European)	Trans-Caucasus	Sunni Hanafi	Armenian
Chalas	less than 1,000	Semites	Central Asia	Sunni Hanafi (crypto Jewish)	Uzbek

II Literary Languages Used by the Muslim People of Soviet Union

Language	Group	Literary since	Alphabet	Remarks
Uzbek	Turkic	Progressively from 1923 and 1937	Arabic until 1927, Latin 1927–40, Cyrillic since 1940	Before the Revolution used Persian and Chagatay or 'Old Uzbek' (literary since 15th cent.)
Kazakh	Turkic	mid-19th cent.	Arabic until 1927, Latin 1927–40, Cyrillic since 1940	Before the 19th cent. used the Chagatay and the Kazan Tatar
Kazan Tatar	Turkic	14th cent. (earlier written monuments in the 11th cent.)	Arabic until 1929, Latin 1927–39, Cyrillic since 1939	Until the middle of 19th cent. a composite language, half Chagatay, half Tatar
Crimean Tatar	Turkic	15th cent.	Arabic until 1929, Latin 1929–40, Cyrillic since 1940	Modern language created by Ismail Gaspraly in late 19th cent., still used by the deported Crimean Tatars in Uzbekistan
Azeri Turkic	Turkic	14th cent.	Arabic until 1927, Latin 1927–39, Cyrillic since 1939	
Tajik	Iranian	9th cent.	Arabic, Latin, Cyrillic	Same as the classical Persian, but different pronounciation and many Russian loan words
Turkmen	Turkic	17th cent. (half Chagatay) modern Turkmen in 1923	Arabic until 1928, Latin 1928–39, Cyrillic since 1939	Before used Persian and Chagatay
Kirghiz	Turkic	1924	Arabic, Latin, Cyrillic	Before 1924 used Kazakh and Chagatay
Bashkir	Turkic	1923	Arabic until 1929, Latin 1929–39, Cyrillic since 1939	Before 1923, the Bashkirs used Kazan Tatar
Chechen	Ibero-Caucasian	attempts in the mid-19th cent. in Cyrillic and Arabic 1925	Latin 1924–38, Cyrillic since 1938	Before 1925, used Arabic

II Literary Languages Used by the Muslim People of Soviet Union (contd)

Language	Group	Literary since	Alphabet	Remarks
Ossetians	Iranian	1924	Latin 1924–38 in two languages, Iron (Christian) and Digor (Muslim), Cyrillic since 1938, Digor disappears	Attempts in 18th cent. in Slavonic script, in early 19th cent. in Georgian, and in Arabic (for the Digor) in 1923
Avar	Ibero-Caucasian	18th cent. semi-literary	Arabic until 1928, Latin 1928–39, Cyrillic since 1939	Before the Revolution used Arabic
Lezghin	Ibero-Caucasian	1928	Latin 1928–38, Cyrillic since 1938	Before 1928, used Azeri and Arabic
Kabardian-Cherkess	Ibero-Caucasian	attempts in mid-19th cent. in Arabic and Cyrillic 1923	Latin 1923–38, Cyrillic since 1938	Used by the Kabardians and the Cherkess. Before used Ottoman Turkish and Crimean Tatar
Karakalpak	Turkic	1930	Latin 1930–40, Cyrillic since 1940	Before the Revolution, used Chagatay and Uzbek
Darghin	Ibero-Caucasian	19th cent.	Arabic until 1928, Latin 1928–38, Cyrillic since 1938	Before the Revolution, used Arabic
Kumyk	Turkic	late 19th cent.	Arabic until 1927, Latin 1927–38, Cyrillic since 1938	Before the Revolution, used Kazan Tatar and Arabic
Uyghur	Turkic	19th cent.	Arabic until 1939, Latin 1939–46, Cyrillic since 1946	Before the 19th cent. used in the Chagatay since the 15th cent. (The Chinese Uyghurs use Arabic script, re-established in 1981)
Ingush	Ibero-Caucasian	1923	Latin 1923–38, Cyrillic since 1938	Before the Revolution, used Arabic and Azeri Turkic
Karachay-Balkar	Turkic	1924	Latin 1924–38, Cyrillic from 1938	Used by both the Karachays and the Balkars. Before the Revolution used Ottoman Turkish and Crimean Tatar
Kurdish	Iranian	1922	Modified Armenian 1922–9, Latin 1929–44, Cyrillic since 1944	Based on the Kurmanji dialect spoken also in Anatolia and different from the dialects used in Iran and Iraq

II Literary Languages Used by the Muslim People of Soviet Union (contd)

Language	Group	Literary since	Alphabet	Remarks
Lak	Ibero-Caucasian	19th cent.	Arabic until 1928, Latin 1928–38, Cyrillic since 1938	Before the Revolution, used Arabic
Adyghe	Ibero-Caucasian	attempt in 1924 in Arabic 1927	Latin 1927–38, Cyrillic since 1938	Before the Revolution, used Ottoman Turkish and Crimean Tatar
Abkhazian	Ibero-Caucasian	attempts in 19th cent. in Cyrillic 1918	Latin 1918–38, Georgian 1938–54, Cyrillic since 1954	Before the Revolution, used Georgian
Tabasaran	Ibero-Caucasian	1936	Latin 1936–9, Cyrillic since 1939	Before 1936, used Azeri Turkic and Arabic
Nogay	Turkic	1928	Latin in two different languages, Aq Nogay and Qara Nogay Cyrillic since 1938	Qara Nogay (spoken in Daghestan) abolished as literary language in 1938. Aq Nogay spoken in Stavropol' basis of the literary language. Before the Revolution, used Kazan Tatar and Crimean Tatar
Dungan	Chinese		Latin 1920–54, Cyrillic since 1954	Chinese script used before 1920
Abaza	Ibero-Caucasian	1938	Cyrillic	Before 1938, used Crimean Tatar and Ottoman Turkish
Tati	Iranian	Middle Ages	Latin from 1928–39, Cyrillic since 1939	Before 1928, the Jewish Tates used the Hebrew script, but the Muslim Tates' language is a non-literary one and they use Azeri Turkic

SELECT BIBLIOGRAPHY

I Russian and Soviet Islam — the Historical Background

Abdullin, Y.G. *Tatarskaia Prosvetitel'naia Mysl'* (Moscow, 1976)
Allen, W.E., and Muratov, P. *Caucasian Battlefields. A History of the Wars on the Turco-Russian Border, 1828-1921* (Cambridge, 1953)
Allworth, E. (ed.) *Central Asia – a Century of Russian Rule* (New York, 1967)
Arsharuni, A., and Gabidullin, Kh. *Ocherki Panislamizma v Rossii* (Moscow, 1931)
Barthold, V.V. *Four Studies on the History of Central Asia*, 4 vols. (New York, 1956–62)
—— *Istoriia Kul'turnoi Zhizni Turkestana* (Moscow, 1927)
—— *Turkestan down to the Mongol Conquest*, 1st edn (London 1928); 2nd edn (1958)
Bazarbaev, Z. *Opyt sotsiologicheskogo Izucheniya Ateizma i Religii* (Nukhus, 1979)
Bennigsen, A., and Lemercier-Quelquejay, Ch. *La Presse et le Mouvement National chez les Musulmans de Russie avant 1920* (Paris, 1964)
Blanch, L. *The Sabres of Paradise* (London, 1960)
Carrère d'Encausse, H. *Réforme et Révolution chez les Musulmans de l'Empire Russe. Bukhara, 1867-1927* (Paris, 1966)
Fisher, A. *The Crimean Tatars* (Stanford, 1978)
Galutzo, M.G. *Turkestan – Kolloniia*, 1st edn (Moscow, 1929); 2nd edn (1935)
Grousset, R. *L'Empire des Steppes* (Paris, 1941)
Holdsworth, M. *Turkestan in the Nineteenth Century* (London, 1959)
Ibragimov, G. *Tatary v Revolutsii 1905 goda* (Kazan, 1926)
Kirimal, E. *Der Nationale Kampf des Krim Türken* (Emsdetten, 1952)
Klimovich, L. *Islam v Tsarskoi Rossii* (Moscow, 1936)
Kraedler, L. *Peoples of Central Asia* (Bloomington, 1962)
Mende, G. von *Der Nationale Kampf des Russlands Türken* (Berlin, 1936)
Pierce, R.G. *Russian Central Asia, 1867-1917 – a Study in Colonial Rule* (Berkeley, 1960)
Safarov, G. *Kolonial'naia Revoliutsiia – Opyt Turkestana* (Moscow, 1921)
Samurskii, N. *Daghestan* (Moscow, 1929)
Schuyler, E. *Turkistan. Notes of a Journey in Russian Turkistan, Kokand, Bukhara and Kuldja*, 2 vols. (New York, 1877); 2nd edn (New York, 1966)
Seydamet, J. *La Crimée* (Lausanne, 1921)
Smirnov, N.I. *Müridizm na Kavkaze* (Moscow, 1963)
Togan, Z.K. *Bugünkü Turkeli (Türkistan) ve Yakin Tarihi (Turkestan Today and its Recent History)* (Istanbul, 1947) (in Turkish)
Tokarev, S.A. *Etnografiia Narodov SSSR* (Moscow, 1958)
Validov, J. *Ocherki Obrazovannosti i Literartury Tatar do Revoliutsii 1917 goda* (Moscow, 1923)
Wheeler, G.E. *The Modern History of Soviet Central Asia* (London, 1964)
—— *The Peoples of Soviet Central Asia* (London, 1966)
Wurm, S. *Turkic Peoples, their Historical Background, their Languages, and the Development of Soviet Linguistic Policy* (London, 1954)

II USSR and the Muslim World Abroad

Boersner, D. *The Bolsheviks and the National and Colonial Questions, 1917-1928* (Geneva-Paris, 1957)

Bräker, H. *Kommunismus und Weltreligionen Asiens, zur Religions und Asienpolitik der Sovjet union, Kommunismus und Islam*, 2 vols. (Tubingen, 1969-71)

Colotti-Pischel, E., and Robertazzi, C. *L'Internationale Communiste et les Problèmes Coloniaux* (Paris-La Haye, 1968)

Compte-rendu Sténographique – Premier Congrès des Peuples d'Orient, Baku, 1920 (Petrograd, 1921)

Cudsi, A.S. (ed.) *Islam and Power* (London, 1981)

Degras, J. *The Communist International – 1919-1943* (Oxford, 1956)

Eudin, X., and North, R. *Russia and the East – 1920-1927, a Documentary Survey* (Stanford, 1964)

Fisher, L. *The Soviets in the World Affairs: A History of the Relations between the Soviet Union and the Rest of the World, 1917-1929*, 2 vols. (Princeton, 1957)

James, C.L.R. *World Revolution, 1917-1936 – the Rise and Fall of the Communist International* (London, 1937)

Hurewitz, J.C. *Diplomacy in the Near and Middle East – a Documentary Record* (Princeton, 1956)

—— *Middle Eastern Politics – the Military Dimension* (New York, 1968)

—— *The Near East and North Africa in World Politics* (New Haven, 1975)

—— *Soviet-American Rivalry in the Middle East* (New York, 1969)

Kazemzadeh, F. *The Struggle for Transcaucasia – 1917-1921* (New York, 1951)

Kolarz, W. *Communism and Colonialism* (London, 1964)

Laqueur, W.Z. *Communism and Nationalism in the Middle East* (New York, 1956)

—— *Soviet Union and the Middle East* (London, 1959)

—— (ed.) *The Middle East in Transition – Studies in Contemporary History* (New York, 1958)

Lederer, I., and Vucinich, W. *The Soviet Union and the Middle East* (Stanford, 1974)

Lenczowski, G. *Russia and the West in Iran, 1918-1948, a Study in Great Power Rivalry* (Ithaca, 1949)

Nollau, G., and Wiehe, H.J. *Russia's South Flank – Soviet Operations in Iran, Turkey and Afghanistan* (New York, 1963)

Rezun, M. *The Soviet Union and Iran* (Geneva, 1981)

Rodisson, M. *Marxism et Monde Musulman* (Paris, 1972)

Schram, S., and Carrère d'Encausse, H. *Le Marxisme et l'Asie* (Paris, 1965)

Zabih, S. *The Communist Movement in Iran* (Berkeley-Los Angeles, 1966)

III Islam in the USSR

Abdülhamitoğlu, N. *Türksüz Kirim, Yüzbinlerin Sürgünü* (Istanbul, 1974) (in Turkish)

Allworth, E. *Uzbek Literary Politics* (New York, 1964)

—— (ed.) *The Nationality Question in Central Asia* (New York, 1973)

Ashirov, N. *Evoliutsiia Islama v SSSR* (Moscow, 1973)

—— *Islam i Natsii* (Moscow, 1975)

—— *Musul'manskaia Propoved'* (Moscow, 1978)

—— *Nravstvennye Poucheniia Sovremennogo Islama* (Moscow, 1977)

Avtorkhanov, A. *Narodoubiistvo v SSSR* (Munich, 1952)

Bacon, E. *Central Asians under Russian Rule* (Ithaca, 1966)

Basilov, V.N. *Kul't Sviatykh v Islame* (Moscow, 1970)

Bayramsakhatov, N. (ed.) *Religioznye Perezhitki i Put' ikh Preodoleniia v Turkmenistane* (Ashhabad, 1977)

Bazarbaev, Zh. *Sekularizatsiya Naseleniya Sotsialisticheskoi Karakalpakii* (Nukhus, 1973)

Bennigsen, A., and Lemercier-Quelquejay, Ch. *The Evolution of the Muslim Nationalities of the USSR and their Linguistic Problems* (London, 1961)

——, —— *Islam in the Soviet Union* (London-New York, 1967)

——, —— *Les Mouvements Nationaux chez les Musulmans de Russie – Le Sultangalievisme au Tatarstan* (Paris, 1960)

——, —— *Les Musulmans Oubliés* (Paris, 1981)

Bennigsen, A. and Wimbush, S.E. *Muslim National Communism in the Soviet Union – a Revolutionary Strategy for the Colonial World* (Chicago, 1979)

Castagné, J. *Les Basmatchis* (Paris, 1922)

—— *Le Turkestan depuis la Révolution Russe, 1917-1921* (Paris, 1922)

Chokaev, M. *Turkestan pod vlast'iu Sovetov* (Paris, 1935)

Davletshin, T. *Sovetskii Tatarstan* (London, 1974)

Demidov, S.M. *Sufizm v Turkmenii* (Ashhabad, 1978)

Dimanstein, S. (ed.) *Revoliutsiia i Natsional'nyi Vopros*, vol. 3 (the only volume published) (Moscow, 1930)

Hayit, B. *Turkestan im XX Jahrhundert* (Darmstadt, 1956)

Istoriia Kommunisticheskikh Organizatsii Srednei Azii (Tashkent, 1967)

Izimbetov, G. *Islam i Sovremennost'* (Nukhus, 1963)

Kadyrov, V. *Prichiny Sushchestvovaniia i puti Preodoleniia Perezhitkov Islama* (Leninabad, 1966)

Klimovich, L. *Islam* (Moscow, 1965)

Kolarz, W. *Russia and her Colonies* (New York, 1952)

Makatov, I. *Islam, Veruiushhii, Sovremennost'* (Makhach-Qala, 1974)

Mamleev, Kh.B. *Nekotorye Osobennosti Islama v Checheno-Ingushetii* (Groznyi, 1970)

—— *Reaktsionnaia Sushchnost' Müridizma* (Groznyi, 1966)

Materialy Nauchnoi Konferentsii Modernizatsiia Islama i aktual'nye Voprosy Teorii nauchnogo Ateizma (Moscow, 1968)

Mavliutov, R.R. *Islam* (Moscow, 1974)

Medlin, W.K., Carpenter, F., and Cave, W.M. *Education and Social Change in Soviet Central Asia* (Ann Arbor, 1965)

Mustafinov, M.M. *Zikrizm i ego Sotsial'naiia Sushchnost'* (Groznyi, 1971)

Nemchenko, M. *Natsional'noe Razmezhevanie v Srednei Azii* (Moscow, 1925)

Nove, A., and Newth, G.A. *The Soviet Middle East – a Model for Development* (New York, 1963)

Park, A. *Bolshevism in Turkestan, 1917-1927* (New York, 1957)

Pipes, R. *The Formation of the Soviet Union* (Cambridge, 1964)

Pivovarov, V.G. *Byt, Kul'tura, Natsional'nye Traditsii i Verovaniia Naseleniia Checheno Ingushskoi ASSR* (Groznyi, 1974)

Rakowska-Harmstone, T. *Russia and Nationalism in Central Asia. The Case of Tadzhikistan* (Baltimore, 1966)

Rasul Zade, M.E. *L'Azerbaydjan en lutte pour l'Indépendance* (Paris, 1930)

Rodinson, M. 'Problématique de l'étude des rapports entre l'Islam et le Communisme', *Correspondance d'Orient* (Brussels, 1961), vol. 5

Rubinstein, L. *V Bor'be za Leninskuiu Natsional'nuiu Politiku* (Kazan, 1930)

Ryskulov, T. *Revoliutsiia i Korennoe Naselenie Turkestana* (Tashkent, 1925)

Rywkin, M. *The Soviet Nationalities Policy and the Communist Party Structure in Uzbekistan* (New York, 1960)

―――― *Moscow's Muslim Challenge – Soviet Cultural Asia* (London, 1982)

Saidbaev, T.S. *Islam i Obshchestvo* (Moscow, 1978)

Sattarov, M. *Islam Dini Galyglary (Islamic Religious Survivals)* (Baku, 1967) (in Aseri)

Sheehy, A. *The Crimean Tatars and the Volga Germans, Soviet Treatment of Two National Minorities* (London, 1971)

Snesarev, G., and Basilov, V. *Domusul'manskie Verovaniia i Obriady Srednei Azii* (Moscow, 1975)

Sukhareva, O.A. *Islam v Uzbekistane* (Tashkent, 1960)

Sultan Galiev, M.S. *Metody Antireligioznoi Propagandy sredi Musul'man* (Moscow, 1922)

Takho-Godi, A.A. *Revolutsiia i Kontrrevolutsiia v Daghestane* (Moscow, 1927)

Teufel-Dreyer, June, 'Ethnic Minorities in the Sino-Soviet Conflict' in McCagg (ed.), *Soviet-Asian Ethnic Frontiers* (New York, 1979)

Trimingham, Spencer, *The Sufi Orders of Islam* (Oxford, 1971)

Tsentral'noe Statisticheskoe Upravlenie pri Sovete Ministrov SSSR, *Itogi Vsesoiuznoi Perepisi Naseleniia 1959 goda* (Moscow, 1962–3)

―――― *Itogi Vsesoiuznoi Perepisi Naseleniia 1970 goda* (Moscow, 1973), especially vol. IV, *Natsional'nyi Sostav Naseleniia SSSR*

―――― *Itogi Vsesoiuznoi Perepisi Naseleniia 1979 goda*, incomplete figures published in *Vestnik Statistiki* (Moscow, vols. 2, 7, 8, 9, 10, 1980)

Wheeler, G. *Racial Problems in Soviet Muslim Asia* (London, 1960)

GLOSSARY

Adat: customary law

Ashura: Shiia festival commemorating the death of Imam Hosein

Dar ul-Islam: the 'Abode of Islam', all Muslim lands as opposed to the *Dar al-Harb*, the 'House of War', which includes non-Muslim lands

fetwa: legal opinion given by a Mufti

ijtihad: the right to individual interpretation of the sacred law

Imam: leader of a congregational prayer

Imam-Khatib: head of a mosque

Ishan: in Central Asia, head of a Sufi *tariqa*

jadid/jadidism: from the Arabic *jadid*, 'new', a loose term used to designate the ideology of the nineteenth-century modernists and reformers

jihad: the Holy War against infidels

kafir: 'infidel'

khütbe: the sermon delivered at the Friday prayer in the mosque. Since it includes a prayer for the ruler, mention in the *khütbe* is a mark of sovereignty

mazar: shrine, tomb of a saint

madrassah: Muslim high school

mektep: Muslim elementary school

millet: Arabic word for nation

mirza: from the Persian *'emir-zade'*, heriditary noble

mollah: general term used to designate Muslim clerics

Mufti: canon lawyer

mürshid: sheikh of a Sufi brotherhood

obkom: regional committee of the party

oblast': region, an administrative unit within some Soviet republics

qadymist: from the Arabic *qadim*, 'ancient', designates the representatives of the conservative trend in Russian Islam before 1917

raykom: district committee of the Party

sadaqa: voluntary contribution of the believers to the upkeep of their mosque

Shariyat: Quranic law

Sufism: a mystical doctrine of Islam based on initiation and leading to personal union with God

tariqa: 'path' (leading to God), Sufi brotherhood

ulema: scholar in theology
ulus: Turkic word for nation
'Umma: the community of believers
waqf: endowment used to support a pious foundation
zakat: alms destined to assist the poor
zikr: individual or collective prayers (silent or loud) of a Sufi brother-
    hood

INDEX

Grousset, René 57
Gurii, Mgr. (bishop of Kazan) 10

Habl ul-Matin 91
Haidar Khan Amu 96
'Hairy Ishans' (*tariqa*) 76
'Harbi Shura' 36
Ho Chi Minh 94
'Holy War' 64–7, 146, 148; *see also* Sufism
Husein (King of Jordan) 106
Husein Zade, Ali 91, 92
'Hümmet' (Azeri Political Party) 81, 92, 96

Ibn Sina (Avicenne) 2, 3, 140
Ibrahimov, Abdurrashid 91–2
Ibrahimov, Veli 85
Idrisi, Galimjan 92
ijtihad 70, 72
Il'minsky, Nicolas 19, 45, 50–1
India (ns) 94, 97, 106
Indonesia (ns) 146; Communist Party 95; Sufism in 65
Ingushe (s) 33–4, 39, 122, 126; deportation of 27, 30–2, 51; language 40; Sufism among 75, 136
Institute of Scientific Atheism 46
Iran (Persia) 94, 95, 100, 102; Baluchis in 111; Communist Party 96, 99; Islamic Revolution 106, 108, 109, 115, 150
Iraq 102, 106, 111, 116
'Iron Curtain' 100–3
Iskhaki, Ayaz 8, 35, 80, 93
Islam Dünyasi 92
Islam Mejmuasi 92
Ismailism 110
Istanbul 90–3, 107
'Ittifaq al-Muslimin' 79
'Ittifaq ve Tarakki' 91
'Ittihad ve Tarakki' 85
Ivan IV, the Terrible (Tsar) 10, 12, 78, 152

'Jadidism', jadids 71–2, 77, 80–2, 90, 109, 144–5
Jengelis 95, 98, 99
Jenming Ribao 119
Jews, Judaïsm 31, 130; among the Khazars 57; in Central Asia 55; in Egypt 102
Jordan 104, 105, 106; Cherkess in 111

Junaid Khan (Basmachi leader) 66

Kabarda (ians) 13, 14, 23, 39, 40, 61–5, 127, 129; deportation 32; Russians in 128
Kabul 91, 113
Kalendariya (*tariqa*) 76
Kalmyks, deportation of 27, 30–1, 61; invasions 15, 56, 59
Karachay (s) 33, 39, 126; deportation of 27, 30–2, 51; Karachay-Cherkess Autonomous Region 40, 127; language 40; Russians in 128
Karakalpak (s) 42, 138, 139, 141–2; language 43, 131; Sufism in 76
Karapapakhs 29
Kasimov (Khanate of) 77
Kasymov, Kenesary (Kazakh Khan) 64
Katayama, Sen 94
Kaufman (General) 23
Kazakh (s), Kazakhstan 42, 52–3, 60, 63, 71, 78, 81, 85, 111, 113, 119, 121–2, 126–8, 130, 131, 134, 138, 140, 149; eighteenth century uprisings 63–4; Hordes 15, 59, 64; in Sinkiang 110, 118–20, 122; language 21, 43; missionaries among 46; 1916 uprising 22, 61; Russians in 20, 127–8; sedentarisation of 22–3, 61
Kazan 13, 16, 19, 37, 78, 85; conquest of 9–10, 60–1, 77, 88; Khanate of 11, 55; Missionary Society of 45; Religious Academy 19; University 85
Kemal, Ataturk 99–101
Keneges (tribe) 136
Kerbela 110
KGB 114, 116
Khal Hoja (Basmachi leader) 66
Khalid (King of Saudi Arabia) 106
Khalqa Doğru 92
Khazar (s) 5, 6, 56–7
Khemshins 29
Khiva 59, 97, 139; Khanate of 18, 41–2, 48, 88
Khojaev, Fayzullah 42–3
'Khomeiniism', its influence on Soviet Islam 115–16
Khwarezm 2, 7, 58; Sufism in 76
Kirghiz, Kirghizia 37, 42, 53, 119, 122, 126-7, 130–2, 140; in Afghanistan 110; in Sinkiang 120;